Parties, Polarization, and
Democracy in the United States

Parties, Polarization, and Democracy in the United States

Donald C. Baumer
Howard J. Gold

LONDON AND NEW YORK

First published 2010 by Paradigm Publishers

Published 2016 by Routledge
2 Park Square, Milton Park, Abingdon, Oxon OX14 4RN
711 Third Avenue, New York, NY 10017, USA

Routledge is an imprint of the Taylor & Francis Group, an informa business

Copyright © 2010, Taylor & Francis.

All rights reserved. No part of this book may be reprinted or reproduced or utilised in any form or by any electronic, mechanical, or other means, now known or hereafter invented, including photocopying and recording, or in any information storage or retrieval system, without permission in writing from the publishers.

Notice:
Product or corporate names may be trademarks or registered trademarks, and are used only for identification and explanation without intent to infringe.

Cataloging-in-Publication Data is available from the Library of Congress.
ISBN 978-1-59451-667-2 (hardcover : alk. paper)

Designed and Typeset by Cynthia Young, Sagecraft, LLC.

ISBN 13: 978-1-59451-667-2 (hbk)
ISBN 13: 978-1-59451-668-9 (pbk)

Contents

List of Tables, Figures, and Appendices   vii
Acknowledgments   xi

1 Political Parties in the Twenty-First Century   1

2 Parties and the Electorate I: Images of the Parties   19

3 Parties and the Electorate II: The Dynamics of Party Polarization   49

4 The Midterm Elections of 1994 and 2006   93

5 Parties in Power: Congress, Presidents, Partisanship, and Gridlock   119

6 Political Parties in Anglo-America   145

7 Looking Backward and Forward: The Election of 2008 and the Future of American Politics   171

Notes   195
Index   229
About the Authors   243

Tables, Figures, and Appendices

Tables

2.1 Modal Images of the Parties in Open-Ended Survey Questions 21
2.2 Public Awareness of Party Differences, 2000 23
2.3 Ideological Placement of the Parties, 1984–2008 23
2.4 Party Identification, Presidential Election Years, 1952–2008 25
2.5 Indicators of Partisanship, 1952–2008 32
2.6 Partisan Identification and Issue Polarization, 1976 and 2008 35
2.7 Identifying Opinion Leaders, 2004 37
2.8 The Impact of Party Image-Holding, Partisan Strength, and Political Interest on Opinion Leadership, 2004 39
2.9 Effects of Persuading Others on Perceptions of Party Polarization, 1976 and 2004 40
2.10 Polarization among Opinion Leaders, 1976 and 2004–2008 42
2.11 How Many Opinion Leaders in 2004? 45
3.1 Predictors of Party Identification, 1960, 1980, and 2000 58
3.2 Three Definitions of "Working Class" 64
3.3 The Effects of Income and Gender on Party Identification and Vote Choice, 1952–2008 (Whites Only) 66
3.4 The Effects of Income and Region on Party Identification and Vote Choice, 1952–2008 68
3.5 The Cultural Divide, Party Identification and Vote Choice, 1972–2008 (Whites Only) 73
3.6 Abortion and Perceptions of the Parties in 2004 and 2008 (Whites Only) 76
3.7 Abortion and Other Non-Cultural Issues, 1972–2008 (Whites Only) 77
3.8 Abortion and Other Cultural Issues, 2004 (Whites Only) 79
4.1 Gender, Race, Independents, and Congressional Voting, 1990–1994 100

4.2 Gender, Marital Status, Independents, and Congressional Voting, 2002–2006   105
4.3 Percentage of Congressional Districts Won by Majority Party in District, 1994–2006   115
6.1 Overview of Anglo-American Party Systems   150
6.2 Perceptions of Ideological Difference between the Major Parties in Anglo-America   163
6.3 Ideological and Partisan Sorting in Anglo-America   164

Figures

2.1   Two Portraits of Party Identification, 2008   28
2.2a Weak versus Independent Democrats   29
2.2b Weak versus Independent Republicans   29
3.1   Income and Party Identification   51
3.2   Region and Party Identification   51
3.3   Gender and Party Identification   52
3.4   Race and Party Identification   53
3.5   Age and Party Identification   54
3.6   Education and Party Identification   56
3.7   Religious Worship and Party Identification   56
3.8a Income Composition of the Parties, 2008   59
3.8b Regional Composition of Parties, 2008   59
3.8c Gender Composition of the Parties, 2008   60
3.8d Racial Composition of the Parties, 2008   60
3.8e Age Composition of the Parties, 2008   61
3.8f Educational Composition of the Parties, 2008   61
3.8g Religious Composition of the Parties, 2008   62
3.9   The "Culture War" in the Press   71
3.10 Influences on Vote Choice, 1972–2008   81
4.1   Abortion and Voting in House Elections, 1972–2008 (Whites Only)   97
4.2   Abortion and Voting in Senate Elections, 1972–2008 (Whites Only)   98
4.3   Region and Voting in House Elections, 1952–2008   99
4.4   Region and Voting in Senate Elections, 1952–2008   99

4.5   Income and Voting in House Elections, 1952–2008 (Whites Only)   106
4.6   Income and Voting in Senate Elections, 1952–2008 (Whites Only)   107
4.7   Party Identification and Voting in House Elections, 1952–2008   111
4.8   Party Identification and Voting in Senate Elections, 1952–2008   112
4.9   Partisan Loyalty in Congressional Elections, 1952–2008   113
4.10 Partisan Loyalty in House Elections, Incumbents versus Open Seats, 1970–2008   114
5.1   Party Polarization in Congress, 1858–2008   137
5.2a Ideological Polarization and Party Unity in the House, 1962–2008   139
5.2b Ideological Polarization and Party Unity in the Senate, 1962–2008   140
6.1   Major Party Support in National Elections   159
6.2   Strong Partisanship in Anglo-America   160
6.3   Nonpartisans in Anglo-America   161
6.4   Partisan Loyalty in Anglo-America   162
6.5   Income and Voting in Anglo-America   165
6.6   Religious Worship and Voting in Anglo-America   166
6.7   Importance of Religion and Voting in Anglo-America   167
6.8   Abortion and Voting in Anglo-America   168
7.1   Partisan Loyalty in Presidential Elections, 1952–2008   184
7.2a Ideological Sorting among Republicans   185
7.2b Ideological Sorting among Democrats   186

Appendices

Tables

A.1   Percent Voting Republican in Presidential Elections, 1952–2008; Percent Voting for a Third Party in Selected Presidential Elections   47
A.2   Effects of Party Image-Holding on Political Knowledge, 2004   48
B.1   Income and Party Identification, 1952–2008   83
B.2   Region and Party Identification, 1952–2008   84
B.3   Gender and Party Identification, 1952–2008   85

B.4 Race and Party Identification, 1952–2008   86
B.5 Age and Party Identification, 1952–2008   87
B.6 Education and Party Identification, 1952–2008   88
B.7 Religious Worship and Party Identification, 1952–2008   89
B.8 Predicting Vote Choice, 1972–2008   90
C.1 Republican Voting in House Elections Broken Down by Party Identification, 1952–2008   116
C.2 Republican Voting in Senate Elections Broken Down by Party Identification, 1952–2008   117

Acknowledgments

This project would not have been possible without the generous sabbatical support available at Smith College. Most of the work that produced this book was done during sabbaticals enjoyed by both authors in the 2006–2008 period. Another valuable resource that came our way due to our association with Smith College was our student research assistant, Shayla Livingston, who helped us greatly during the 2006–2007 academic year, extending into the summer.

After the bulk of the manuscript had been completed, we contacted Jennifer Knerr at Paradigm Publishers, who Howard had worked with on a previous book project, and we were fortunate enough to get a positive response from her about our project. She has been all we could have hoped for in an editor—supportive, efficient, and, most importantly, enthusiastic about the project. Our production editor, Lori Hobkirk, was also a pleasure to work with as the final manuscript took shape. We also wish to thank Professor Nick Horton of the Smith College Department of Mathematics and Statistics who provided us with valuable statistical advice. Finally, Kelly Slough provided some much needed technical assistance at the very end of the process. Of course, none of this would have been possible without the love and support of our families—Polly, Ben, and Maggie, and Jennifer, Sarah, Annie, and Bobby.

CHAPTER 1

Political Parties in the Twenty-First Century

Polarization, especially in the form of partisan polarization, has been the dominant theme of American politics over the last twenty years. It has been written about in numerous books and articles, and talked about extensively by politicians, media pundits, and ordinary citizens. Our most recent presidents, George W. Bush and Barack Obama, made frequent statements deploring the state of partisan relations, both as candidates and while in office. In the judgment of most scholars, Bush never fulfilled his promise to be a "uniter, not a divider," and Obama's early efforts at bipartisan policymaking were not particularly successful.[1] In his first major legislative test, his economic stimulus proposal, Obama managed to get all of three Republican votes in the Senate and none in the House of Representatives.[2]

Numerous political observers have linked partisan polarization to deeper cultural divisions within American society. Sociologist James Davison Hunter was the first scholar to put forth the notion that America was riven by deeply rooted political and cultural differences:

> The heart of the culture war argument was that American public culture was undergoing a realignment that, in turn, was generating significant tension and conflict. These antagonisms were playing out not just on the surface of social life (that is, in its cultural politics) but at the deepest and most profound levels, and not just at the level of ideology but in its public symbols, its myths, its discourse, and through the institutional structures that generate and sustain public culture.[3]

An especially memorable partisan expression of Hunter's culture war thesis came in the form of a speech by Patrick Buchanan at the 1992 Republican convention, where he said, among other things:

> The agenda Clinton and Clinton would impose on America—abortion on demand, a litmus test for the Supreme Court, homosexual rights, discrimination against religious schools, women in combat—that's change, all right. But it is not the kind of change America wants. It is not the kind of change America

needs. And it is not the kind of change we can tolerate in a nation that we still call God's country . . .

My friends, this election is about much more than who gets what. It is about who we are. It is about what we believe. It is about what we stand for as Americans. There is a religious war going on in our country for the soul of America. It is a cultural war, as critical to the kind of nation we will one day be as was the Cold War itself. And in that struggle for the soul of America, Clinton & Clinton are on the other side, and George Bush is on our side. And so, we have to come home, and stand beside him.[4]

To be sure, not all analysts share the Hunter/Buchanan position that America is fundamentally divided over political and cultural issues. In their acclaimed book *Culture War? The Myth of a Polarized America*, political scientist Morris Fiorina and his colleagues accept the notion of a major divide between partisan elites, but they do not believe that this extends to the mass public.[5] Most Americans, they believe, are somewhere in the middle on the leading political and cultural issues, which means that their true preferences are not reflected in the choices presented to them by partisan elites. In this book we will argue that American political parties represent sharply different values, policies, and constituencies, that the American public recognizes these sharp differences, and that this partisan polarization runs deeply into the electorate. We will also argue that there are many reasons to believe that the current state of party politics is healthy for the American republic.

Political parties exist to win elections; thus fierce competition between parties should be expected. Rival parties offering contrasting positions on vital issues of public policy is an essential element of a functioning democracy. Most voters need the kind of guidance that contending parties provide in order to make sense out of the choices they are offered in elections. Although citizens are turned off by public displays of personal animosity by politicians, they also want and expect elected officials to vote their consciences and to stand up for the political principles and policy positions they espoused during election campaigns.[6] Whether they recognize it or not, people's attitudes and beliefs about politics and politicians contribute to political conflict. Without conflict there is no meaningful democracy.

The logic of conflict expansion and its relationship to democracy is explained cogently and persuasively by political scientist E. E. Schattschneider.[7] He argues that politics is much like a street fight: it attracts attention and draws people in. Soon the original combatants get lost, as those in the audience become participants. Conflict is contagious, and the outcome of political battles is ultimately determined by the size of the contending sides, or the "scope of conflict." Thus most of politics is about trying to draw more people into the fray to change the balance between the winning and losing sides. If a political system is open, and thus democratic, conflicts should expand to the point that anyone who wants to participate will have a chance to do so. Often those with political power try to limit the scope of conflict to maintain their competitive advantage. For example, white Southerners prevented black Southerners from voting for many years as part of an effort to stop them from gaining the political power necessary to change their situation of oppression. A similar analysis can be used to explain most of the great political battles in American history, which basically involve some interests (usually powerful ones) trying to "privatize" conflict, while others (aspiring interests) try to "socialize" it. For Schattschneider, conflict expansion and democracy are synonymous, and political parties are the primary engines of conflict expansion.

If political conflict among major parties is essential to democracy, what does this say or imply about polarization? Using standard definitions of the two terms, polarization would appear to be an extreme form of conflict—one in which political actors congregate at opposite ends (or poles) of political or ideological spectrums.[8] And, while the image of increasing congregation at the extremes does fit many aspects of contemporary politics, not every important political battle in American government is a reflection of a state of polarization. However, the thrust of our argument, which we support with copious amounts of data, is that the political differences among Americans are real and important, and the parties have captured (perhaps exploited) these differences in ways that are understandable to most citizens.

Political Parties and American Democracy

E. E. Schattschneider, who was perhaps the best known political science expert on political parties in his day, is often quoted as stating, "Political parties created democracy, and modern democracy is unthinkable save in terms of political parties."[9] What Schattschneider had in mind in making this assertion are the crucial functions parties perform in democratic political systems. These functions distinguish parties from all other political actors in fundamentally important ways.

First, political parties serve as integrative agents for the electorate. This means that they help citizens and groups to band together in broad coalitions to pursue their mutual interests. Since the days of Alexis de Tocqueville (circa 1830) Americans have been known for their propensity to form groups, or "associations," to protect and/or advance specialized interests.[10] The multiplicity of groups in this country tends to fragment, rather than integrate, the political community. Parties provide the most important and effective counterforce to the tendency toward fragmentation. For the contemporary Republican party, this means bringing together religious and socially conservative groups, who are primarily interested in issues such as abortion, gun control, and gay marriage, with big and small business interests for whom taxes and government regulatory policy are the most important concerns. For Democrats the integrative task involves linking blue collar workers/unions with certain professionals, especially teachers and lawyers, and with liberal cause groups, such as those interested in civil rights, women's rights, and environmental protection. In Chapters 2 and 3 we examine the constituent parts of each party in some detail.

Second, and perhaps most fundamentally, parties serve as electors. This is the sine qua non of their existence; parties that cannot elect their own to public office soon disappear. National, state, and local party organizations try to identify promising candidates around the country to run for elected positions, and then try to help such candidates in a variety of ways. This help includes everything from supplying them with consultants, who conduct polls and develop media advertisements, to providing them with money, which can be given directly to candidates or spent indirectly on their behalf.[11] Although the literature on American elections emphasizes the "candidate centered" nature of the electoral process and the limited control that party organizations have over who runs for office under their labels around the country, both major parties have developed elaborate machinery for helping their candidates win office (see Chapter 4). Much of this machinery is devoted to establishing a connection between voters and candidates. In recent elections, most Democratic and Republican candidates have staked out discernibly different positions on the key issues of the day, which has enabled large numbers of voters to make rational decisions about which candidate they prefer. Parties are by far the most important source of voting cues for the average voter. We will explore this connection in depth in Chapter 2.

Third, parties play a central role in the governing process. After the election results are tallied, and legislatures and chief executives set out to organize themselves to conduct business, the influence of party in these organizing decisions is pervasive. At the national level, the party organizations in the House and Senate are the backbones of their respective institutions. Voting on all matters of organization, such as who will be Speaker of the House and who will chair the legislative committees, goes strictly along party lines. The leaders of the majority party are the most powerful actors in each institution; and the different facets of the legislative process, from committee/subcommittee deliberations to floor voting, are heavily influenced by, if not controlled by, the majority party leadership (particularly in the House). In recent years, Republicans and Democrats have shown an increasing tendency to vote in unison, or near unison, on key policy matters. Much the same is true in many state legislatures.[12] On the executive side, the nominations and appointments presidents and governors make to high-level positions in their administrations, and to the judiciary, go overwhelmingly to members of their party. Not surprisingly, the relationship between legislatures and chief executives is dominated by partisan considerations. The role of parties and partisanship in the governing process is analyzed in Chapter 5.

A Brief History of Political Parties in the United States

The history of political parties in the United Sates is usually told by identifying five (or six) different party systems that have held sway at different points in time.[13] The first party system, which emerged during George Washington's presidency (1789–1797) featured the debate over Alexander Hamilton's (Secretary of Treasury under Washington) various initiatives for building up our new nation. Hamilton's program consisted of instituting protective tariffs to protect America's fledgling industry from British imports; an ambitious set of public works projects to facilitate trade, transportation, and western expansion; the development of a strong military for protection against hostile foreigners; and the establishment of a sound currency policy by instituting a National Bank and paying off Revolutionary War debts. These initiatives were opposed by southern and agricultural interests led by Thomas Jefferson and James Madison, who argued for limited government (laissez faire) and states' rights. Washington's and Hamilton's group were known as the Federalists, Jefferson's as the Republicans (or Democratic-Republicans).

By the early 1800s, Jefferson's party dominated, although once in power (under presidents Jefferson, Madison and Monroe) they retained many of Hamilton's programs. The Federalists faded out of existence by 1816, and the Democratic-Republicans enjoyed one-party rule until 1824. Modern-day Democrats trace their roots to Jefferson's party, even though the party did not drop the "Republican" part of its name until the 1820s. Neither of these early parties had much of a grassroots base or public following; they were largely elite-level organizations.

The second party system ran from 1824 to just before the Civil War. The key figure in the early part of this period was Andrew Jackson, who is generally credited with opening up national politics to rank and file voters, especially those residing in states outside of the Atlantic seaboard. Jackson whipped up, and then rode, popular resentment against the "Eastern aristocrats" to the presidency in 1828. He then teamed with his vice president, Martin Van Buren, to build the first truly national political party in the country's history. Their party-building efforts culminated in the staging of the first national political party convention, held in Baltimore in 1832 (to renominate Jackson for president). Another important manifestation of "Jacksonian democracy" was that more and more states opened up voting eligibility in presidential elections to white male citizens, thus creating a national electorate. (Prior to this, most states chose their Electoral College delegations by vote of the state legislature.) The percentage of the eligible electorate voting in presidential elections rose from around 20 percent in 1820 to more than 75 percent by 1840.[14]

The opposition to the Democrats, the Whigs, led originally by Henry Clay and Daniel Webster, succeeded in winning the presidency on two occasions: the elections of 1840 and 1848. The campaign of 1840 was quite colorful, with the Whigs promoting their candidate William Henry Harrison, the hero of the Battle of Tippecanoe, as a man of the people against incumbent President Martin Van Buren, whom they accused of rampant corruption. The public pageantry that accompanied this campaign was very elaborate.[15] Harrison, of course, died shortly after taking office. In 1848, the Whigs nominated another war hero, Zachary Taylor, who beat Democrat Lewis Cass. (The ever persistent Martin

Van Buren ran as the nominee of the newly created Free Soil Party, but received few votes.) The Whigs stood for many of the same policies as Hamilton, thus favoring northern commercial interests over southern agricultural interests. Neither party knew exactly what to do with the most important and explosive issue of the era: slavery.

The third party system was mainly about the emergence of the Republican Party as a dominant national political force. The Republicans began in 1854 as a party unified in opposition to the expansion of slavery outside of the South. This position was unacceptable to Southern Democrats, and when Abraham Lincoln was elected to the presidency in the 1860, the Civil War broke out. During and after the Civil War, the Republicans were able to consolidate and hold power over national government until 1876. In the famous election of 1876, Democrat Samuel Tilden won the popular vote over Republican Rutherford B. Hayes, but eventually lost the presidency when the Electoral College votes from several Southern states were disputed, and a specially appointed electoral commission voted for Hayes strictly along party lines. Democrats in Congress finally agreed to this outcome after they made a deal with Republicans to accept the Hayes presidency in exchange for a pledge to end Reconstruction by removing U.S. troops from the South.[16] Perhaps the most significant outcome of this agreement was that white Southerners were able to deny Black Americans in the South the civil rights and voting rights they had supposedly been guaranteed by the Fourteenth and Fifteenth amendments, which Republicans had passed during their period of dominance following the war.

For most of the remainder of the nineteenth century the two major parties, Democrats and Republicans, were fairly evenly matched at the national level. Republicans won three of five presidential elections (Hayes in 1876, Garfield in 1880, and Benjamin Harrison in 1888) and controlled the Senate for eight of the ten Congresses (45th through 54th). Democrats had a majority in the House of Representatives in eight out of the ten Congresses, and elected Grover Cleveland to the presidency twice (in 1884 and 1892).

During the latter part of the nineteenth century, and continuing into the twentieth century, party politics revolved around the activities of organizations known as "party machines," which existed in most large cities in the United States, including New York, Boston, Philadelphia, Pittsburgh, and St. Louis.[17] The machines were built on the backs of newly arrived immigrants from Europe who welcomed the favors—in some cases even the employment—the machine politicians offered in exchange for political loyalty. Exploiting this loyalty, machine "bosses" could control elections in municipalities around the country, and then use their access to public officials to create even more benefits for their followers. The machines, and a group of super-rich industrialists called "Robber barons," were two sources of extensive corruption that typified the politics of the late nineteenth-century America. Two new movements arose in reaction to this unchecked power and corruption: the Populist Movement and the Progressive Movement. The former included mostly farmers and had a strong base of support within the Democratic Party; the latter harnessed the energies of urban, white, middle-class activists and eventually made deep inroads into both parties.

The Populists argued most vociferously for currency reform: in particular the coinage of silver, which would have moved the country from having one currency standard (gold) to having two (gold and silver). The basic idea was to make more currency available to farmers who suffered from chronic debt in an era of gold standard–induced deflation. The other major villain (besides bankers) in the Populist world was the railroad industry, whose pricing policies (long haul versus short haul) were widely viewed as being detrimental (even discriminatory) to farmers. The Populists called for government regulation of railroad pricing policies to correct these problems. (The Interstate Commerce Act was enacted in 1887.)

The Populists formed their own party, held a national convention in 1892 and nominated their own presidential candidate (James Weaver), who got more than 1 million votes (9 percent) in the presidential election. Populists then fell into disarray as the Northern and Southern wings of the movement split apart, largely over whether African Americans should be included. However, agrarian/Populist elements still had enough strength within the Democrat Party to nominate one of their own, William Jennings Bryan, for president in 1896, 1900, and 1908. He lost all three elections. Republicans encouraged fear of many Populist reform proposals, especially those dealing with monetary policy, and were eventually able to gain political control in most Northern states. Still Populists should be given credit for being the first large national movement that eschewed laissez-faire in favor of an active role for government in promoting social welfare.[18]

The Progressive Movement struck consistently, and for the most part successfully, at the heart of machine politics—patronage, rigged elections, public corruption, etc. One of their most effective innovations was the introduction of the so-called Australian ballot in voting precincts around the country. This allowed citizens to vote in privacy with ballots that listed all candidates of both parties, rather than being forced to make a public decision about which party to take a ballot from (only one per voter) as they entered the polling area. Many other election reforms followed, such as the use of primary elections, rather than party conventions, to select party nominees for important offices; making various local elections nonpartisan, so party labels did not appear next to candidates on ballots; and the introduction of additional electoral tools for citizens, including initiatives, referenda, and recall elections. Another very important Progressive success was the enactment of civil service reform at the national level (the Pendleton Act of 1883) and in many states and municipalities.[19]

Progressives also sponsored and eventually enacted several important constitutional amendments, including those that legalized federal income taxes (Sixteenth), brought about the direct election of senators (Seventeenth), and guaranteed women's suffrage (Nineteenth). Indeed, by the first and second decade of the twentieth century the Progressive Movement had become so pervasive that almost any politician, regardless of party, with national political aspirations called himself a Progressive. Presidents as different in outlook and philosophy as Theodore Roosevelt and Woodrow Wilson shared the Progressive profile.[20]

The fourth party system (1896–1932) was a by-product of the events just described, especially the success of Progressives in breaking the monopoly power of the party machines (most of which were Democratic and operated in Northern urban areas), and the split between Northern and Southern Populists. One of the defining features of the fourth party system was Republican control of national politics (Democrats held the South). Republicans elected presidents McKinley (in 1896 and 1900), Roosevelt (in 1904), Taft (in 1908), Harding (in 1920), Coolidge (in 1924), and Hoover (in 1928); and maintained majorities in both houses of Congress during most of this period. The only Democratic interlude (1912–1920) was in part a result of Republican in-fighting. Theodore Roosevelt decided he didn't like the way his successor, William Howard Taft, was governing. After losing the Republican nomination to Taft, he formed his own Progressive or "Bull Moose" Party and ran for president in 1912 against Taft and Woodrow Wilson. Roosevelt got more votes than Taft, but Wilson won. Democrats also secured majorities in both houses of Congress for the first six years of Wilson's two-term presidency. Of course, the seminal event of the Wilson presidency was America's entry into World War I.

An aspect of progressive reforms and Republican dominance during this period of American political history that political scientists like to point out is the fact that voter turnout in presidential elections declined from around 80 percent in the 1880s to roughly 60 percent in the 1920s because of registration and other voting requirements, and the reduced role of parties in elections.[21] Of course, one has to wonder how many of the 80 percent of those considered eligible, who the parties delivered to the polls in late nineteenth century, were actually voting legally.

Parties in the Twentieth Century: The New Deal to Great Society

The Great Depression was perhaps the most important development of the twentieth century. Herbert Hoover and Republicans in Congress were unable to formulate an effective response to the economic downturn that followed the stock market crash in 1929, and they were swept from power in 1932 by Franklin D. Roosevelt and large Democratic majorities in both houses of Congress. With the national unemployment rate hovering around 25 percent, and unemployment rates in many cities reaching nearly 50 percent, the challenges facing Roosevelt and his Democratic team were immense.[22]

They responded first with short-term relief programs, followed by large public employment programs; they also enacted numerous long-term structural change policies including Social Security, unemployment insurance, agricultural price supports, labor relations laws, rural electrification projects, and others. The laissez-faire approach that had characterized federal government policy since Jefferson was finally set aside in favor of Roosevelt's "New Deal," with one result being enormous growth in the size and scope of the federal government. Although economic historians still debate the ultimate effectiveness of New Deal programs and policies as remedies for the ailing economy of the 1930s (unemployment rates remained high, roughly 15 percent, through the late 1930s), there is general agreement among political scientists that the New Deal brought about permanent changes in the nature of government and government policy in the United States.[23]

The fifth party system in the United States was all about Roosevelt's "New Deal Coalition," which would dominate national politics for most of the rest of the century. This new and invigorated Democratic Party coalition included white Southerners, for whom the Civil War legacy of the Republican Party still loomed large, and who benefited greatly from many New Deal programs; Catholics and Jews in large, Northern cities; union members, who grew rapidly in number at this time; poor people, including small farmers and African Americans; and intellectuals with liberal values. This was the political base that emboldened Roosevelt and congressional Democrats to institute numerous groundbreaking programs and policies. Over time the conflicts and tensions (especially between white Southerners and the others) embedded in this coalition would lead to its demise, or at least to its transformation, but it held together pretty well from the 1930s to the early 1960s. The experience of economic depression, World War II, and postwar prosperity engendered deep loyalty to Roosevelt, the New Deal, and the Democratic Party in many citizens.

The vulnerabilities of the New Deal coalition became apparent to many in the period following World War II. Republicans parlayed unhappiness with the Truman administration, some of which even came from labor unions, into majorities in the House and Senate after the midterm election of 1946. This helped to reestablish them as full rivals to the Democrats in national politics. Any lingering doubt about Republican competitiveness was laid to rest with the election and reelection of Dwight Eisenhower in 1952 and 1956. At the governance level, the 1950s was a period in which a bipartisan force known as the "conservative coalition" was very formidable, if not dominant. Conservative Southern Democrats would often join with conservative Republicans in Congress to either block progressive legislation or promote conservative policies in areas such as civil rights, labor relations, health care, and foreign and defense policy.

The conservative coalition had actually been an important factor in national politics since the late 1930s (most of Roosevelt's key New Deal policies were passed in his first term), but it drew increasing attention in the 1950s and 1960s. Indeed, the failure of the parties to deliver a coherent set of policies in the aftermath of national elections led the American Political Science Association (APSA) to issue a report entitled "Toward a More Responsible Two-Party

System" in 1950.[24] The thrust of the report was that American parties were failing to carry out their essential function in a democratic society because they were not presenting the public with clear, competing choices about national policy, and they were not delivering on the policies they had promised after a majority of the public had chosen one party over the other in a national election.

Before and after the publication of the APSA report, many of the writings of party scholars, journalists, and even politicians made these same points. The basic argument was that responsible or "strong" parties should have the internal means and mechanisms (conventions, primaries, caucuses, etc.) for developing coherent policy platforms and selecting candidates who will run for office based on the issue positions called for in the platform. If elected to office in sufficient numbers to control the legislature, party members were then expected be able to work together with enough cohesion to turn their electoral success into a set of policies that mirrored the platform. This would give the public a chance to experience those policies and express its reaction to them at the next election. This type of party system (very much like the British parliamentary model) was thought by many to represent the most effective kind of democracy a large, modern nation-state could be expected to have.

Judged against this standard, American parties have usually been found to be wanting, and thus they are described as "weak" or irresponsible. Major party platforms are often vague or silent on key policy questions, most candidates around the country are selective about which platform positions they support, and once in office policymakers do not work systematically to enact their party's platform. This was certainly the prevalent view of American parties in the 1950s through the 1970s. The tendency toward weakness notwithstanding, scholars do recognize two twentieth-century episodes in which the Democratic Party acted in the strong party mode: Roosevelt's New Deal (1933–1936) and Lyndon Johnson's "Great Society" (1965–1966). In both cases, sweeping programs of breakthrough policies were put in place by a president, acting in concert with a large majority of his party in Congress, after decisive victories in national elections.

Johnson's Great Society was a political "Perfect Storm," at least from a Republican perspective. With the nation still in shock after John Kennedy's assassination, and Johnson running as an incumbent president with solid political strength in the South, Democrats crushed the Republicans in the national election of 1964. Johnson received 61 percent of the popular vote and 90 percent of the Electoral College vote, as Goldwater won in only six states (five Southern states and Arizona). Of equal or greater importance was the Democrats' sweep of Congress: their majority in the House in 1965 was 295–140, and in the Senate it was 68–32 (both more than two-thirds).[25] Furthermore, there was a mandate (the "Great Society" and "War on Poverty"), much of which had been handed down to Johnson from Kennedy. That mandate was to help those left behind by the otherwise prosperous post–World War II economy. This included African Americans, who sought both civil rights and antipoverty policies; and several other categories of poor Americans, including young people, the unemployed, the rural poor, and the elderly.

Unelected President Johnson and a Democratic Congress had a good deal of success in launching the War on Poverty and Great Society in 1964 when they passed the Civil Rights Act of 1964, the Economic Opportunity Act, the Food Stamp Act, and others. After the election, the floodgates burst with the enactment of legislation that created new and very significant programs such as Medicare and Medicaid, the Elementary and Secondary Education Act (ESEA—currently No Child Left Behind) and the Voting Rights Act of 1965. In addition, existing programs, most notably Social Security, were amended several times during this era to increase benefits and coverage to both the elderly (in the main Social Security program, Old Age Survivors and Disability Insurance or OASDI) and to the nonelderly poor, more and more of whom received cash assistance from the main welfare program of the day known as AFDC (Aid to Families with Dependent Children).[26] In retrospect, the magnitude of this policy undertaking, much of which was not fully appreciated at the time, was truly phenomenal.

The Great Society and War on Poverty soon generated many critics, especially among Republicans. The essence of much of the criticism was that Johnson and Congress had done too much too fast, and that the new programs would lead to higher taxes and larger deficits without solving the problems for which they were created. Democrats lost nearly fifty seats in the House in 1966 midterm elections, and Republican Richard Nixon won the presidency in 1968 and again in 1972. Indeed, much of what we have experienced in national politics since the Great Society has been a series of reactions to its programmatic and fiscal legacies. It is worth remembering, however, that the national poverty rate in the late 1950s and early 1960s was persistently above 20 percent, and that it declined rapidly in the late 1960s to the 12 to 15 percent range, where it has remained ever since. Policies enacted in the Johnson era, especially changes to Social Security, were largely responsible for this decrease in the poverty rate. War on Poverty engineers understood the so-called cycle of poverty and directed their efforts at treating all aspects of poverty from education, to employment, to housing, to health care, to income support, to economic development. Many of the programs spawned at this time, including Medicare and Medicaid, Food Stamps, Head Start, and ESEA have survived repeated attacks, and have long constituted part of the core of America's social safety net.

Party Decline and Resurgence: Sixth-Party System?

The Great Society, though very potent, was short-lived, and the political era that followed was one that was widely considered to not be good for political parties. The dominant theme in the political science literature on parties in the 1970s was one of "decline."[27] The weak or irresponsible parties of the 1950s were now said to have sunk even lower, failing ever more miserably against the standard (or ideal) of how strong or responsible parties should behave in a democratic society. The causes and symptoms of this decline were multiple and various.

First, party organizations (national and state party committees) were experiencing a diminishing role in the decisions about who would run for office under their labels. This was caused in part by reforms initiated mainly by Democrats (led by George McGovern) in the aftermath of their tumultuous national convention in Chicago in 1968. These reforms opened up the presidential candidate selection process to ordinary voters by imposing requirements that led most states to institute primary elections, as opposed to using state conventions, to choose delegates (pledged to candidates) for the national nominating convention. State decisions to hold presidential primaries affected the Republicans as well as the Democrats. In the 1950s and 1960s, fewer than twenty states held presidential primaries, by 1980 more than thirty states held them, and most other states used party caucuses, which were also open to the rank and file.[28] Taken as a whole, these reforms took power and influence over the presidential candidate selection process away from party leaders and professionals, while empowering activists and ordinary party members. The choice of McGovern by Democrats in 1972, and his subsequent resounding defeat, led many to question whether intraparty democracy was actually an asset for a party that sought to field competitive candidates in general elections.

Second, parties were losing their role in the staffing of major national campaigns. Beginning with Richard Nixon's formation of the Committee to Re-elect the President (CREEP) in 1971, presidential candidates, and more and more congressional candidates, formed their own campaign committees, rather than relying on state or national party organizations for campaign work. By the end of the decade candidate campaign committees were nearly universal, and recognized as such in campaign law. The Federal Election Campaign Act (FECA), as amended in 1974, set up regulations for how, and in what amounts, individuals, groups, and parties could contribute to campaigns of candidates, thus clearly placing the campaign committees of candidates at the center of the electoral process.

Third, parties were no longer an important conduit of political information. Voters were relying increasingly on television for political news, and the voice of the party was difficult to discern over the rest of the political chatter for all but the most committed partisans. It is interesting in this context to look back upon American politics in the early nineteenth century (from Jefferson to Jackson) when many newspapers were owned or controlled by political parties, and these party mouthpieces were vital sources of political information for citizens.

Fourth, parties were losing their role as financers of political campaigns. FECA set forth provisions that enabled parties to contribute directly to the campaigns of candidates, and to "coordinate" a limited amount of spending with candidates, but it also legalized a way for interest groups to channel money to candidates through the formation of "Political Action Committees" (PACs). By the late 1970s, PACs were playing a bigger role than parties in the financing of congressional campaigns.[29] In addition, FECA's creation of a public financing scheme for presidential elections marginalized the parties in this arena as well. These four changes, taken together, were a major part of the shift in the United States toward "candidate-centered" as opposed to "party-centered" elections.

On the citizen side of the equation, party decline revealed itself in several forms. First, more citizens began to describe themselves as "Independents" rather than identifying with the Democratic or Republican parties. From 1950 to 1965, surveys found that on average about 22 percent of the electorate identified themselves as Independents. Between 1965 and 1980 Independents rose to about 35 percent of the electorate. Second, those who did identify with the major parties showed a weakened connection with their party. Using these same two time periods (1950–1965 and 1965–1980), those who described themselves as "strong," rather than "weak," Democrats or Republicans decreased from an average of about 36 percent to about 26 percent.[30] Third, this weakened partisanship translated itself into voting behavior. The percentage of the electorate who voted for national candidates (presidential, House, and Senate) from different parties in the same election rose from an average of around 15 percent in the 1960s to roughly 25 percent in the 1970s and 1980s.[31] All of this, combined with high levels of public distrust of the parties,[32] led to a pretty bleak picture of party health by the late 1970s.

By the end of the 1970s, with FECA having been in place for about five years, the prevailing view was that the combination of public financing for presidential elections and the encouragement the law gave to interest groups to form PACs, ended up favoring candidates and interest groups over political parties in the financing system. One indicator of this was the rapid rise in the number of PACs, the growing amount of money PACs were spending in elections, and the increasing reliance of some congressional candidates, especially House candidates, on PAC contributions to finance their campaigns.[33] Between 1975 and 1985, the number of PACs rose from around five hundred to more than four thousand, their spending went from less than $50 million to nearly $200 million, and their contributions to House candidates rose from an average of about 20 percent of the total amount such candidates raised to more than 35 percent.[34] Another indicator of imbalance in the system was the reduced role state and local party organizations played in the 1976 presidential election.

But the parties had sympathetic observers in high places, and Congress came to the rescue in 1979 by adding a little-noticed provision to FECA that allowed parties to raise and spend unlimited amounts of money, from contributions that were also not limited in amount, for state and local "party building" activities. Such funds were quickly dubbed "soft money," and stood in contrast to "hard money," which was the limited and regulated public and private funds that individuals, PACs, and parties could contribute and spend in presidential and congressional elections.[35] Hard money was supposed to be the heart and soul of the FECA system; however, by the 1990s the flexibility (the Federal Election Commission was very lenient about what it allowed to qualify as a "party building" activity) and availability (especially in the form of large donations from wealthy individuals) of soft money made it the most talked about aspect of election financing. And, the ballooning amounts of soft money put the parties back in the middle of the action in both presidential and congressional elections.[36]

Although soft money was by no means the only factor that contributed to the reinvigoration of parties in the 1980s and 1990s, it did help to breathe new strength into party organizations throughout the country. At the national level, each party had a three-headed organization apparatus consisting of: *a national committee*, the Democratic National Committee (DNC), and the Republican National Committee (RNC); *a House campaign committee*, the Democratic Congressional Campaign Committee (DCCC), and the National Republican Congressional Committee (NRCC); and *a Senate campaign committee*, the Democratic Senate Campaign Committee (DSCC), and the National Republican Senatorial Committee (NRSC). During the 1980s and 1990s all of these organizations became bigger, more sophisticated and thereby more important in the overall electoral process. An appreciation for this growth can be gained by noting the changes in each organization's staffing levels over time. In the early 1970s, the two national committees had staffs of 30, while the congressional campaign committees on each side had staffs of fewer than 6. By 2000, the DNC staff had grown to 150, the RNC staff to 250; the smallest staff of a congressional campaign committee was DSCC at 40, the largest the DCCC and the NRSC at 75.[37]

The Republicans led the way toward party reinvigoration with new fund-raising techniques, in particular, carefully developed lists of likely donors. Initially these lists were used to collect large numbers of limited hard money donations, but later more specialized lists were employed to solicit large soft money donations. The Democrats were a little slow to catch on, but under the leadership of California Representatives Tony Coelho, Leon Pannetta, and Vic Fazio, the DCCC instituted some effective fund-raising tactics of their own.[38] Although the Republican committees enjoyed a fund-raising advantage throughout these two decades, the difference between the parties in this area gradually narrowed, especially after President Clinton came to the White House.[39]

As the 1990s unfolded, the national committees became more and more involved in congressional races around the country. This involvement started from the ground floor and extended all the way through the campaign and election process. Thus committee officials would identify and groom promising candidates for races they thought their party could win. They would then help these candidates by hosting seminars that taught them how to organize and run political campaigns and by supplying them with much needed up-front funding so that they could assemble a campaign staff, which, among other things, enabled these candidates to raise more money. National organizations also supplied technical expertise for polling constituents, putting together media ads, conducting "opposition research," and even developing basic campaign strategies. Funding for much of this came under FECA provisions allowing party organizations to make both direct contributions to candidates and "coordinated expenditures" on their behalf.[40]

By the late 1990s, the parties were also spending large amounts of money on "independent" activities designed to help all their candidates, but these could not be undertaken "in consultation" with any of the candidates' campaigns.[41] In both congressional and presidential elections party soft money, much of which was passed down to state party organizations, became a big factor in efforts to promote candidates (with signs, posters, and the like) and to contact and turn out voters in the days and weeks leading up to national elections. These activities also were not supposed to have been undertaken with the active involvement of candidates and/or their campaign committees.

State and local party committees also grew larger and more involved in fundraising, voter registration, and providing services to candidates during the 1980s and 1990s. In most states each major party has organization structures (normally called committees) that begin at the neighborhood or precinct level, rise to the city and/or county level, then to the congressional district level, and finally to the state "central committee" level. Many local organizations were very powerful in the machine era, while most of the state organizations were weak. By the 1970s, both the state and local party organizations were struggling, but there were signs of new energy, especially in Republican organizations in the South. By the 1990s, most state central committees had money, staff, and lots of work to do. State and local committees were also plugged into their national organizations in new and effective ways; and, while not exactly constituting a hierarchy, there was an important sense in which the party organizations from the national to the local level operated in unison in support of their candidates for national office.[42]

At the same time the parties were battling their way back into the processes of nominating, supporting, and electing candidates to public office, party leaders in Congress were gaining more power and influence over the legislative process. Much of this was caused by the perceived need among Democrats to form a common defense against the highly partisan policies and approaches of the Reagan administration. Reagan's twin successes in 1981, passing major income tax cut legislation and redirecting budget priorities away from social welfare spending and toward defense, set the stage for conflict over the budget for the remainder of his administration. Faced with rapidly growing deficits and repeated proposals from Reagan to balance the budget by cutting deeply into domestic social welfare spending, Democrats felt the need to band together to preserve cherished health, education, and income support programs they had instituted in the 1960s and 1970s. In addition, the Reagan administration's continuous attacks on environmental programs and polarizing judicial nominations, particularly the highly visible but ultimately unsuccessful nomination of Robert Bork for the Supreme Court, stoked partisan fires in Congress.

However, to be successful in acting as a unified front against Reagan's policies meant that congressional Democrats had to move away from the decentralized, committee-based legislative system that had served the reelectoral ambitions of their members so very well throughout the 1970s and adopt a more centralized, party-based approach to legislating. Speaker Jim Wright (Texas) is widely credited with having achieved notable advances in the power of the majority party leadership in the House in the late 1980s, but interestingly enough he soon found himself attacked and eventually brought down by a newly emerging Republican firebrand by the name of Newt Gingrich.[43] Since then intense partisan fighting over policy and appointments has typified the congressional process.

With the parties strengthening themselves as electoral organizations, and national political leaders (presidents, prominent members of Congress, and party chiefs) increasingly emphasizing partisan differences, it should come as no surprise that rank and file voters began to get the message. The same indicators that party decline proponents had used to argue that the parties had become irrelevant to large numbers of voters now began to point in the opposite direction. That is, beginning in the late 1980s and continuing to the present, voters were increasingly able to describe accurately the differences between the parties on policy matters, and held distinct images of the parties. These images, in a nutshell, were that the Republicans were conservative, antigovernment, favorable to big business/wealthy, strong on national security, supportive of tax cuts, and against abortion; Democrats were liberal, in favor of active government, aligned with the working class, and supportive of expanded health care, education spending, and environmental protection. The ability of voters to recognize differences between the parties led more and more of them to favor one party over the other (as opposed to being neutral toward the parties). In addition, straight party voting was on the rise, and the percentage of the electorate describing themselves as "strong" Democrats or Republicans returned to the levels registered in the 1950–1965 period.[44]

The resurgence of political parties in the United States is, perhaps, the most noteworthy political development of the late twentieth and early twenty-first centuries. As outlined above, this resurgence is in large part due to the parties' increasing propensity to stake out distinctive positions on the leading political issues of the day, which has enabled large numbers of citizens and groups to align themselves with one party or the other in order to both uphold shared political values and pursue commonly held policy objectives. Much of this has been driven by political elites—politicians and activists—at the state and national level who are genuinely at odds with one another across party lines, and who act with high levels of cohesiveness when they gain governmental power. By pitting broad coalitions with differing political views against one another, the parties offer voters fairly simple and understandable choices in elections.

Furthermore, this clarifying of party positions has been accompanied by a significant realignment, as white Southerners deserted the New Deal coalition in the 1970s and 1980s and relocated to the Republican Party. This, in turn, has resulted in the two national party coalitions becoming much more equal in size, which led to two extremely close presidential elections in 2000 and 2004. To be sure, the current partisan alignment is far from perfect, largely because a substantial portion of the public does not affiliate with either party. Indeed, the movement of white, male Southerners to the Republican Party and the enlarged number of Independents has led some party scholars to speculate that we may be in the midst of a sixth party system in the United States, one in which "dealignment" is a significant feature.[45] There is no real scholarly consensus on the question of whether the fifth party system, dominated by the New Deal Coalition, has actually given way to a sixth system; however, it is clear to us that the most common criticisms from the 1960s and 1970s—that the parties did not take distinctive stands on the issues and/or that they were ineffective in communicating their respective messages to voters—are no longer accurate.

It is also important to note that the parties face significant obstacles in attempting to accomplish their core mission in a large republic like the United States. State and regional diversity makes forming a cohesive national political coalition difficult, winner-take-all elections encourage candidates and parties to take centrist positions, and the separation of powers and check and balances at the national and state level make it difficult for elected officials to deliver on promised policies. All of these factors and forces favor inertia and status quo policy-making, which is often dispiriting to voters. Nevertheless, if the major political parties have become forces that emphasize conflict and the importance of the differences that elected officials of one party, as opposed to the other, bring to policy debates, we see some considerable value in this. It seems to us that American democracy in the twenty-first century has more to fear from widespread elite consensus than from genuine disputes over policy directions and values. Could it be that American democracy has rarely, if ever, been healthier?

Plan for the Book

The subsequent chapters are designed to follow up on the themes and developments introduced in this first chapter. Thus, Chapter 2 describes the "images" of the parties in some detail, examines the patterns of party identification in several ways, revisits the party decline and resurgence themes, compares the political attitudes of different types of partisans, and seeks to identify likely "opinion leaders" within the electorate. Chapter 3 examines in some depth the constituent parts of each major party, and looks at the effect of income and attitudes on cultural issues, such as abortion, on partisanship and on voting behavior. Chapter 4 looks at the midterm elections of 1994 and 2006, with special emphasis on the partisan nature of those elections. In Chapter 5 we analyze the role of partisanship in Congress, past and present, and how it affects the relationship between Congress and the president. Chapter 6 compares American political parties to those found in the other Anglo-American countries. Finally, Chapter 7 provides a brief description of the 2008 presidential election and early actions taken by the Obama administration and concludes by offering a series of observations about the current state of partisan relations.

CHAPTER 2

Parties and the Electorate I: Images of the Parties

Political parties, and what they stand for, are so much a part of American political rhetoric that they sometimes go almost unnoticed. For example, we have become so accustomed to the kinds of negative campaign ads run against Democrats and Republicans that we don't even have to inquire as to the party affiliation of the candidate being attacked. Democratic candidates are routinely scorned for being weak on defense, national security and terrorism; for wanting to tax middle-class voters to death and spend the money on wasteful programs that create large bureaucracies; and for trying to ban God from the classroom and/or undermine heterosexual marriage and the nuclear family. Republicans are attacked for catering to the rich and powerful; for wanting to turn back the clock on equal rights for African Americans, women, and other minorities; for never encountering a military weapons program they didn't like; for being insensitive to the needs and suffering of the poor and working class; and, most recently, for encouraging public fear of terrorists. Party labels don't need to be explicitly identified in these kinds of communications; everyone knows which attacks go with which party.

Much the same is true for the speeches given by politicians. Republican candidates almost always say something about tax cuts, the need for a strong defense, and the importance of religion and family. Democrats pitch their knowledge of, and sympathy for, the plight of ordinary Americans, the need to be welcoming, inclusive of people from all types of backgrounds and belief systems, and the belief that the government has an obligation to provide for the elderly and the sick. To be sure, politicians of both parties will try to align themselves with popular issues/themes associated with the other party—Republicans appeal to ordinary American "common sense," and Democrats invoke God and family—but these kinds of crossover statements are almost always appetizers or desserts, rather than the main course. Our point here is that the images the voters have of the parties, and their candidates, are deeply ingrained and widely understood, in part because they are what people are constantly exposed to by politicians and the media. These images form the heart and soul of American political discussion and debate. As much as many Americans decry the ugliness of partisan political warfare, it is hard to imagine what political discourse in this country would be like without it.

Party Images

To support our claim that images of the two major parties are recognized widely by citizens, we turn to the National Election Study (NES) series.[1] Most of the NES survey consists of closed-ended questions in which respondents are given a limited number of choices in answering questions posed by interviewers. For example, people are asked what they think about the level of spending in the Social Security program, with the answer options being "too high," "too low," or "about right." However, since 1952 the NES has asked a series of open-ended questions about the political parties. Respondents are first asked what they like about each party, and then what they dislike about each party. They can give up to five responses to each question, so a single respondent could offer as many as twenty observations about what he/she likes or dislikes about the parties. This gives researchers a treasure trove of raw data, but bringing coherence to these data certainly poses a challenge.

The advantage of open-ended questions in a survey is that they allow respondents to express their views freely, without prompting or cues from the interviewer. This makes it very unlikely that the responses obtained represent nonopinions.[2] On the other hand, with open-ended questions there is a much greater likelihood that respondents will be daunted by the prospect of offering numerous responses to a battery of questions and will opt to offer no response at all. It is also the case that the better educated people in the sample will be more likely than others to give answers to open-ended questions.[3] Taking all of this into account, we offer our summary and analysis of the open-ended party like/dislike data, which include some 114,000 responses given over a fifty-four-year period.

Table 2.1 displays the most commonly expressed (modal) images of each party, grouped by decade, starting with the 1950s.[4] These data show that a large proportion of respondents articulate similar images of the parties, that these images are distinct thus reflecting partisan differences, and that the most commonly articulated characteristics of each party capture nicely each party's respective identity. In the 2000s, for example, about 14 percent of respondents perceived the Democrats as pro–common/working man, while almost 20 percent of respondents offered an image of the Republicans as the party of the rich and big business. Taking into consideration the three modal images of each party since the 1990s, we find that citizens express a common portrait of the parties: the Democrats are for working people and the poor, they support government activity and social programs, and they are liberal; the Republicans are for big business and the rich, they are conservative, and they are antigovernment. In 2004, fully 15 percent of respondents offered at least one of these three images for each party.

Looking at the modal images over a longer stretch time, we see that voters have long perceived the Democrats as the party of the poor and working class, as a liberal party that sought to use government to solve social problems, but also as

TABLE 2.1 Modal Images of the Parties in Open-Ended Survey Questions

	Democrats	Republicans
1950s	Pro–common man/working people (22%) Express party loyalty (8%) Economic prosperity (8%)	Pro–big business/rich (15%) Dwight Eisenhower (11%) Spend less money (5%)
1960s	Pro–common man/working people (20%) Express party loyalty (11%) Spend more money (7%)	Pro–big business/rich (11%) Conservative (8%) View party as generally good or bad (6%)
1970s	Pro–common man/working people (14%) Liberal (6%) Pro-poor/needy people (5%)	Pro–big business/rich (15%) Conservative (8%) Richard Nixon (3%)
1980s	Pro–common man/working people (15%) Pro-poor/needy people (8%) Pro-government activity/aid (7%)	Pro–big business/rich (17%) Conservative (7%) For a strong military (7%)
1990s	Pro–common man/working people (12%) Pro-poor/needy people (8%) Liberal (8%)	Pro–big business/rich (16%) Conservative (8%) Against government activity/social programs (5%)
2000s	Pro–common man/working people (14%) For government activity/social programs (10%) Pro-poor/needy people (6%)	Pro–big business/rich (19%) Conservative (8%) Against government activity/social programs (7%)

Source: American National Election Studies.

a party that was somewhat prone to wasting public money. The Republicans have long been viewed as the party of big business and the wealthy, as a conservative (family values) party that opposed more aid for the poor while favoring tax cuts and balanced budgets. Republicans have also gotten a good deal of credit for being better at protecting the country from foreign enemies through its support of the military. In recent years, Democrats have been associated with the pro-choice position on abortion; Republicans with the pro-life position.[5] The percentage of the electorate articulating these distinct images of the parties decreased in the 1970s, but has increased since then, with the most noticeable upturn in the number of responses occurring in the 1990s.[6]

If one takes into account all the open-ended party like and dislike responses, there are certainly some that convey a misunderstanding of the parties—respondents who associate Republicans with pro-choice in the 1990s, for example. But the vast majority of the responses are consistent with the basic images of the parties outlined above, even if they are not expressed with great frequency.[7] The central finding that emerges from an analysis of this vast set of data is that party images are substantive, well established in the mind of the public, and fairly accurate. On this last point, compare our description of party images (above) to what a leading American Government textbook has to say about the parties: " . . . party labels still carry valuable information about candidates. . . . In general, Republicans tend to favor smaller, cheaper government; they advocate lower taxes, less regulation of business, lower spending on social welfare. They would be more generous only when it comes to the Defense Department. Democrats are more inclined to regulate business in behalf of consumers and the environment and more supportive of programs designed to improve domestic welfare; they would spend less on defense. Democrats are more concerned with "fairness" and equality, Republicans with letting free enterprise flourish. Republicans would ban abortion and gay marriage and allow official prayer in public schools; Democrats would not."[8] When it comes to describing what the parties stand for, it seems that voters and scholars agree.

This awareness of what the parties represent can be seen in two other sets of indicators. In 2000, the NES asked respondents not only whether they saw important differences between the parties but also to express, in open-ended format, what these differences were.[9] The most common (modal) responses with regard to party differences for 2000 are displayed in Table 2.2, and they echo our findings with respect to the open-ended party likes and dislikes. When asked to articulate differences between the parties, these are the most popular responses: Democrats support big government, Republicans prefer smaller government; Democrats are good for the common man, Republicans support big business; Democrats are liberal, Republicans are conservative; Democrats are pro-choice, Republicans are pro-life. Overall, 35 percent of the 2000 sample offered at least one of the modal differences presented in Table 2.2.

Finally, since 1984, the NES has asked respondents to place the parties on a 7-point ideological scale. In the 20-year period from 1984–2004, public awareness of ideological differences between the parties rose consistently. The proportion of Americans who correctly placed the Republicans to the right of the Democrats on this scale exceeded 75 percent in 2000 and 2004 (see Table 2.3). Similarly, the mean perceived difference between the two parties reached new highs (2.25 and 2.14) during these two presidential election years. In 2008, the perceived ideological differences between the parties blurred just a bit.

TABLE 2.2 Public Awareness of Party Differences, 2000

References to Democrats	Percentage of respondents
Democrats are for big government	8.0%
Democrats support abortion	6.7
Democrats are good for common man	5.1
Democrats are good for the people	4.6
Democrats are liberal	4.4
References to Republicans	
Republicans oppose big government	8.6%
Republicans are good for big business	8.5
Republicans are good for the wealthy	7.6
Republicans oppose abortion	7.4
Republicans are conservative	5.0

Source: American National Election Studies.

TABLE 2.3 Ideological Placement of the Parties, 1984–2008

	Places Republicans to Right of Democrats	Places Parties at Same Point on Scale	Places Republicans to Left of Democrats	Mean Difference on 7-Point Scale
1984	68.4%	11.0%	20.6%	1.52
1986	66.7	12.7	20.6	1.40
1988	70.9	10.0	19.1	1.73
1990	63.9	14.4	21.7	1.34
1992	72.7	11.7	15.7	1.94
1994	71.4	12.9	15.8	1.87
1996	74.7	8.9	16.4	1.94
1998	70.3	11.9	17.8	1.68
2000	78.6	9.1	12.3	2.25
2004	76.2	9.2	14.6	2.14
2008	71.4	11.6	17.0	2.07

Source: American National Election Studies.
Note: No data available for 2002 and 2006.

Party Identification

As pervasive as parties and partisanship are in American political life, one would think that defining partisanship would be rather easy. However, this is not necessarily the case. When systematic political science studies of the American electorate began, in the late 1940s and early 1950s, partisanship or party identification was thought to consist of a psychological attachment to a party, an affiliation that included a sense of loyalty to a party. This reflected the experience of many voters, especially Democrats, with the Depression and New Deal because such voters recognized and appreciated many tangible benefits that resulted from programs Roosevelt and Democratic Congresses created in the 1930s. They were grateful for these benefits and felt a sense of loyalty to the party that provided them. On the other side, many steadfast Republicans were struck by what they saw as the negative aspects of the Roosevelt era—new taxes, bigger government, more support for unions, etc. They resented the liberal drift of American policy and were committed to stopping it. Thus, loyalty, as a psychological attachment, was an important component of partisan identification for this age cohort.

The baby boom generation (1946–1964) did not experience nearly the same level of suffering and deprivation as the Depression and World War II generations. For most of the boomers, the Civil Rights Movement and the Vietnam War were the formative influences on their political thinking, and neither major party had an unambiguous stand on these issues. By the 1970s, the parties became important for some boomer voters because of the causes they supported (not the benefits they provided). For others, the parties served mainly as orienting devices, or as guides for determining which politicians were more likely to share their political beliefs and values. As this group got older and became a larger and more dominant force within the American electorate (in the 1980s and 1990s), the nature of partisanship also changed. It became less about loyalty/attachment and more about utility. Parties were valued because they made political choices simpler for voters, and because they provided avenues through which citizens could make demands. Gratitude and psychological loyalty were still around, but in significantly smaller quantities. Parties adapted to this new environment by marketing themselves aggressively to likely supporters.

The way the NES, and many other polling organizations, have measured partisan identification is fairly straightforward, and has been consistent over time. Survey respondents are asked first whether they think of themselves as a Democrat, a Republican, or an Independent. Those who respond by saying they are a Democrat or a Republican are then asked whether they consider themselves to be a "strong" or a "not very strong" Democrat or Republican. Those who answered the first question by declaring themselves to be an Independent are then asked whether they think of themselves as being "closer" to one party or the other. This set of questions yields the eightfold classification of partisans shown in Table 2.4.

TABLE 2.4 Party Identification, Presidential Election Years, 1952–2008

	1952	1956	1960	1964	1968	1972	1976	1980	1984	1988	1992	1996	2000	2004	2008
Strong Democrat	22%	21%	23%	27%	20%	15%	15%	18%	17%	18%	18%	19%	19%	17%	19%
Weak Democrat	25	23	24	25	25	26	25	23	20	18	18	20	15	15	15
Independent Democrat	10	6	6	9	10	11	12	11	11	12	14	14	15	18	17
Independent	6	9	9	8	11	13	14	13	11	11	12	9	12	10	8
Independent Republican	7	8	6	6	9	11	10	10	12	13	12	11	13	12	11
Weak Republican	14	14	14	14	15	13	15	14	15	14	14	15	12	13	13
Strong Republican	14	15	15	11	10	10	9	9	12	14	11	13	13	16	13
Apolitical	3	4	2	1	1	1	1	2	2	1	1	1	1	0	3
Democratic ID	57	50	53	61	55	52	52	52	48	48	50	53	49	50	51
Independent	6	9	9	8	11	13	14	13	11	11	12	9	12	10	8
Republican ID	35	37	35	31	34	34	34	33	39	41	37	39	38	41	37

Source: American National Election Studies.

Bearing in mind the way partisan identification is measured and defined, a very important point about partisanship and the electorate is clear at the outset. If all self-declared Independents are treated as falling outside the ranks of partisans, then the number and proportion of partisans has fallen rather significantly over the last fifty to sixty years. Indeed, Independents as a group would appear to outnumber both Democrats and Republicans in recent years. If, on the other hand, Independent partisans or "leaners" are included among the ranks of Democrats and Republicans the electorate looks largely partisan, as the percentage of "pure" Independents has always been fairly small (see bottom panel of Table 2.4). What is the best way of looking at the partisan landscape? Clearly, if psychological loyalty is thought to be a defining quality of partisans, Independents should not be counted among them. However, if parties are viewed mainly as sources of voting cues, then it may make sense to treat Independent leaners as partisans, at least for some analytical purposes.

Before examining the data in Table 2.4 in further detail, several additional observations about the nature of American political parties and partisanship in the late twentieth and early twenty-first centuries are in order. First, American political parties are rather odd entities in that all it takes to be a member of one is to say that you are, and/or to register as one. You don't have to pledge to believe anything, to pay any money, or to go to any meetings, and you can enter or leave whenever you want. Given that there are virtually no constraints on someone becoming a partisan, we should expect party members to exhibit widely varying degrees of commitment, loyalty, and affiliation to the party. On the loyal and committed end of the spectrum would be those who actually do go to meetings and are involved in national, state, or local party organizations (party activists). On the other end would be large numbers of people with relatively weak ties to their party.

Second, parties are not very popular with average citizens and voters. For example, a 2005 Harris Poll found that while distrust of political institutions was widespread among Americans (only 27 percent and 22 percent "tended to trust" the government and Congress, respectively), distrust of the parties was nearly universal: only 8 percent "tended to trust" them.[10] In an earlier paper, we likened the parties to the late comedian Rodney Dangerfield because they, like Rodney, "can't get no respect."[11] Most voters express the view that parties are inclined to confuse issues, promote conflict, and, when in power, to govern badly. Not surprisingly then, most Americans say they like to assess candidates independently of party affiliation.[12] Still, amid all the criticisms and protestations a very large percentage of the public associates itself, in one manner or another, with the parties and, as we will show, this association seems to have a direct and powerful effect on their voting behavior.

Third, there is a lot of appeal to declaring oneself to be an Independent. It fits with the American cultural value of being a free thinker, or at least someone who is not bound to accept the political thinking of someone else, especially a large organization. It is also a way of distancing oneself from the ugly sides of political business: fund-raising, attack ads, unappealing leaders within a party, confrontational legislative or executive governing tactics, etc. On a practical level, the main disadvantage of registering as an Independent would be the possibility that you would be prevented from voting in primary elections. However, most states do allow Independents to vote in party primaries; indeed, Independents often have the option of choosing the party primary in which they will vote, while many partisans do not.[13]

Returning to Table 2.4, several noteworthy trends and developments in partisan identification are evident. The first, as noted previously, is the steady growth in the proportion of Independents (all three categories); this group increases from just over 20 percent of respondents in the early 1950s, to 40 percent by 2000. The second most obvious trend is the decline in Democratic partisans, from roughly 50 percent of the NES sample in the 1950s and 1960s, to roughly 35 percent in recent years. A third less noticeable trend is the rather steady level of Republican partisans at 25 to 30 percent of the sample. Given the greatly expanded number of Independents, the Republican steady state is probably best read as signifying a slight increase in their ranks over time. The basic picture then is one of increasing numbers of Independents, decreasing numbers of Democrats, and Republicans holding steady or increasing slightly. A fourth and final trend shown in Table 2.4 is the dip and then rise in the percentage of "strong" partisans. This group falls from a high of roughly 38 percent in the 1960s to a low of 24 percent in 1976, but then rebounds to 32 to 33 percent since the mid-1990s.

As pointed out earlier, the big picture looks somewhat different if Independents with a partisan leaning are grouped with partisans (see bottom panel of Table 2.4). Using this type of grouping, we see the Democratic portion of the sample declining from a high of 61 percent in 1964 to a low of 48 percent in 1984–1988, but then leveling off at roughly 50 percent after 1992. The Republican share rises noticeably from a low of 31 percent in 1964 to a high of 41 percent in 1988, then holds pretty steady after that. Pure Independents fluctuate up and down around an average of 10 percent.

Which is the better picture of the electorate: the 34(D)–36(I)–26(R), or the 51(D)–37(R)–8(I)? (See Figure 2.1.) One way to make some headway on this question is to compare the voting behavior of partisans and Independent partisans in national elections since 1952 (see Figures 2.2a and 2.2b, and Appendix A.1). The key finding here is that the voting behavior of weak partisans and Independent partisans is pretty similar, especially among Republicans. When there are large differences between the two groups it is usually the Independent partisans who are more inclined than weak partisans to support the candidates of their preferred party, at least until recently. Take the election of 1960, for example. John F. Kennedy received 90 percent of the vote of Democratic leaners, but only 69 percent from weak Democrats. In 1988 nearly the same pattern occurred among Democrats, although this time the Republican candidate (George H. W. Bush) won the election (see figures in Appendix A.1).

Figure 2.1 Two Portraits of Party Identification, 2008

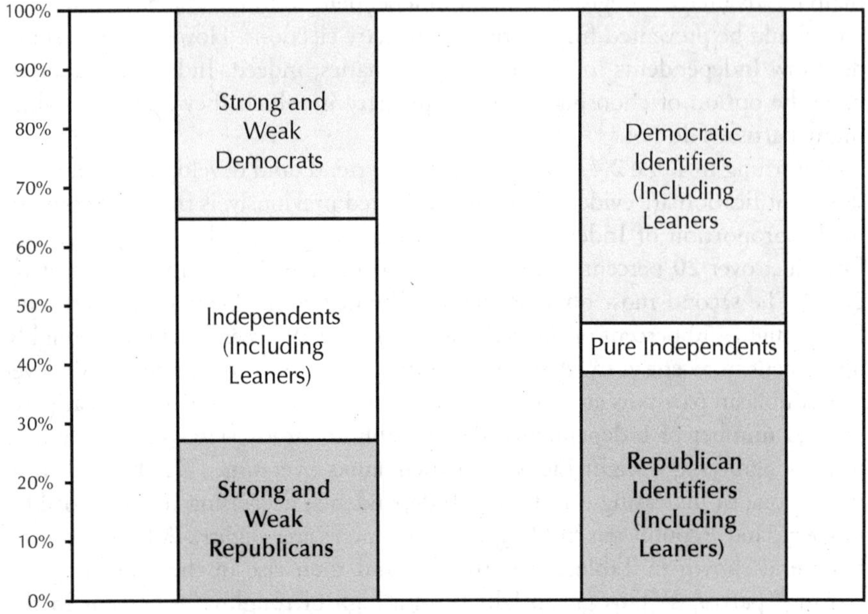

Strong and Weak Democrats	Democratic Identifiers (Including Leaners)
Independents (Including Leaners)	Pure Independents
Strong and Weak Republicans	Republican Identifiers (Including Leaners)

Source: American National Election Studies.

Most of the significant differences in the voting behavior of Independent partisans and weak partisans appear to be related to three intertwined trends and conditions. First, from the 1950s until the late 1980s, the Democrats (weak and leaners) were almost always less loyal partisan voters than were the Republicans (the exception being in 1964). This no doubt reflected the presence of a fairly large number of conservative Democrats (many of whom were white, male Southerners), who often voted for Republican presidential candidates (or George Wallace in 1968). Many of these conservatives left the party during the 1970s and 1980s, and the Democrats became a smaller, but more cohesive, party as a result. In the 1990s, the partisan loyalty of Democratic leaners and weak identifiers actually exceeded that of Republicans (the Ross Perot factor), while in the 2000 and 2004 elections, weak and leaning Republicans were slightly more loyal than their Democratic counterparts. In 2008, Democratic leaners voted for Obama at a very high rate.

A second factor that has contributed to significant disparities in the voting behavior of Independent partisans and weak partisans is the presence of particularly appealing or unappealing major party candidates. Barry Goldwater drove an unusually large number of weak Republicans (but fewer Republican leaners) to vote for Lyndon Johnson in 1964. A similar dynamic occurred in 1972, when the candidacy of George McGovern led many weak Democrats to vote for

Figure 2.2a Weak versus Independent Democrats

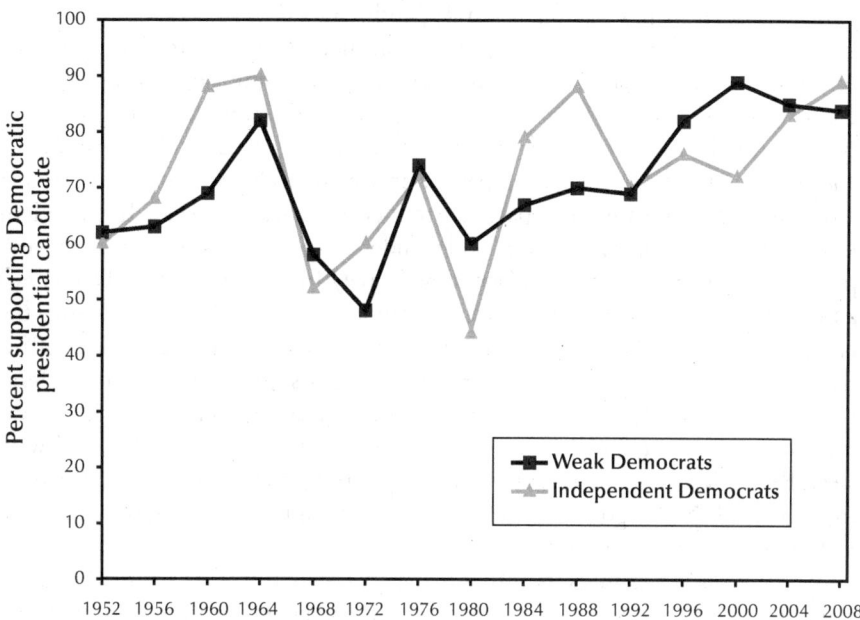

Source: American National Election Studies.

Figure 2.2b Weak versus Independent Republicans

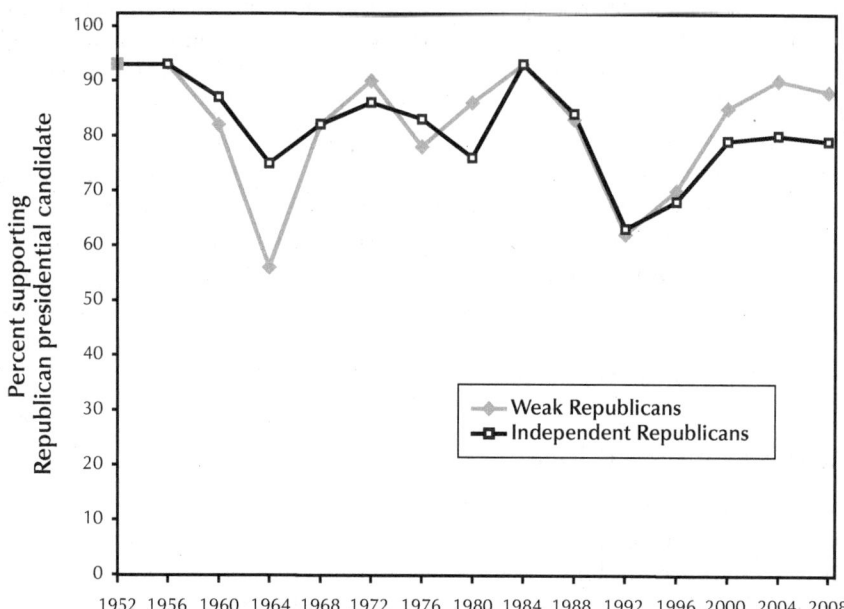

Source: American National Election Studies.

Richard Nixon. Ronald Reagan's success in 1980 and 1984 was a combination of his appeal to weak Democrats and his extraordinary popularity among Republicans of all stripes (see figures in Appendix A.1).

The third, and most interesting, condition that contributes to unusual voting patterns among partisan groups is the appearance of significant third party candidates (1968, 1980, 1992, 1996, and 2000; see bottom panel of Appendix A.1). This reduces the partisan voting of Independent leaners quite substantially and typically results in the voting pattern in which weak partisans are somewhat more likely to vote for their party's presidential candidate than Independent leaners. Still, the appeal of strong Independent candidates is often felt by weak partisans. In 1968, George Wallace drew heavily from Independent Democrats and Republicans, but also from weak Democrats, which helped to swing the election to Richard Nixon. John Anderson in 1980 was mainly a product of Independents (all three categories), with his strongest support coming from Democratic leaning Independents (Reagan won the election easily). Ross Perot was very popular among all kinds of Independents in 1992, but also did well with weak Republicans, which helped to swing the election to Clinton. In 2000, even though Ralph Nader got few votes, his candidacy did have significant appeal for Independents (of all varieties).

What this analysis suggests is that being an Independent, as opposed to a declared partisan, means something, but that meaning gets expressed most clearly when there is a viable Independent candidate in the election. In such circumstances, Independent voters are somewhat more inclined to vote for Independent candidates than partisan voters.[14] However, in presidential elections that boil down to a choice between the major party candidates, there is no consistent and/or significant difference in the voting behavior of Independent leaners and weak partisans. In fact, since 1952 the average loyalty of weak Republicans and Republican Independents has been exactly the same (81.6 percent); among Democrats, Independent leaners were 2 percent more loyal than weak partisans (71.6 percent compared to 69.9 percent). This analysis also makes it clear that partisanship is far from being everything in American elections. Although strong partisans of both parties are very loyal, weak partisans and Independents are clearly influenced by the qualities of candidates, the nature of the times, and other factors. To win a presidential election, a party must choose the right candidate, someone who has the ability to draw votes from weak partisans and leaners of the other party; or, at the very least, to avoid choosing the wrong candidate, someone who drives marginal partisans to the candidate of the other party.

Party Decline and Resurgence

As described in Chapter 1, the "decline" of American political parties has been a major theme of the political science literature since the 1970s. Those who have advanced the party decline thesis have relied on a series of NES indicators that measure the salience of parties among the mass public to make their case. We have taken these various indicators, updated through the 2008 election, and compiled them in Table 2.5. Careful inspection of the figures in the table reveals that the parties did go through a period of decline, which seemed to bottom out in the mid-1970s, but by roughly the mid-1990s all of the measures of partisan salience had strengthened and a partisan renewal in the minds of citizens ensued, which has continued through 2008.

We have reviewed one measure of the state of partisanship already (in Table 2.4): the percentage of the public who think of themselves as being strongly partisan. The size of this group declines noticeably from the 1950s to the 1980s, but then increases significantly after that. By 2002, one in three citizens identified as a strong partisan, compared to roughly 25 percent in the mid-1970s. In fact, on a four-point NES scale (strong partisans, weak partisans, Independent leaners, and pure Independents), strong partisan was the modal category from 2000 to 2008—marking the only times this has happened since the NES began measuring party identification in 1952 (see Table 2.4).

All of the other measures displayed in Table 2.5 follow a similar pattern. Looking at straight party voting, we see that since 1996 it has exceeded 80 percent in presidential and House elections, reaching levels close to those seen in the 1950s and 1960s. Also since 1996, perceptions of party difference have grown such that in 2004 and 2008 the proportion of Americans who saw important differences between the Democrats and Republicans (78 percent) was higher than it has been since the question was first asked by NES in 1952. That so many Americans now see important differences between the parties should come as no surprise given the intensity of partisan battles in Congress, and among party activists, from the 1980s to the present.

One of the main arguments made by party decline scholars had to do with the salience or relevance of the parties. Using the open-ended party like and dislike data (discussed previously), party decline advocates showed that a growing segment of the public seemed to be neutral about the parties.[15] For example, respondents would point out something they liked (or disliked) about both parties, and thereby not indicate a clear preference for one party over the other. Here again, party neutrality appears to have peaked in the mid 1970s. Since then a steadily increasing proportion of voters has been showing partisan preferences in their responses. In 2004, 36 percent of respondents were "positive-negative;" that is they made, on balance, positive assessments of one party and negative assessments of the other. In that same year, about a quarter of the sample was neutral toward both Republicans and Democrats. By way of contrast, in 1980 more than one-third of the respondents were neutral about the parties, while roughly a quarter showed a preference for one party over the other (see Table 2.5).

The NES introduced a new measure of partisan salience in 1978, which uses a "feeling thermometer" to gauge people's sympathies for one party or the other. These thermometers have an explicit point of neutrality—50 degrees, and thus may provide a more accurate reading of partisan neutrality.[16] We used the feeling thermometers to construct a second measure of neutrality and found that

TABLE 2.5 Indicators of Partisanship, 1952–2008

	Strong Partisan ID	Straight Ticket Voting	Important Differences between Parties	Likes/ Dislikes Positive-Negative	Likes/ Dislikes Neutral-Neutral	Feeling Thermom. Positive-Negative	Feeling Thermom. Neutral-Neutral
1952	36%	88%	50%	50%	13%		
1954	35						
1956	36	85		40	16		
1958	38			36	23		
1960	38	86	51	42	17		
1962	35						
1964	38	85	55	38	20		
1966	28						
1968	30	82	52	38	17		
1970	29						
1972	25	70	46	30	30		
1974	28						
1976	24	75	47	32	32		
1978	23			19	46	25%	25%
1980	27	72	58	27	37	33	16
1982	30			35	29	39	15
1984	29	75	63	31	36	35	16
1986	28		48	28	37	34	15
1988	32	75	60	34	30	35	16
1990	30		46	27	39	30	20
1992	29	78	60	35	31	42	13
1994	31		52	34	31	43	13
1996	32	82	65	35	28	49	10
1998	30					46	10
2000	32	82	67	36	26	43	12
2002	33						
2004	33	83	78	36	26	49	11
2008	32	81	78	NA	NA	51	12

Source: American National Election Studies.

from 1992 to the present, the proportion of "neutral-neutral" respondents was between 10 percent and 13 percent (compared to 26 percent using the open-ended measure); and more importantly, that the proportion of respondents who expressed a positive view of one party and a negative view of the other has averaged about 45 percent, reaching a high of 51 percent in 2008.

Of course, we are not alone in suggesting that the parties had become more salient to voters since the mid-1980s. Important studies have documented the increased impact of partisanship on voting behavior in both congressional and presidential elections and established a connection between this renewed sense of partisanship on the part of voters and partisan polarization among political elites.[17] Indeed, something resembling a new consensus has emerged among party scholars, which marks the Reagan administration as the beginning of a new era of American politics; an era in which bitter battles over policy (and nominations), contested largely along partisan/ideological lines, began to define the political landscape.[18] Beginning in the late 1980s and continuing through the 1990s, voters became more aware of the issue and ideological differences between the parties and established a higher level of consistency between their own issue and ideological preferences and those of the parties. Two events that accelerated this partisan differentiation process were the Gingrich-led revolution in 1994, and the Clinton impeachment in 1998.[19] Even though the policy and ideological battles may have been best understood and felt most intensely by political elites, it didn't take long for the battle lines to filter down to voters.[20] One simple, yet powerful, indicator of this filtering down is the fact that in 2004 straight ticket voting reached its highest level (of 83 percent) since 1964.

Voters, Issues, and Partisanship

Our goal in this chapter is to show that partisanship is a central element in a divide among the American electorate that has become the most important feature of American politics. We are not claiming that partisanship is more fundamental to this divide than genuine differences among citizens about the leading issues of the day. Indeed, we suspect that the issue and ideological differences are more fundamental because, as we have indicated above, the parties themselves and partisan conflict are not particularly appealing to most people. Nevertheless, parties are useful instruments for political leaders and citizen activists who are looking to mobilize a following, and for average citizens seeking to understand what all the hollering and bad feeling they see on TV is about. Large numbers of voters look to the parties as their basic political compass, which is rational because the parties and their candidates do represent importantly different political and governance viewpoints. The parties are crucial in helping people connect their political beliefs to choices among candidates that reflect those beliefs, and in this sense contribute mightily to democratic elections. Although many imperfections in this process remain, we believe the parties have become somewhat better at helping to clarify the political terrain for average voters in recent elections than in many past elections.

To examine the issue/ideological divide in American politics we assembled the information presented in Table 2.6. As we have shown in several of the preceding tables and figures, according to a variety of measures the low point in partisanship and partisan differences was the mid-1970s, so Table 2.6 compares the attitudes of the different categories of partisans on a series of issue and ideological indicators in 1976 (the heyday of decline), and in 2008 (period of party resurgence).[21] Looking first across categories, in 1976 strong Republicans, as expected, are consistently the most conservative group; however, strong Democrats are only slightly more liberal than Independent Democrats on most of the measures. Weak Republicans and Independent Republicans display similar attitudes on most of the issues, and the same is true, to a somewhat lesser degree, for the comparable categories of Democrats. By 2008, the Democrats had sorted themselves more like the Republicans, with strong Democrats being more liberal than Independent Democrats (and weak Democrats) in ideological self-placement and on all of the issues, except the role of women. (It should be noted that the variation across all the partisanship categories with regard to the role of women is not statistically significant in either 1976 or 2008, but that during this thirty-two-year period support for an equal role for women increased greatly.)

The key finding in Table 2.6 is that the differences between Democrats and Republicans of all varieties became much more pronounced between 1976 and 2008. Take ideological self-placement, for example. In 1976 the difference between strong Democrats and strong Republicans was 1.71 on a seven point scale with 4 as the midpoint. That is, strong Democrats placed themselves just left of center (3.61), while strong Republicans were decidedly conservative (5.32). By 2008, strong Democrats had become noticeably more liberal and strong Republicans even more conservative, as the difference between them increased to 2.58 points. This same comparison for weak partisans shows a 0.77 difference in 1976 increasing to 1.66 by 2004. A similar pattern is exhibited on almost all of the issue measures.

Another way of looking at these data is to compare the attitudes of strong partisans to the full sample means (the middle of the road) on these different questions. In 1976, there were two measures (ideological self-placement and support for government guaranteed health insurance) where strong Republicans were more than one point away from the mean, and none for which strong Democrats strayed that far from the mean. By 2008, both strong Republicans and strong Democrats were more than one point away from the mean on several measures. All of this adds further support to the claim that partisanship has become much more meaningful, and partisan differences have become significantly more pronounced, over the last thirty years.

One of the principal difficulties with the picture we are presenting of the American electorate is that it seems incompatible with the widespread political ignorance and apathy that surveys have shown to pervade the public. How can we argue that voting behavior can be understood as a set of rational calculations voters make about candidates using partisan orientation as their main political compass when many voters admit to not paying much attention to politics, as illustrated by the fact that only a quarter of the public can even name their two home-state senators?[22] We believe an important part of the explanation lies with the activities of "opinion leaders." Although a sizeable portion of Americans

Table 2.6 Partisan Identification and Issue Polarization, 1976 and 2008

(Entries are mean score on 7-point issue scales)

1976

	Strong Democrats	Weak Democrats	Independent Democrats	Independents	Independent Republicans	Weak Republicans	Strong Republicans	Full Sample
Ideology**	3.61	3.91	3.70	4.13	4.62	4.68	5.32	4.23
Health Insurance**	3.31	3.58	3.42	3.89	4.49	4.56	4.99	3.95
Jobs/Standard of Living**	3.52	4.03	4.32	4.76	4.83	4.79	5.38	4.41
Aid to Blacks**	3.93	3.99	4.04	4.42	4.45	4.65	4.71	4.26
Role of Women	3.21	3.16	2.94	3.13	2.87	3.45	3.39	3.18

2008

	Strong Democrats	Weak Democrats	Independent Democrats	Independents	Independent Republicans	Weak Republicans	Strong Republicans	Full Sample
Ideology**	3.19	3.43	3.48	4.27	4.85	5.09	5.77	4.24
Health Insurance**	2.83	3.09	3.07	3.24	3.77	4.56	5.28	3.63
Jobs/Standard of Living**	3.10	3.83	4.15	4.18	4.81	5.25	5.55	4.33
Aid to Blacks**	3.85	4.34	4.48	5.13	5.46	5.56	5.65	4.82
Role of Women	1.80	1.72	1.65	1.91	1.93	1.67	2.04	1.81

Source: American National Election Studies.

** $p < .01$ (ANOVA)

may know (and care) very little about politics, another sizeable portion of the electorate knows quite a bit about politics, candidates, and parties. The latter group is well equipped to provide cues and direction to others who prefer to remain "rationally ignorant."[23] We now turn our attention to trying to describe/identify this group of cue givers, or opinion leaders

Looking for Opinion Leaders

Who are these potential opinion leaders? In their classic study of the 1940 presidential election, Paul Lazarsfeld and his colleagues found that opinion leaders were knowledgeable and politically engaged individuals who communicated ideas from the media to less active segments of the population.[24] More recent work has continued to find strong connections between political knowledge and certain kinds of political behavior, including giving political cues to fellow citizens.[25] Political information flows through a multistep process that usually begins with politicians and issue activists, goes through media sources, and is then conveyed to the public; however, a subset of the public (opinion leaders) plays an important role in transmitting (and translating) what political and media elites are saying about political subjects.

We begin our search for likely opinion leaders with the NES question that would seem to most directly tap this type of political behavior. Survey respondents are asked whether they have engaged in any of a number of activities during election periods—from attending meetings or rallies, to making political contributions. One of the activities covered is talking to other people in order to persuade them to vote for a particular party or candidate. We believe that those who say that they have done this constitute a group that serves as a good starting point in a search for opinion leaders; such a collection of individuals might be viewed as the universe of possible opinion leaders. (This group represented roughly 33 percent of the 1976 NES sample, and 45 percent of the 2008 sample.)

Taking the work of Lazarsfeld and others into account, we would expect opinion leaders to be both knowledgeable of, and interested in, politics. We hypothesize that a series of factors ought to help explain who exactly these opinion leaders are. Toward that end, we have constructed a simple multivariate model that explores the relationship between attempts at voter persuasion in 2004 (dependent variable) and four explanatory variables (see Table 2.7).[26] The first explanatory variable is a measure of political knowledge that we constructed from the open-ended party likes and dislikes questions. We expect that citizens with greater knowledge of the parties will be more able and likely to try to persuade others how to vote. There is plenty of evidence that most respondents who articulate likes or dislikes make substantive and accurate comments about the parties' respective images.[27] Proceeding, therefore, from the finding that respondents tend to get it right when they evaluate the parties, we sorted respondents according to the number of party like or dislike comments that they offered to survey interviewers. Indeed in 2004, those who offered numer-

TABLE 2.7   Identifying Opinion Leaders, 2004

(Entries are logistic regression coefficients)

Independent variables[b]	Dependent variable:[a] Persuade others to vote
Number of party images	.12**
Partisan strength	.21**
Education	.06
Follows Politics	.23**
Constant	–2.29
Goodness of fit[c]	.95
Percentage correctly predicted	63.9
N	1046

Source: American National Election Studies.

** $p < .01$

[a] Measurement of dependent variable:

Persuade: 0 = does not attempt to persuade others how to vote; 1 = attempts to persuade others how to vote.

[b] Measurement of independent variables:

Number of Party Images: Number of open-ended party images expressed by respondent; ranges from 0 to 20.

Partisan strength: 1 = independent; 2 = independent-leaner; 3 = weak partisan; 4 = strong partisan.

Education: 1 = 8 grades or less; 2 = 9–11 grades; 3 = high school diploma; 4 = more than 12 years of schooling; 5 = junior or community college degree; 6 = BA level degree; 7 = advanced degree.

Follows Politics: 1 = follows politics hardly at all; 2 = follows politics now and then; 3 = follows politics some of the time; 4 = follows politics most of the time.

[c] Goodness of fit measure is corrected Aldrich-Nelson pseudo r^2.

ous responses ("image holders") possessed much higher levels of political knowledge than those who offered few or no responses (see Appendix A.2). It also stands to reason that strong partisans who have a deep commitment to their parties would be especially motivated to offer voting cues to others. Our model includes two other independent variables as predictors of opinion leadership: education and interest in politics. We expect that better educated respondents and those more interested in politics would be more likely to attempt to persuade others how to vote.

Our results, presented in Table 2.7, confirm the impact of both the image-holding and partisan strength variables on the likelihood of persuading others. The coefficients on these variables are strong and significant and suggest that each of these factors has an independent effect on the likelihood of persuading others how to vote. We also find that political interest is positively related to the dependent variable but that the effect of education is not significant.

To illustrate the impact of these explanatory variables, we converted the logistic regression coefficients shown in Table 2.7 into probabilities that are more easily interpreted.[28] These probabilities are displayed in Table 2.8. Our model predicts, for example, that a typical respondent (four images of the parties, weak partisan, follows politics some of the time, and has little schooling beyond high school) has a 44 percent chance of being an opinion leader (that is, attempting to persuade others how to vote). If we vary the number of party image comments for this same respondent but hold everything else constant, the probability of persuading others varies accordingly. A respondent who offers eight comments about the parties but is typical in every other way has a 56 percent chance of persuading others. Other such scenarios are presented in Table 2.8 and show the cumulative impact of the explanatory variables. At one end, a fairly apolitical respondent has only a 17 percent chance of being an opinion leader. At the other end, a highly political respondent sees that probability rise to two-thirds.

Another test for this group of likely opinion leaders is to examine their perceptions of the parties at different points in time. We would expect that opinion leaders would view the parties differently during periods of low partisanship (1976) as opposed to high partisanship (2004). These perceptions about the degree and intensity of party differences would then be expected to manifest themselves in the broader electorate, and help explain the heightened partisanship displayed in Table 2.5, and the partisan-based issue differences shown in Table 2.6.

Table 2.9 compares the perceptions of partisan difference among persuaders (cue givers), nonpersuaders, persuaders who are also party image holders (those who offered more than eight responses to the party like/dislike question), and the full sample, in 1976 and 2004.[29] In 1976, as in 2004, persuaders were more likely than others to believe that there are important differences between the parties. In 1976, 60 percent of the cue-giving group saw important differences between the parties, while only 40 percent of non-cue-givers recognized these differences, with the sample mean being 47 percent. The subset of especially knowledgeable cue-givers (image holders) shows a greatest awareness of party differences in 1976. By 2004, recognition of party differences had increased significantly in all four groups; it now stood at 89 percent among persuaders, 96 percent among persuader-image holders, 69 percent among nonpersuaders, and 78 percent for the full sample.

What is especially striking about the comparisons presented in Table 2.9 is that all of the perceptions of difference and of ideological distance are much weaker in 1976 than in 2004. Thus when rating the two parties on ideology and on issues, persuaders in 1976 placed Republicans less than two points to the right of Democrats on eight of the ten issues measured; the persuader-image holders did so on seven of the ten issues. By contrast, in 2004, persuaders as a whole placed Republicans more than two points to the right of the Democrats on five of the six issue/ideology measures, and the especially knowledgeable persuaders separated

TABLE 2.8 The Impact of Party Image-Holding, Partisan Strength, and Political Interest on Opinion Leadership, 2004

	Number of Party Images	Strength of Party Identification	Follows Politics	Probability that Respondent is an Opinion-Leader*
Apolitical	0	Independent	Hardly at all	.17
Typical	4	Weak	Some of the time	.44
Typical but a strong partisan	4	Strong	Some of the time	.49
Typical but follows politics most of time	4	Weak	Most of the time	.50
Typical but 8 images of the parties	8	Weak	Some of the time	.56
Highly Political	8	Strong	Most of the time	.66

Source: American National Election Studies.

*Probabilities are calculated for a respondent that has done some years of schooling beyond high school but does not have a college degree.

the two parties by more than three points on four of the six measures. When those who try to persuade others how to vote see fewer differences between the parties, it stands to reason that the signals and cues they communicate will produce an electorate that views the parties as less relevant; when opinion leaders view politics largely in partisan terms (as in 2004), so will a large portion of the public.

We have established that the pool of potential opinion leaders viewed the parties as being farther apart on issues and ideology in 2004 compared to 1976. How about the views of the opinion leaders themselves? Did they become more polarized? To explore this we added strong partisanship to cue-giving and produced two groups of potential Democratic and Republican opinion leaders so as to compare their mean scores on the NES series of issue/ideological measures in both 1976 and 2004–2008. For additional points of comparison we also included the mean scores for all Democratic and Republican identifiers and the mean scores for the entire NES sample (see Table 2.10).[30] As expected, the degree of polarization between Democratic and Republican opinion leaders is quite a bit higher in 2004–2008 than in 1976.

On the basic ideological measure, the difference between Democratic and Republican opinion leaders in 1976 is 1.82; by 2004 it increases to 2.89.

TABLE 2.9   Effects of Persuading Others on Perceptions of Party Polarization, 1976 and 2004

1976	Never Persuade Others How To Vote	Persuade Others How To Vote	Persuaders With 8 or More Party Images	Full Sample
Important differences between parties* (%)	40%	60%	75%	47%
Mean difference on Ideology*	1.82	2.15	2.75	1.94
Mean difference on Health Insurance*	1.45	2.32	2.80	1.83
Mean difference on Jobs and Standard of Living*	1.36	1.95	2.22	1.60
Mean difference on Aid to Minorities*	0.91	1.47	1.90	1.11
Mean difference on Role of Women*	0.37	0.68	0.83	0.51
Mean difference on Rights of Accused*	0.46	0.91	1.41	0.65
Mean difference on Busing	0.58	0.90	1.88	0.67
Mean difference on Urban Unrest*	0.93	1.27	1.39	1.08
Mean difference on Legalization of Marijuana*	0.27	0.63	1.27	0.42
Mean difference on Progressive Tax*	0.82	1.40	1.89	1.08

Mean difference between persuaders and non-persuaders across issues is 0.47 points.

Mean difference between persuaders with 8 or more images and non-persuaders across issues is 0.94 points.

Continued

**TABLE 2.9
(Continued)**

2004	Never Persuade Others How To Vote	Persuade Others How To Vote	Persuaders With 8 or More Party Images	Full Sample
Important differences between parties* (%)	69%	89%	96%	78%
Mean difference on Ideology*[a]	1.82	2.54	3.41	2.14
Mean difference on Services/Spending*	1.53	2.15	3.12	1.73
Mean difference on Defense*	1.58	2.18	2.72	1.80
Mean difference on Jobs and Standard of Living*	1.74	2.53	3.19	1.98
Mean difference on Aid to Blacks*	1.62	2.36	3.08	1.86
Mean difference on Role of Women*	0.87	1.48	2.12	1.11

Source: American National Election Studies.

Mean difference between persuaders and non-persuaders across issues is 0.68 points.

Mean difference between persuaders with 8 or more images and non-persuaders across issues is 1.41 points.

* Difference between the persuaders and non-persuaders is statistically significant ($p < .01$).

[a] Mean differences for all issues were calculated by subtracting respondent's placement of Democrats on issue from respondent's placement of Republicans on issue. All scales run from liberal (point 1) to conservative (point 7).

A similar change occurs between partisan identifiers, as the ideological gap between them widens from 1.07 to 1.93. In 1976, out of the nine issues NES measured on a seven-point scale, the difference between Democratic and Republican opinion leaders is less than one point on five of the issues, and close to two points on only two (whether government should provide health insurance and guarantee jobs for all Americans). These two issues, both government/economic rather than social, would appear to have defined the partisan

TABLE 2.10   Polarization among Opinion Leaders, 1976 and 2004–2008

(Entries are mean score on 7-point issue scales that run from liberal to conservative)

1976	Democratic Opinion Leaders*	Democratic Identifiers	Full Sample	Republican Identifiers	Republican Opinion Leaders
Ideology	3.52	3.77	4.23	4.84	5.34
Health Insurance	3.05	3.46	3.95	4.66	5.07
Jobs/Standard of Living	3.55	3.95	4.41	4.97	5.50
Aid to Minorities	3.93	3.99	4.26	4.60	4.50
Role of Women	3.14	3.12	3.18	3.26	3.30
Rights of Accused	3.62	4.07	4.26	4.52	4.89
Busing	5.64	5.85	6.07	6.31	6.35
Urban Unrest	2.68	2.95	3.20	3.6	3.49
Marijuana	4.97	4.7	4.82	5.0	4.87
Taxation	3.41	3.92	4.18	4.56	4.44

1976: Average difference between Democratic and Republican opinion leaders across nine policies is 0.96 points.

2004 and 2008					
Ideology (2004)	2.85	3.3	4.2	5.12	5.74
Ideology (2008)	2.89	3.35	4.24	5.28	5.75
Services/Spending (2004)	2.76	2.91	3.48	4.17	4.57
Services/Spending (2008)	2.58	2.97	3.62	4.53	4.94
Health Insurance (2004)	2.62	3.05	3.66	4.36	5.12
Health Insurance (2008)	2.76	2.99	3.63	4.56	5.37
Defense Spending (2004)	4.11	4.06	4.57	5.15	5.61
Defense Spending (2008)	3.53	3.81	4.22	4.82	5.40

Continued

TABLE 2.10 (Continued)

2004 and 2008	Democratic Opinion Leaders*	Democratic Identifiers	Full Sample	Republican Identifiers	Republican Opinion Leaders
Jobs/Standard of Living (2004)	3.03	3.55	4.21	5.01	5.65
Jobs/Standard of Living (2008)	3.19	3.66	4.33	5.21	5.67
Aid to Blacks (2004)	3.28	3.91	4.54	5.25	5.54
Aid to Blacks (2008)	3.82	4.19	4.82	5.56	5.80
Environment/jobs (2004)	2.98	3.16	3.59	4.0	4.30
Environment/jobs (2008)	3.37	3.59	3.99	4.46	4.89
Role of Women (2004)	1.51	1.72	1.92	2.14	2.54
Role of Women (2008)	1.71	1.73	1.81	1.88	2.01

Source: American National Election Studies.

2004: Average difference between Democratic and Republican opinion leaders across seven policies is 1.86 points

2008: Average difference between Democratic and Republican opinion leaders across seven policies is 1.87 points

*Opinion leaders are strong partisans who try to persuade others how to vote.

faultline at the time. The aggregate mean difference on the issues in 1976 was just less than one point (.96). In 2004, among the seven issues measured on a seven-point scale, there is not a single one where Democratic and Republican opinion leaders are separated by less than one point; on several of them the difference exceeds two points, with the aggregate mean difference being nearly two points (1.86). The corresponding figures for 2008 are very similar to those of 2004, with the aggregate mean difference between the views of Democratic and Republican opinion leaders being 1.87. Presently, we see significant differences between partisans not only on government/economic issues, but also social issues.

Another point of interest in Table 2.10 is the fact that in 2004–2008 Democratic and Republican opinion leaders were farther apart than regular party identifiers on all of the displayed measures. Thus the voting cues they conveyed no doubt emphasized partisan differences. In contrast, in 1976 not only are Democratic and Republican opinion leaders closer to their respective party identifiers than they are in 2004–2008, there are several instances where one or the other party's opinion leaders are actually closer to the full sample mean than are partisan identifiers (aid to minorities, role of women, urban unrest, legalization of marijuana, and taxation). This suggests that some of cues being sent out by opinion leaders may have served to mute rather than emphasize partisan differences. In 2004–2008 there is only one instance in which identifiers are closer to the sample mean than opinion leaders (Democrats on defense spending in 2004); the progression from left to right runs consistently from Democratic opinion leaders through Democratic and Republican identifiers to Republican opinion leaders (recall that a similar pattern appears in Table 2.6).

We believe that the evidence we have presented supports the notion that there is a segment of the electorate that acts as opinion leaders or cue-givers, and that the nature of the cues they have given out about the parties has varied over time. More specifically, during the party decline period (1970s) opinion leaders viewed the parties as being less divided than in more recent times. We believe that opinion leaders constitute one of the links between elite-level polarization, which became widespread in the 1980s, and the resurgence of partisanship in the minds of voters from the mid-1980s to the present. The definition of an opinion leader is somewhat amorphous. The NES question about efforts to persuade others does not distinguish between cue-givers (or persuaders) and opinion leaders, but presumably not all of the people who report giving out voting cues are actually viewed as opinion leaders by those to whom the cues are directed. Some people may think of themselves as, or aspire to be, opinion leaders, but never quite make the grade. Thus the size of the opinion leader group is difficult to pin down with precision.

We began our search for opinion leaders with the assumption that all those who claim to try to persuade others how to vote in elections are potential opinion leaders. We then offered up two subsets of persuaders as high probability opinion leaders—party image holders who reported attempts to persuade, and strong partisans who were persuaders (see Tables 2.9 and 2.10). In 2004, 44 percent of the NES sample, which translates into about 88 million people, claimed to have given out voting cues. The size of the party image holder group in 2004 was roughly 20 percent of the sample (about 40 million people). The intersection of persuaders and party image holders includes about 12 percent of the sample (about 24 million people). The combination of persuaders and strong partisans produced a group that represented about 17 percent of the 2004 sample (34 million Americans). These scenarios and others are displayed in Table 2.11, and although the precise definition of opinion leaders may be difficult to pin down, there certainly are plenty of them. We invite readers to ask themselves how many people they know who give out voting advice that they take seriously, and extrapolate to the larger U.S. population.

TABLE 2.11 How Many Opinion Leaders in 2004?

Possible Opinion Leaders	Share of NES Sample	Numbers of Opinion Leaders
Try to persuade others to how vote	44%	88 million
Strong partisans	33%	66 million
Express eight or more party images	20%	40 million
Strong partisans who try to persuade others how to vote	17%	34 million
People who express 8 or more party images and who try to persuade others how to vote	12%	24 million
Strong partisans who express 8 or more party images and who try to persuade others how to vote	7%	14 million

Source: American National Election Studies.

We offer these tentative estimates of the size of the opinion leader group in the U.S. because there is a good deal of debate among political scientists and journalists about the nature and extent of partisan polarization in the United States, and the role of political activists in shaping it. Prominent political scientist Morris Fiorina and his colleagues, for example, describe what they call the "Hijacking of American Democracy" in the book *Culture War?*[31] This hijacking is allegedly the work of a group of ideological partisans who they refer to as "purists" and "activists." These people are said to set the agenda and frame the terms of public debate in ways that accentuate extreme positions and conflicting ideologies. Fiorina et al. express great concern about what they call "the present disturbing state of American politics" because they see the purists and activists as stifling the voice of the moderate majority.[32] One of the difficulties in assessing the argument of Fiorina at al. is that they are never entirely clear about how large a group these activists and purists are. Although the thrust of their argument is that the cadre of activists and purists within the population is rather small, their own examples suggest otherwise. Our rough calculation, based on their specific comments on this point, is that "purists" and "activists" could easily include about 20 percent of the population, or about 40 million people.[33] With that many people involved, the activities of the purists and activists seem to us to be more like a ground war than a hijacking.

As in a ground war, there are leaders and followers in American politics. With the exception of elected officials and a few party officials, most of those who are most active in politics today live "for politics," not "off politics."[34] They are people who are motivated by passionate beliefs about political issues and, therefore, are likely to hold more extreme positions on the issues than others.[35] Such extremism does contribute to political conflict, but this conflict often clarifies what is at stake for poorly informed, modestly interested, middle-of-the-road voters.[36] Thus while Fiorina draws attention to the coercive effect that purists and activists can have on those in the middle, we place emphasis on the greater informational clarity conflictual political dialogue can bring about. In recent national elections most voters have had a pretty good sense of what they were likely to get when they voted for a Democrat or a Republican, which is an important element of democratic accountability. By focusing public attention on the conflict between their competing ideologies and policy positions (political and cultural liberalism vs. conservatism), we believe the parties are performing a crucial function for U.S. democracy, and performing better than they have in the past.

Assessing the Big Picture

Although we have presented a good deal of data and analyzed it in a variety of ways, the message we are trying to convey is rather simple. Armed with some basic information about partisanship we (and you) can explain a lot about American politics. Why were the 2000 and 2004 presidential elections so close? Using what we have shown about partisan affiliation, it first appears that the Democrats should have won both elections. After all, Democratic identifiers and Independent Democrats represented roughly 50 percent of eligible voters in both elections, while the same combination of Republicans was only about 40 percent (see Table 2.4). But, two other factors serve to reduce the apparent Democratic advantage: turnout and loyalty. Republicans turn out to vote at a rate that is higher than Democrats (6 percent on average since 1984), and are somewhat more loyal in voting for their party's candidate (5 percent in 2000 and 4 percent in 2004, according to exit polls).[37] The combination of these two factors more or less evens the partisan odds among voters. This is not to say that there aren't many other factors that play a role in election outcomes—presidential debates, Swift Boat ads, and foreign wars come to mind—but one can go a long way toward understanding and explaining recent national elections with a limited amount of information organized around parties.

In 2008, the partisan balance tipped farther in the Democratic direction, with the gap between identifiers reaching 14 percent (Table 2.4). Add to this the Bush administration's unpopularity and a slumping economy, and the 7 percent Democratic victory (Obama 53 percent, McCain 46 percent) becomes the more or less expected result. Democrats did manage to narrow the loyalty gap in 2008, but Republicans continued to have an advantage with regard to turnout.[38]

Even though most Americans do not think of themselves as loyal soldiers marching to a partisan tune, much of their political behavior can be explained as if they were. Drawing on the work of other political scientists, we are convinced that partisan conflict among elites has been transmitted to ordinary voters through a steadily enlarging group of knowledgeable political intermediaries, who understand what the elite-level conflict was about and can convey this information to others.[39] As this has been taking place, the media has also been communicating a message emphasizing partisan conflict.[40] All of this has enabled more and more voters in the elections of 2000, 2004, and 2008 to understand that the parties, and the candidates running under their labels, stood for importantly different political goals and values. We believe that this awareness of partisan differences is healthy for democracy. Even one of the longest-standing shortcomings of American democracy, low voter turnout, was partially overcome in 2004 (60 percent) and 2008 (62 percent) because citizens were interested in the outcome and aware of the differences between the two major parties and their candidates.[41]

Appendix A

TABLE A.1 Percent Voting Republican in Presidential Elections, 1952–2008

Year	SD	WD	ID	I	IR	WR	SR
1952	16	38	38	79	93	94	99
1956	15	36	33	84	94	93	99
1960	11	31	10	52	87	82	99
1964	5	18	10	23	75	56	90
1968	8	27	30	55	82	82	96
1972	27	51	39	66	86	90	97
1976	9	25	23	57	83	78	96
1980	11	33	29	64	76	86	92
1984	11	32	21	71	93	93	96
1988	6	27	12	61	84	83	98
1992	3	15	6	23	63	62	86
1996	2	9	6	37	65	70	94
2000	2	11	20	44	79	85	97
2004	3	17	13	45	83	89	98
2008	5	13	9	40	79	88	96

SD = Strong Democrat; WD = Weak Democrat; ID = Independent who leans Democrat; I = Independent; IR = Independent who leans Republican; WR = Weak Republican; SR = Strong Republican

Continued

TABLE A.1 (Continued)

Percent Voting for a Third Party in Selected Presidential Elections

Year	SD	WD	ID	I	IR	WR	SR
1968	8	15	19	21	14	8	2
1980	4	8	26	14	13	10	4
1992	4	17	24	37	26	25	11
1996	2	9	18	27	12	10	1
2000	1	1	8	13	8	1	1

Source: American National Election Studies.

SD = Strong Democrat; WD = Weak Democrat; ID = Independent who leans Democrat;
I = Independent; IR = Independent who leans Republican; WR = Weak Republican;
SR = Strong Republican

TABLE A.2 Effects of Party Image-Holding on Political Knowledge, 2004

	0 images	1–2 images	3–4 images	5–7 images	8+ images
Places Republicans to the right of Democrats on ideology scale	57%	62%	78%	85%	95%
Identifies Republicans as majority party in House	29	46	59	67	77
Identifies Republicans as majority party in Senate	25	39	52	62	74
Correctly identifies Hastert	2	4	6	15	25
Correctly identifies Cheney	69	82	91	91	98
Correctly identifies Blair	42	49	64	78	89
Correctly identifies Rehnquist	10	23	33	38	51
Percentage of sample	23	17	19	21	20

Source: American National Election Studies.

CHAPTER 3

Parties and the Electorate II: The Dynamics of Party Polarization

In the preceding chapter, we presented a good deal of data to substantiate a simple point: Republicans and Democrats are different. They tend to have different opinions on the leading issues of the day, different ideological moorings, and different voting patterns. These points of difference are not trivial; indeed, they represent a fundamental divide in American political life that both motivates and orients a great deal of political behavior. Furthermore, these partisan differences have become somewhat better defined and more widely recognized in recent years (since the late 1980s). The last three presidential elections have been close and contentious, not because voters didn't understand or care about the choices they were presented with; on the contrary, they understood what the candidates stood for quite well. As a nation, we simply find ourselves importantly divided over the policies and values we would like to see our political leaders espouse in campaigns and implement in office.

In this chapter, we will attempt to clarify the foundations of the political and partisan differences among Americans. As suggested in Chapter 2, the choices most voters make about the parties are the products of rational calculations based on voters' political beliefs and their perceptions of what the parties stand for, the latter being informed by the enduring images of the parties we have described.[1] But a person's political beliefs and ideological orientation are at least partially influenced by certain social, economic, and demographic factors. These include age, education, income/social class, race, region, and religion. This means, for example, that the region of the country in which a person grows up may affect the likelihood that he/she will think of himself/herself as a liberal versus a conservative. Being a woman, as opposed to a man, may affect one's political perspective, as does being black rather than white. The goal of the analyses that follow is to examine the nature of the relationship between each of the characteristics listed above and partisanship and voting, and in so doing further illuminate the basic, politically relevant divisions among the American public.

Composition of the Parties

Figures 3.1 to 3.7, and Figure 3.8 (a through g) lay out the composition of the Democratic and Republican parties in two somewhat different, but also complementary, ways. In Figures 3.1 to 3.7, the propensity of subgroups of Americans to affiliate with one party as opposed to the other over time is displayed. For each group, we calculated the Republicans' partisan advantage or disadvantage—the percent that identify with the Republicans (partisans and leaners) minus the percent that identify with the Democrats (the data for these figures are in the Appendices B.1 to B.7, at the end of this chapter). Then we compared the Republican advantage within that subgroup to the level of Republican identification among all respondents. In Figures 3.1 to 3.7, positive numbers on the "Partisanship Scale" mean that a particular subgroup's party identification is more Republican than the population at large; negative numbers indicate that a subgroup's party identification is more Democratic than the population at large.[2] In Figure 3.8 (a through g) the contribution of the various economic and demographic subgroups to the overall makeup of each party is shown. Taken together these figures reveal a good deal about the composition of the parties. For example, Figure 3.4 shows us that African Americans were split very disproportionately in favor of Democrats in 2008, while Figure 3.8d shows us that African Americans made up about 20 percent of the full body of Democrats at that time.

Turning first to Figure 3.1, we see the marked and enduring effect of income on partisanship. Low-income Americans have long favored the Democratic Party and high-income Americans have long favored the Republican Party, as can be seen by comparing top and bottom lines. An examination of these lowest and highest income groups also suggests that the relationship between income and partisanship became somewhat stronger in the 1990s, diminished a bit in 2000–2004, but returned emphatically in 2008. The middle income category is more or less evenly split between the two parties. This finding is certainly consistent with our emphasis on rational, self-interested choices Americans make about politics. Republican emphasis on tax cuts has a natural appeal for upper income citizens, while Democratic emphasis on government services has a similar appeal for lower income citizens.[3]

Figure 3.2 shows the regional contours of partisanship. The most evident and important finding here is the change in the South, from being heavily tilted toward the Democrats to favoring the Republicans. This change was somewhat gradual, but each decade shows a noticeable rise in Southern Republican affiliation. When the focus is sharpened to consider only whites, the change in the partisanship of Southerners is even more dramatic and unmistakable, with the majority crossing over to the Republican side during the Reagan administration (and never coming back).

The so-called gender gap is plainly seen in Figure 3.3. Interestingly enough, women actually favored the Republican Party through 1960, but beginning in the 1980s they switched their allegiance to the Democrats. Men did more or less the opposite. Even though the partisan gaps between men and women are smaller than some of those in other figures, they are quite significant since each category represents roughly half the sample. Women's preference for the Democrats is

Figure 3.1 Income and Party Identification

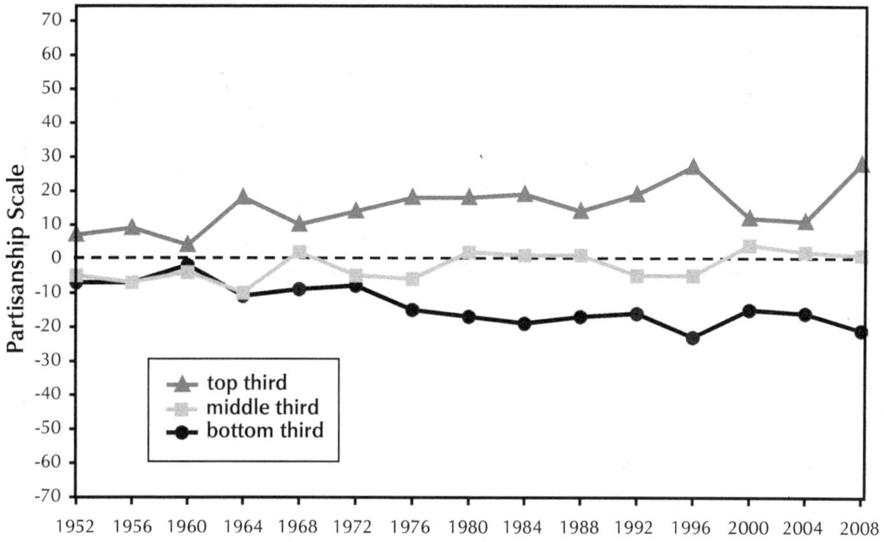

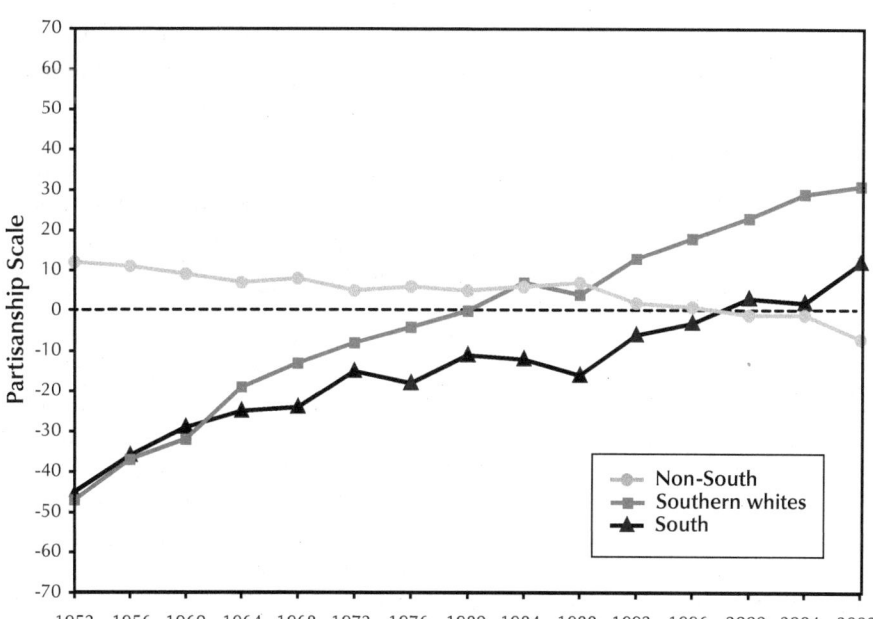

Source: American National Election Studies.

Figure 3.2 Region and Party Identification

Source: American National Election Studies.

Figure 3.3 Gender and Party Identification

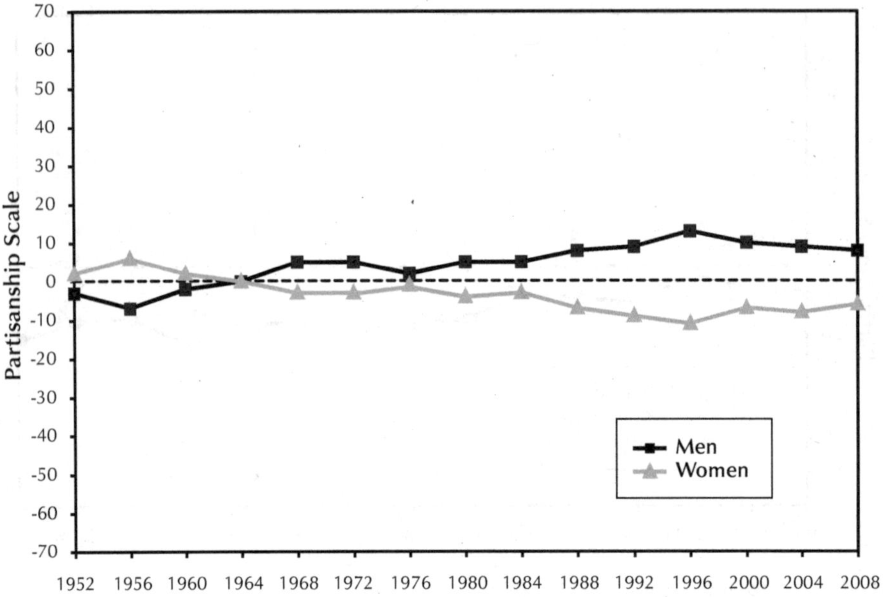

[Line chart showing Partisanship Scale for Men and Women from 1952 to 2008. Men's line trends upward from near 0 to about +10. Women's line trends downward from near 0 to about -5 to -10.]

Source: American National Election Studies.

largely a reflection of the emphasis the party places on issues such as health care, education, equal rights, and others that have special appeal to women.[4] In 2000–2008, there was some movement of women toward the Republicans (the "security moms"). Indeed among white married women in the South, fully 74 percent supported President Bush in 2004 and 77 percent voted for John McCain in 2008.

The partisan breakdown by race (Figure 3.4) is pretty straightforward. African Americans are a very loyal (the most loyal) Democratic contingent. Since 1964, they have favored the Democrats by very large margins. Whites, on the other hand, have shown a preference for the Republican Party, and this preference has become somewhat more pronounced over time. The division is by no means coincidental. Issues relating to race have been an important part of each party's approach to voters, with Democrats emphasizing policy stands that appeal to African Americans and Republicans pitching many of their policy stands toward whites.[5]

It is important to note that the NES did not create a separate category for Hispanics until 1972. From 1972 through 1996, Hispanic respondents were disproportionately likely to identify as Democrats. During these years, the average level of Democratic identification among Hispanics was 65 percent; only 22 percent of Hispanics identified as Republicans. Beginning in 2000 there was noticeable movement of Hispanics toward the Republicans, as their identification levels rose to 30 percent in 2000 and 33 percent in 2004. Democratic identification ranged

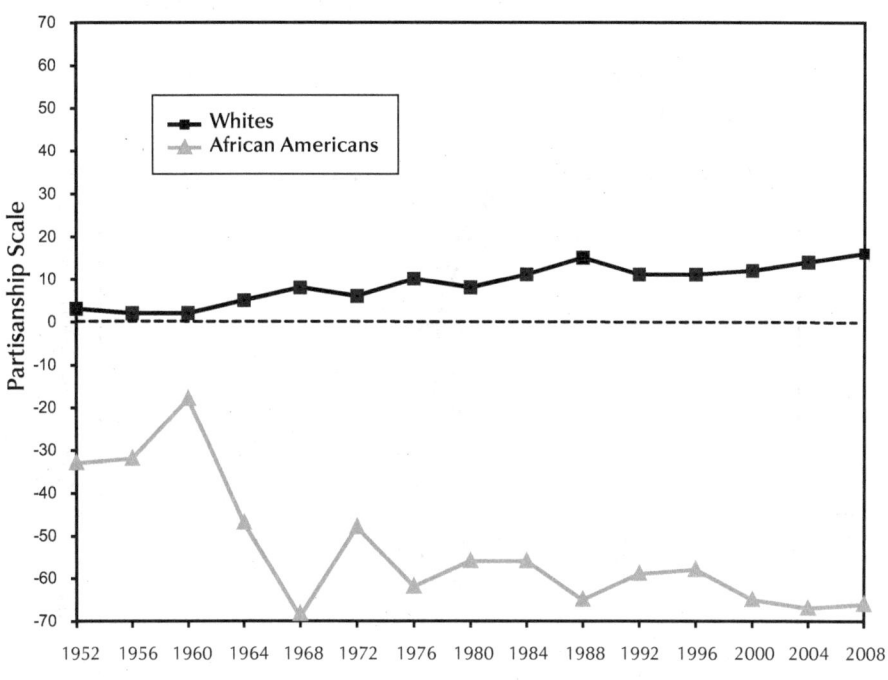

Figure 3.4 Race and Party Identification

Source: American National Election Studies.

from 52 to 59 percent during these years. Hispanics returned to the Democrats in 2008, with Republican identification down to 24 percent and Democratic identification up to 67 percent. However, two important caveats should be noted when assessing these figures. First, the NES samples have consistently underrepresented Hispanics, many of whom select white or black as their racial identification. In 2004, for example, only 7.3 percent of the NES sample identified as a Hispanic (7.9 percent in 2008), whereas the 2005 U.S. Census reported that about 15 percent of Americans were Hispanic.[6] Second, whereas African Americans tend to be homogeneous in their partisan identification, there are important differences in partisanship among Hispanic subgroups. Cuban Americans, for example, tend to identify more strongly with the Republican Party. Mexican and Puerto Rican Americans are more likely to identify as Democrats.[7]

The distribution of partisans by age (Figure 3.5) is very interesting and a bit complicated. In the 1950s and '60s there was a clear pattern in which young people were consistently more likely than older people to be Democrats. The relationship between age and partisanship became muddied in the 1970s when age seemed to have had very little relevance to partisan choice. In the 1980s, the pattern of the 1950s was turned on its head, as Democratic affiliation was now

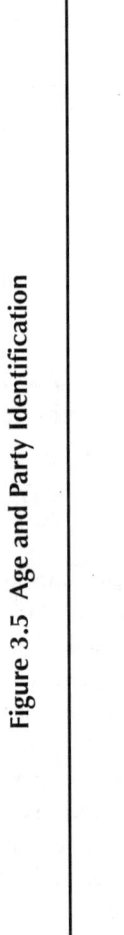

Figure 3.5 Age and Party Identification

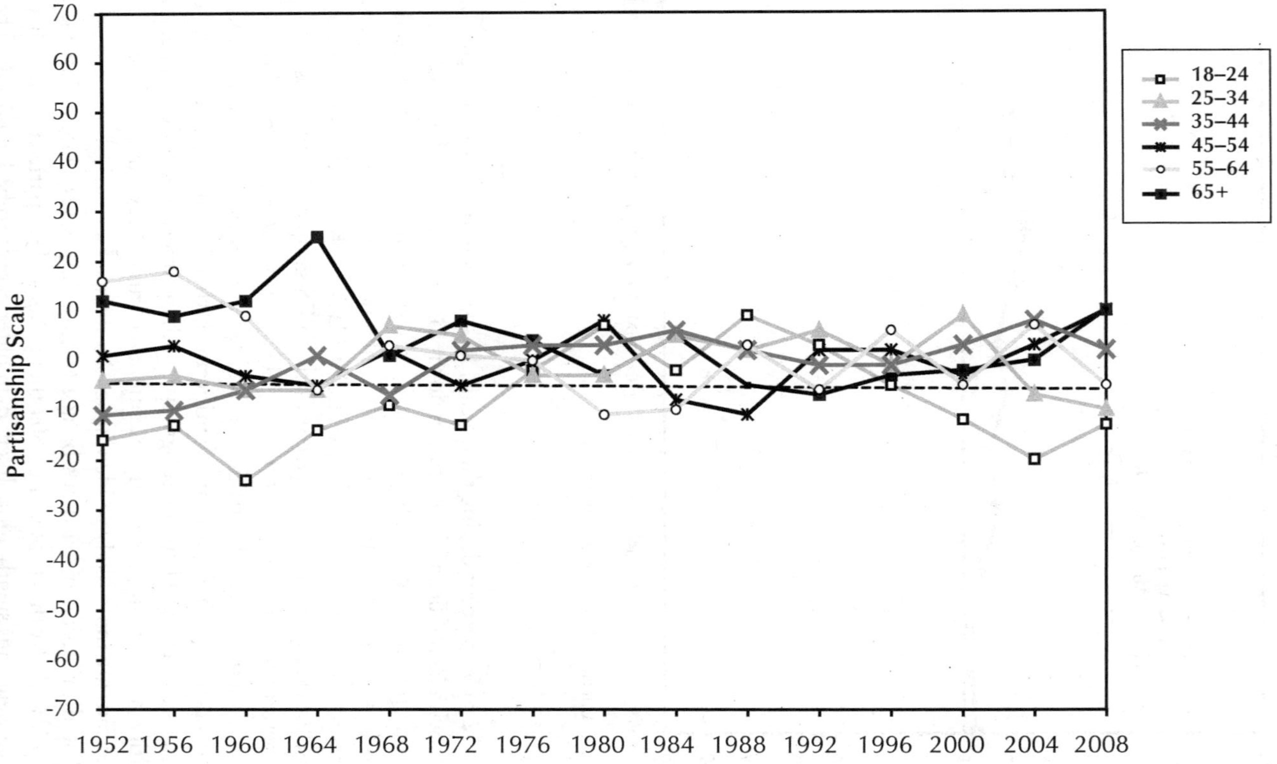

Source: American National Election Studies.

disproportionately exhibited among older voters (who were the youth voters of the 1950s and '60s), whereas the younger voters of this era became increasingly Republican. By 2000, a new crop of young voters appeared and showed a strong preference for the Democratic Party, as 25- to 44-years-olds (the young people of the 1980s) favored the Republicans, and older people exhibited a mild preference for the Democrats. In 2004, young voters were even more Democratic, but the groups between the ages of 35 and 65 included a disproportionate number of Republicans. In 2008, the 35 to 54 group stayed with the Republicans, but the 55 to 64 cohort went Democratic, and those over 65 favored Republicans to Democrats. The underlying dynamic seems to be some combination of maturational effects (middle-age people being somewhat more likely to be Republican than young people), and generational effects (New Dealers, baby boomers, and the children of baby boomers being somewhat more likely to be Democrats; those who came of age during the Reagan administration being inclined toward the Republicans).

The relationship between education and partisanship (Figure 3.6) is fairly consistent over time: less well educated citizens are disproportionately Democratic and the best educated are disproportionately Republican. The latter relationship becomes somewhat weaker over time, which appears to be a product of two factors/trends. First, the entire sample gets better educated during the period from the 1950s to 2000, and thus the number of respondents with some college education or a college degree increases, and becomes more heterogeneous.[8] Second, those with college degrees, especially those with advanced degrees, are also somewhat more likely to be liberal since the 1980s, in particular on social issues and on foreign policy.[9] The 2004 election was somewhat unusual in that it shows the least pronounced pattern of partisanship by education.

One of the most talked about aspects of partisanship in recent years is its relationship to religion. Republicans are widely viewed as the party of those who care most about religion, while Democrats are often portrayed as the party of nonbelievers. These perceptions are backed up by the positions the parties, especially the Republicans, have taken on major religious issues, such as prayer in schools, abortion, and public displays of religious symbols.[10] Our measure of religiosity is the number of times respondents report attending religious services. Figure 3.7 presents data covering the entire period from 1952 to 2008, but it should be noted that the way this question was asked changed in 1972.[11] The pattern is pretty clear: the most religious Americans show a marked preference for the Republican Party, particularly in recent years (since the 1990s). It was not always this way. In the 1950s and early '60s, the most regular worshippers were inclined toward the Democrats, and Republicans were actually disproportionately represented among the least religious Americans. But, beginning in the 1970s and continuing to the present, Democrats do well among those who are more occasional religious observers and those who do not observe at all, while the Republicans dominate among the more observant.

Independents with no partisan leaning are not included in Figures 3.1 to 3.7. There are few strong or consistent patterns across the economic and demographic

Figure 3.6 Education and Party Identification

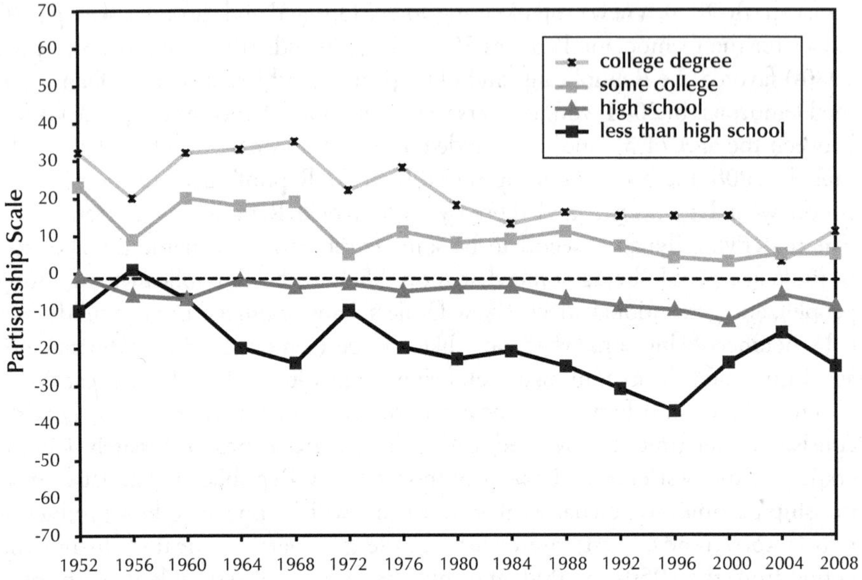

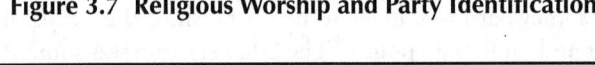

Source: American National Election Studies.

Figure 3.7 Religious Worship and Party Identification

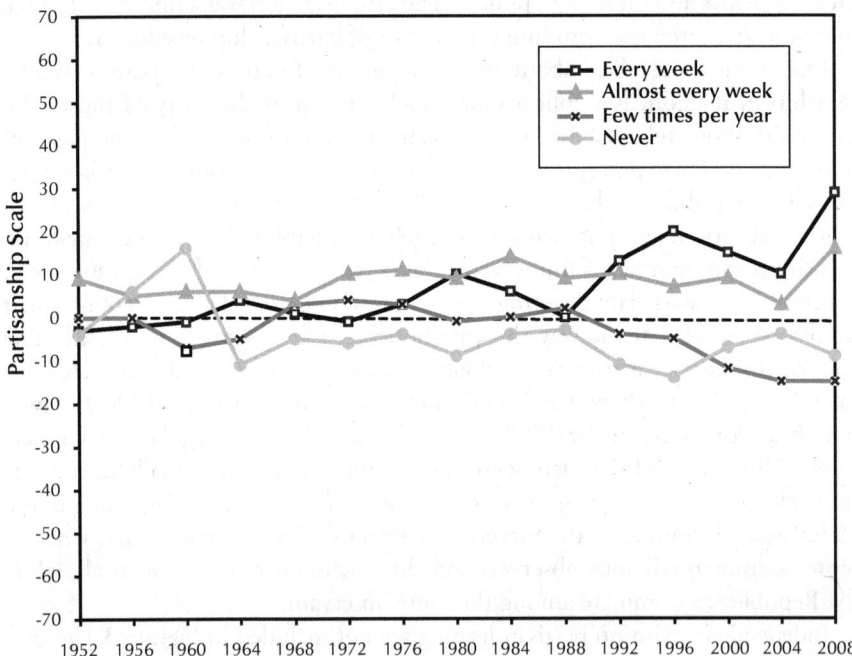

Source: American National Election Studies.

variables just covered among pure Independents. The weak and inconsistent tendencies were for Independents to be low income, non–African American, young, not well-educated, and nonreligious (see Appendices B.1 to B.7).

The bivariate relationships just reviewed tell us a lot about the patterns of partisanship in the United States, but several of the variables we have analyzed are also related to one another. For example, both higher incomes and higher levels of education are associated with the propensity to affiliate with the Republican Party, but income and education also affect one another. How can we isolate the effect of each variable on partisan identification? Table 3.1 shows the results of multivariate models designed to determine the independent effect of the various social and demographic characteristics we have covered on partisan identification at three distinct points in time: 1960, 1980, and 2000. We have marked the statistically significant (nonchance) relationships with asterisks. The results clarify much of what was observed in Figures 3.1 to 3.7.

Turning first to income, we see that the relationship between income and partisanship in 1960 was weak (not statistically significant). However, by 1980 and 2000, higher-income Americans are much more likely to be Republicans than middle- and lower-income Americans. There is, in short, a strong and independent effect of income on partisan affiliation. The regional effect is also as we have described it previously. Being from the South inclined one toward the Democratic Party in 1960, but by 2000 it had a strong effect in the opposite direction (toward Republicanism). Age had an independent effect on partisanship in 1960, as older people were more likely to be Republicans, but that effect disappears by 1980 and remains submerged in 2000. Race has mattered, particularly since 1964. Being black regardless of one's income, age, level of education, gender, or the region of the country in which one lives makes one highly likely to be a Democrat; and the relationship between race and party identification has grown stronger over time. Gender was not related to partisanship in 1960, but there was a strong relationship between the two (women favoring Democrats) by 1980, and it continued through 2000. Education has run a course that is more or less the opposite of income: higher levels of education had a strong and independent effect on partisanship (favoring Republicans) in 1960; this relationship diminished by 1980, and disappeared by 2000. Religiosity was not related to partisanship in 1960 but achieved a clear and consequential relationship with it by 1980 and 2000 (the more frequently one worships, the more likely one is to be a Republican, all other things being equal).[12]

Figure 3.8 (a through g) is an attempt to depict the major building blocks of each party as they appear in 2008. Several important differences stand out. Democrats have significantly larger groups of low-income (3.8a), young (3.8e), and non-college-educated people (3.8f), within their ranks. They also have fewer Southerners (3.8b) and larger numbers of women (3.8c) and those who do not attend church (3.8g). Most conspicuously, Democrats have a much larger African American contingent than the Republicans (3.8d). Indeed, Republicans do not have a racial or ethnic minority larger than 5 percent of their total, while

TABLE 3.1 Predictors of Party Identification, 1960, 1980, and 2000

(Cell entries are logistic regression coefficients)

	1960	1980	2000
Age	.19**	.01	−.07
Region	1.02**	.30*	−.43**
Income	−.02	.17**	.19**
Education	.39**	.21**	.09
Gender	.15	−.26*	−.32*
Race	−.08	−1.95**	−2.52**
Religiosity	.02	.18**	.21**
Constant	−3.90	.02	2.39

Source: American National Election Studies.
* $p < .05$
** $p < .01$

Dependent variable
Party Identification: 0 = Democratic ID; 1 = Republican ID.
Independent variables
Age: 1 = 18–24; 2 = 25–34; 3 = 35–44; 4 = 45–54; 5 = 55–64; 6 = 65–74; 7 = 75 or older.
Region: 1 = South; 2 = Non-south.
Family Income: 1 = 0–16 percentile; 2 = 17–33 percentile; 3 = 34–67 percentile; 4 = 68 to 95 percentile; 5 = 96 to 100 percentile.
Education: 1 = 8 grades or less; 2 = 9 to 12 grades; 3 = Some college; 4 = College degree.
Gender: 1 = Male; 2 = Female.
Race: 1 = White; 2 = Black.
Religiosity (1960): 1 = Never; 2 = Seldom; 3 = Often; 4 = Regularly.
Religiosity (1980 & 2000): 1 = Never; 2 = Few times a year; 3 = 1–2 times per month or almost every week; 4 = Every week.

Democrats have two—African Americans and Hispanics. Thus common stereotypes about the parties—that Republicans are the party of wealthy, white males and the religious, while Democrats are the party of women, racial minorities, the poor, and secularists—have a considerable basis in fact. In 2008, white males accounted for 44 percent of all Republicans, but only 26 percent of all Democrats. Indeed, African Americans and white males made up a similar portion of the Democratic Party while white males outnumbered African Americans among Republicans by more than twenty to one.

The remainder of this chapter extends the analysis of the relationships identified in Table 3.1. This follow-up analysis is grouped under two headings; one that features income and class; the other featuring culture and religion. However, issues related to region, race and gender (the other important determinants of partisanship emerging from Table 3.1) are also explored.

Figure 3.8a Income Composition of the Parties, 2008

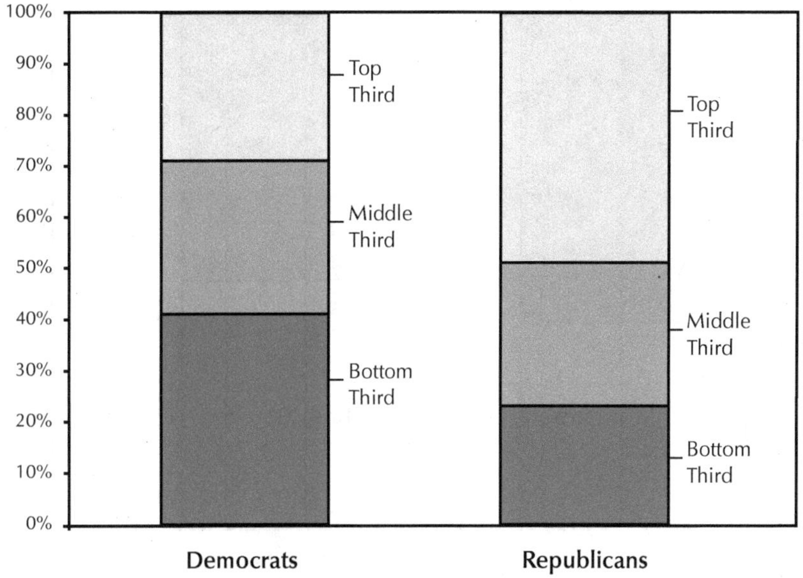

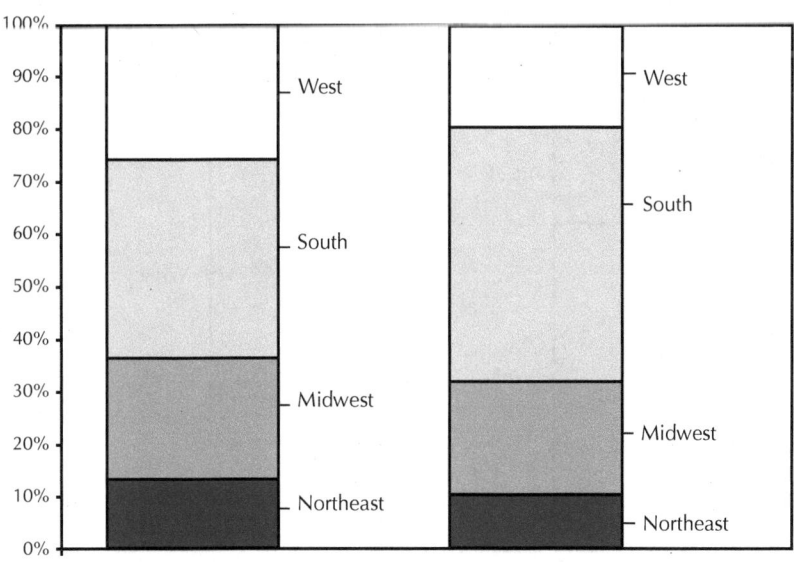

Source: American National Election Studies.

Figure 3.8b Regional Composition of the Parties, 2008

Source: American National Election Studies.

Figure 3.8c Gender Composition of the Parties, 2008

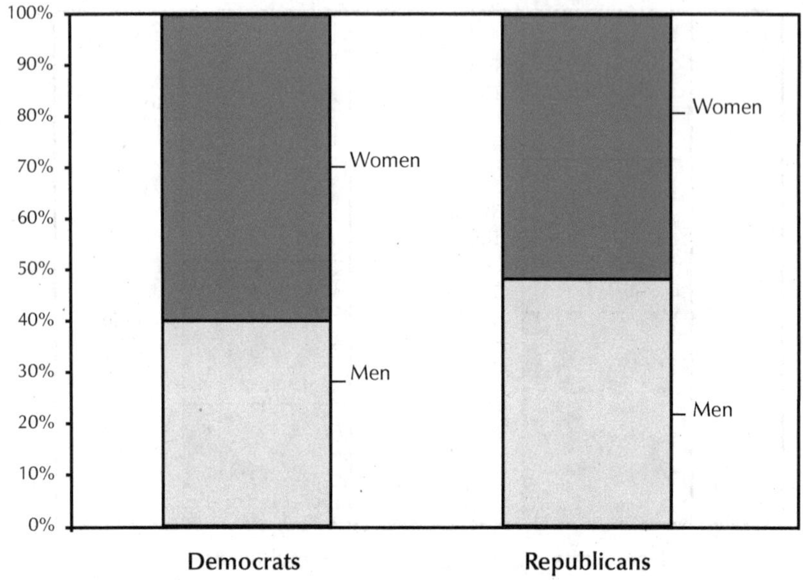

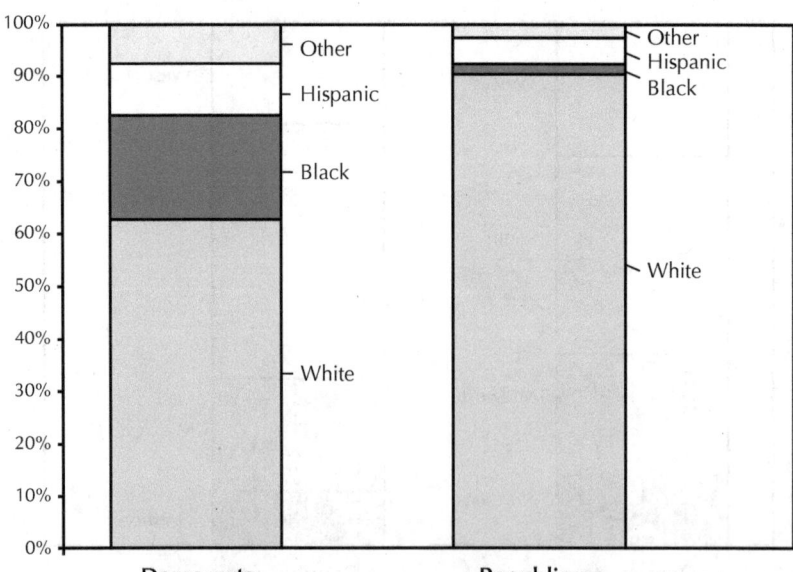

Source: American National Election Studies.

Figure 3.8d Racial Composition of the Parties, 2008

Source: American National Election Studies.

PARTIES AND THE ELECTORATE II: THE DYNAMICS OF PARTY POLARIZATION   61

Figure 3.8e Age Composition of the Parties, 2008

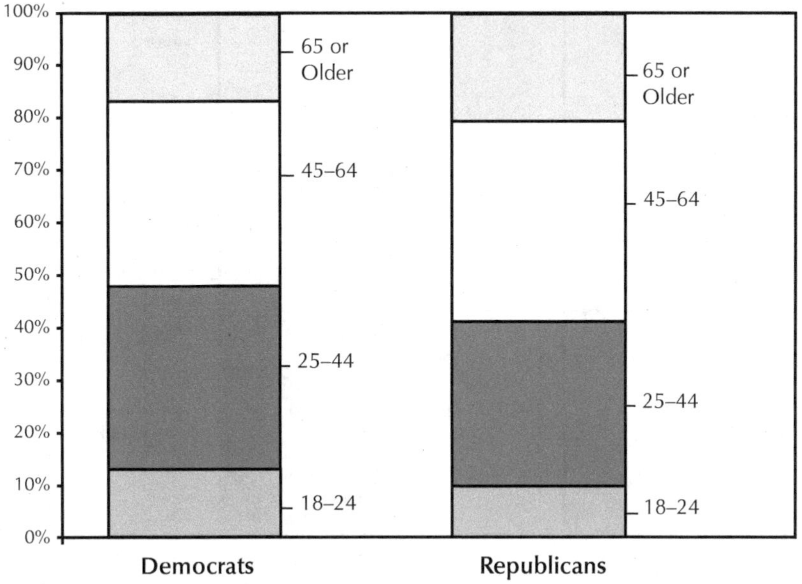

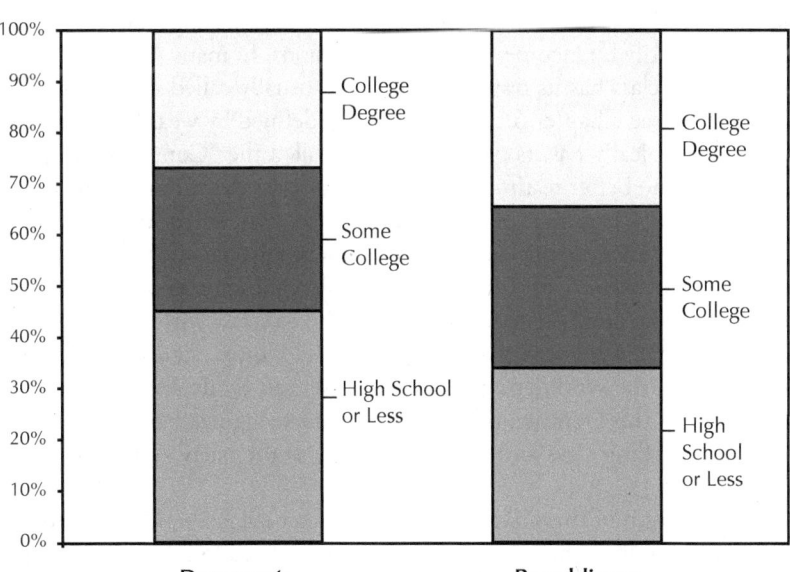

Source: American National Election Studies.

Figure 3.8f Educational Composition of the Parties, 2008

Source: American National Election Studies.

Figure 3.8g Religious Composition of the Parties, 2008

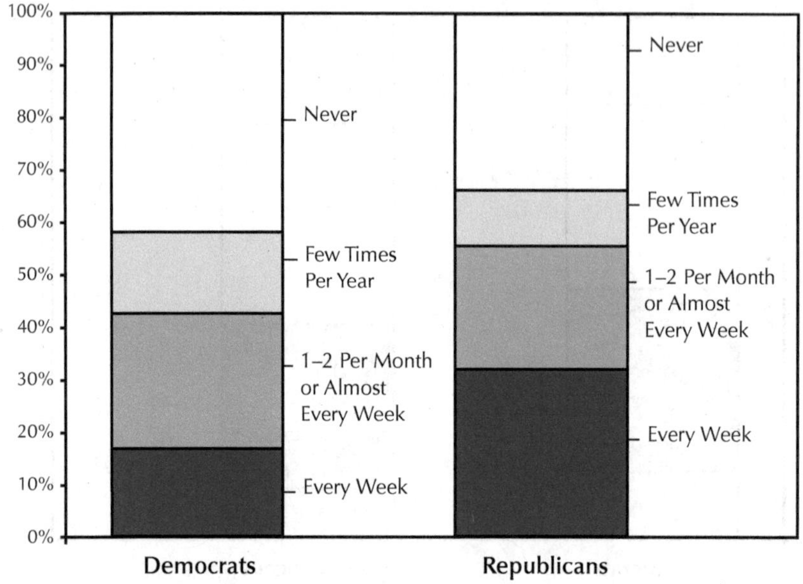

Democrats:
- Never
- Few Times Per Year
- 1–2 Per Month or Almost Every Week
- Every Week

Republicans:
- Never
- Few Times Per Year
- 1–2 Per Month or Almost Every Week
- Every Week

Source: American National Election Studies.

Income and Social Class

American political parties are often contrasted with European parties for not being defined primarily by income and/or class divisions. In many European countries the working class has its own political party, usually called the "Labour" or "Socialist" party (see Chapter 6); the upper class (defined by wealth and in some cases privilege) typically has its party too, often called the "Conservative" party. There is perhaps no better testimony to the lack of class definition of our parties than the status of Franklin Roosevelt as the most renowned and beloved of twentieth-century Democratic presidents. Roosevelt led his party into a close and enduring association with labor unions, while hailing from one of the most prominent patrician families in America. Still, the contrast with Europe should not be exaggerated. While the major parties in the United States look for support among both the working and middle classes, as we demonstrated in the previous chapter, the Democratic Party has been recognized by many as the party of labor/working class and the Republicans as the party of business since the 1950s.

In the first section of this chapter we saw that income is a powerful predictor of partisan affiliation. Although low-income people have long favored the Democrats and high-income people the Republicans, the divisions along income lines became significantly more pronounced in the 1980s and 1990s (see Figure

3.1 and 3.8a).[13] Thus there is a good deal of evidence pointing to income (and/or social class) as one of the primary definers of our contemporary party system; indeed, some have argued it is the most important force behind party cleavages.[14] Others, however, have argued that cultural issues, many of which are linked to religious faith, are at least as important as income in determining election outcomes and party affiliations.[15] In this and the next section of this chapter we take a stab at sorting out these competing claims.

Social or economic class has never had the same meaning or significance in the United States as it has in Europe. By the late eighteenth century, when the United States was founded, class had come to the fore as the central political issue in Europe. European nations had emerged from a long period of feudalism during which class divisions were deeply ingrained and nearly immutable, and were transforming themselves into capitalist democracies. In these transformations, the rights and privileges of classes (upper class/nobility, middle class/bourgeoisie, and lower class/workers/proletariat) were the driving forces of politics (and revolutions). This country was simply too young for class divisions of the European sort to have taken hold. Nevertheless, by the late nineteenth century, and continuing through the twentieth century, the position of wage laborers and blue-collar workers in the United States relative to entrepreneurs and corporate managers was certainly similar to that of their counterparts in Europe. Still, the level of class consciousness (an outlook on politics in which class divisions are paramount) never reached the same height in this country as in Europe. Part of the reason for this is both the myth and reality of American upward economic mobility.

The goal of this brief (indeed, inexcusably brief) discussion of class in modern history is to make the point that awareness of class distinctions can be a very powerful force in politics. Why don't the have-nots in American society band together in a more conscious and organized way to oppose the haves, particularly in light of growing economic inequality over the last thirty years?[16] The most common answer is that the American working class (and lower class) have been distracted and divided by other issues: first, race, which divided working-class whites and blacks, especially in the South; and second, cultural issues, which divided working people along religious lines. The fact that common economic interests can be sidetracked by these other issues again raises the question of how important issues of class are in this country.

One of the difficulties associated with incorporating the concept of class into an analysis of American politics is defining it for operational use. One approach is simply to ask people what class they see themselves belonging to (lower, working, middle, or upper). The NES has used the following question since the 1950s: "There's quite a bit of talk these days about different social classes. Most people say they belong to either the middle class or to the working class. Do you ever think of yourself as being in one of these classes?" Those who respond affirmatively are then asked to place themselves in the middle or working class. Those who respond negatively are presented with a follow-up question that asks

TABLE 3.2 Three Definitions of "Working Class"

(Cell entries are percentage identifying as Democratic)

	Self-reported working class	Self-reported working class + income in bottom two thirds	Bottom third of income distribution
1960	59%	58%	56%
1970	59	58	59
1980	59	59	63
1990	55	56	59
2000	57	57	57

Source: American National Election Studies.

them which class they would choose "if they were forced to." The result is that most people end up in the working or middle class, but some volunteer either lower class or upper (or upper-middle) class. Some of the problems with this approach should be apparent. Typically, between one-quarter and one-third of respondents initially decline to put themselves in a social class; and, even when pushed, some choose something other than working or middle class. Others offer answers that are suspect—high-income people claiming to be working class, or low-income people claiming to be middle or even upper class.[17] These kinds of difficulties have led some analysts to use more objective indicators of class, such as occupation, income, or education.[18]

Table 3.2 examines the relationship between partisanship and class using three different definitions of social class. The first defines working class according to self-reports (all those who describe themselves as "working class" or "lower class" are included). The second combines self-reported class with income, and defines working class as those who describe themselves as working class and have incomes in the lower two-thirds of the sample. The third ignores self-reported class status and defines the working class as the third of the sample with the lowest income. As is readily apparent, all three definitions yield essentially the same result over five decades. Therefore, because of the subjective component inherent in class self-identification, we have chosen to use income as our measure of social class for the remainder of this chapter.

What additional light can income/class shed on the relationships identified in Table 3.1? We already know that since the 1980s women and African Americans are decidedly more likely to identify with the Democrats than white men (Figures 3.3 and 3.4). Do these propensities vary by income? Table 3.3 shows the difference (Republican Class Advantage) between high-income white men and women (top third of sample) and low-income men and women (bottom third) with regard to both partisanship and presidential vote choice.[19] Also displayed are percentages of high-income respondents (white men and women) who identified with the Republicans and voted for Republican candidates for president. (The corresponding percentage for the low-income groups can be derived by subtracting the differences listed from the high-income percentages shown.) There is in short a good deal of information packed into this table.

Let's look at election year 2000 as an example of what can be gleaned from the figures in this table. We see (top panel of Table 3.3) that 46 percent of high-income white women identified with the Republican Party, and that this was 13 percentage points higher than the proportion of low-income white women who identified as Republican (which would make the rate among this group 33 percent). In the bottom panel, we find that in 2000, 52 percent of upper-income women supported the Republican candidate, and that this was nine percentage points higher than the Republican support level among low income women. For white men, the upper income group was fourteen percentage points more likely than the lower-income group to affiliate with the Republican Party; on voting, the gap was seven percentage points. Notice also that high-income white men were more likely than high-income white women to identify with the Republican Party (53 percent versus 46 percent) and to support their candidate (56 percent versus 52 percent).

One of the main findings in Table 3.3 is that income has mattered a lot when it comes to partisanship and voting among white men in certain election years. In 1984, for example, higher-income white men were heavily Republican and voted massively for Reagan, while lower-income white men favored the Democrats. Looking across election years, we see what by now should be recognized as a familiar pattern: smaller income effects in the 1950s–1970s, and larger effects in the 1980s and 1990s. All this suggests that income and/or class differences have been (and still are) very significant factors in American politics. Of special interest is the fact that the 2000 and 2004 elections showed a reduced effect of income on partisanship and vote among white men. This was due in part to the higher than usual support for Republicans among low-income white men; their level of Republican identification and vote in these election years was equal to the sample and national averages. (Of course, the level of such support among high-income white males was quite a bit higher than average.) Clearly the Republican Party in the Bush years had a special attraction for white men. In 2008, class-based partisanship and voting made something of a comeback in the sense that high-income white men were even more supportive of the Republicans than in 2000–2004; still, once again, low-income white men voted for McCain at a level that matched the national average (47 percent).

Income has mattered somewhat less when it comes to the political affiliations and behavior of white women. Higher-income white women are more likely to favor Republicans than low-income white women, but the differences between the two groups are smaller than those among men in most presidential election years. Although the overall (1952–2008) difference in average support for the

TABLE 3.3 The Effects of Income and Gender on Party Identification and Vote Choice, 1952–2008 (Whites Only)

	PARTY ID—White Men		PARTY ID—White Women	
	% Republican ID in top third of income	Republican Class Advantage*	% Republican ID in top third of income distribution	Republican Class Advantage*
1952	38%	+6	41%	+5
1956	41	+8	48	+9
1960	39	+6	39	0
1964	40	+14	42	+13
1968	42	+7	39	+9
1972	47	+14	43	+6
1976	43	+14	46	+10
1980	50	+23	43	+11
1984	58	+27	52	+13
1988	57	+13	55	+14
1992	56	+23	49	+13
1996	61	+24	49	+18
2000	53	+14	46	+13
2004	58	+17	47	+9
2008	65	+29	55	+20
1952–2008	50%	+16	46%	+11

Continued

Republican Party and its candidates among high-income men and women is not huge (50 percent versus 46 percent, and 60 percent versus 56 percent respectively), since the 1980s high-income white women have become significantly less Republican-inclined than their male counterparts (on average, 7 percent less Republican on identification and 9 percent less likely on voting). If one separates married women from single women, one finds that married women actually vote more like men (that is, they display large differences in partisan affiliation and voting based on income) than single women.[20]

Table 3.4 displays the results of a similar data presentation, focusing on region. As in the previous table, the figures listed are both the differences between the high- and low-income respondents in terms of partisan affiliation and voting, and

TABLE 3.3 (Continued)

	VOTE—White Men		VOTE—White Women	
	% Republican ID in top third of income	Republican Class Advantage*	% Republican ID in top third of income distribution	Republican Class Advantage*
1952	63	+1	62%	+7
1956	63	+13	63	0
1960	52	+4	53	−6
1964	45	+18	40	+6
1968	54	+5	51	−1
1972	74	+6	68	+2
1976	58	+17	63	+14
1980	63	+12	56	+5
1984	76	+31	68	+11
1988	69	+14	61	+3
1992	42	+14	40	+3
1996	55	+22	47	+18
2000	56	+7	52	+9
2004	64	+12	57	+9
2008	72	+25	60	+22
1952–2008	60%	+13	56%	+7

Source: American National Election Studies.

*Republican class advantage is percentage of respondents in top third of income distribution identifying as or voting Republican minus percentage of respondents in bottom third of income distribution identifying as or voting Republican.

the percentage of high-income respondents who affiliate with and vote for Republicans. We see, for example, that 68 percent of high-income Southerners (white and nonwhite) voted for President Bush in 2004, and the difference between high-income Southerners and low-income Southerners in this respect was 32 percent (only 36 percent of low-income Southerners voted for Bush). Outside of the South, the difference between high- and low-income voters in their preference for Bush over Kerry was only 10 percent. Thus, income had a much larger effect on vote choice in the South in 2004 than in other parts of the country. In fact, this same pattern has been in evidence for voting going back to the 1960s; for partisan affiliation it has been present since 1980. What this clearly suggests is that in the last twenty-five years Southerners with higher incomes have developed

TABLE 3.4 The Effects of Income and Region on Party Identification and Vote Choice, 1952–2008

	PARTY ID—Non-South		PARTY ID—South	
	% Republican ID in top third of income distribution	Republican Class Advantage*	% Republican ID in top third of income distribution	Republican Class Advantage*
1952	43%	+4	13%	–6
1956	48	+8	23	–3
1960	43	+2	21	–3
1964	41	+11	36	+23
1968	43	+11	23	+3
1972	43	+7	41	+20
1976	45	+14	30	+10
1980	43	+15	45	+23
1984	52	+18	48	+26
1988	52	+15	46	+19
1992	48	+17	52	+25
1996	51	+21	58	+35
2000	43	+13	52	+24
2004	44	+9	62	+36
2008	48	+20	63	+35
1952–2008	46	+12	41	+18

Continued

a marked preference for most things Republican (before that they were conservative, but not necessarily Republican). Outside of the South, the preference for Republicans among high-income citizens has become gradually less pronounced; in other words, in the last eight elections high-income Southerners were significantly more supportive of Republicans than non-Southerners with high incomes. If one narrows the focus to whites only, the differences by income diminish somewhat (that is, income is less predictive of partisanship and vote), but the basic pattern remains—greater income effects in the South.[21]

The preceding analysis shows that income is an important, but not overriding factor in American political life. Overall, the party of business (Republicans)

TABLE 3.4 (Continued)

	VOTE—Non-South		VOTE—South	
	% Republican ID in top third of income distribution	Republican Class Advantage*	% Republican ID in top third of income distribution	Republican Class Advantage*
1952	62%	+2	59%	+17
1956	65	+3	49	+8
1960	53	−1	47	0
1964	39	+12	54	+28
1968	50	0	52	+19
1972	67	+8	75	+20
1976	58	+18	55	+25
1980	52	+5	70	+38
1984	67	+21	79	+43
1988	60	+15	66	+30
1992	37	+10	44	+17
1996	45	+19	55	+37
2000	47	+13	60	+17
2004	53	+10	68	+32
2008	51	+20	70	+38
1952–2008	54	+10	60	+25

Source: American National Election Studies.

*Republican class advantage is percentage of respondents in top third of income distribution identifying as or voting Republican minus percentage of respondents in bottom third of income distribution identifying as or voting Republican.

is preferred by those with higher incomes and the party of government (Democrats) by those with lower incomes. However, the effect of income on the political preferences and behavior of different groups in the United States varies a good deal. Minorities and women, for example, have an attraction to the Democratic Party that is not explainable on the basis of income alone. The Republicans have been able to attract some support from low-income Americans, especially white men, presumably through their positions on certain cultural issues. At the same time, Democrats have been able to attract some support among high-income Americans, especially outside of the South, presumably for the same reason. We take up the cultural divide in the next section.

The Cultural Divide

There has been much discussion in recent years of a cultural divide in American politics. The 2004 election campaign was regarded by many pundits as a victory for cultural conservatism over secular liberalism. The number one exhibit in defense of this interpretation were the eleven referenda on gay marriage held during the 2004 campaign. In all eleven states, gay marriage initiatives were defeated; in most of these states, the margin of victory was large.[22] Even though Barack Obama won the 2008 presidential election, cultural conservatives had some things to celebrate, most notably, the passage of California's Proposition 8, which banned same-sex marriage that had been legalized several months earlier by the state's supreme court.[23]

The failure of the gay marriage initiatives is only one piece of the evidence cited by proponents of the culture war view of American politics. The extraordinarily close elections in both 2000 and 2004, alongside the consistent divisions in the Electoral College (Red State versus Blue State) are also put forward as evidence of polarization rooted in cultural differences. (Although the electoral map changed importantly in 2008, with the key states of Ohio, Florida, Virginia, and North Carolina going to Obama, much of the regional division persisted.) Pundits have been quick to pit coastal America against Middle America—secular, latte-drinking liberals against God-fearing, NASCAR-loving conservatives.[24] Exit polls did reveal a religious divide in voting in 2004: 64 percent of those who worship more than once a week voted for Bush; 62 percent of those who never worship voted for Kerry. A whopping 78 percent of white evangelicals voted for Bush.[25] And when Americans were asked in 2004 what mattered most in deciding how they voted for president, the modal response was "Moral Issues" (22 percent), adding additional credibility to the image of a nation concerned with, and divided over, cultural issues.

However, others have taken issue with the interpretation of the 2004 election as evidence of a cultural backlash. Abramowitz and other election analysts attributed Bush's victory to incumbency, the war, and an economy that was just good enough to get a president reelected.[26] Exit polls revealed that relative to 2000, Bush's gains were concentrated among women (security moms) and Hispanics, two groups whose interests do not mesh with the culture war perspective.[27] Nevertheless, the media coverage of the 2004 campaign certainly bought into the idea of a culture war; major newspapers were far more likely to use the term than they had been in the past (see Figure 3.9). Interestingly enough, by 2008 the media had backed away (somewhat) from the culture war theme.

The notion of a culture war is nothing new in American politics. Back in the 1960s, some analysts believed that cultural conflict had joined economic security as an important dividing line within the public. For example, Kevin Phillips argued that civil rights and the Great Society programs of the 1960s alienated many "Middle Americans" who felt that their values and interests were no longer being promoted by Democrats.[28] Scammon and Wattenberg

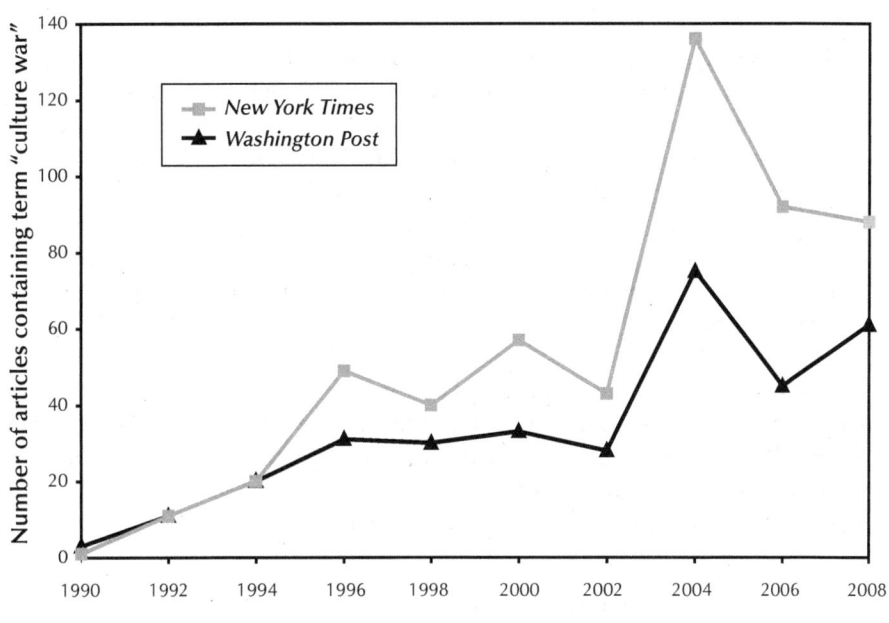

Figure 3.9 The "Culture War" in the Press

Source: Lexis-Nexis.

echoed this view in their book *The Real Majority*. As they put it, the majority of Americans were "unyoung, unpoor and unblack," and they objected to civil rights, antiwar protests, and a sense of growing lawlessness.[29] Although the issues may have been different (crime, civil rights, patriotism), the basic idea was the same. Cultural liberals, housed within the Democratic Party, were advancing the interests of minority groups and doing so at the expense of traditional American values.

The contemporary culture war is an extension of that basic theme. As we described in our discussion of party images (Chapter 2), the Democrats are widely regarded as the party of social liberalism and all that that has come to entail: pro-choice, pro–gay rights, secular values; the Republicans are viewed as prolife, anti–gay rights, and advocates of traditional values. To be sure, not all analysts accept the depiction of an America fundamentally divided over cultural issues. As we mentioned in the previous chapters, Fiorina and his colleagues believe the cultural divide is confined largely to partisan elites and activists.[30] Most Americans, they believe, are somewhere in the middle on these cultural issues, which means that their true preferences are not reflected in the choices presented to them by partisan elites.

Thomas Frank, who is perhaps the best known contemporary proponent of the view that cultural issues have transformed American politics, argues in his book, *What's the Matter with Kansas?*, that Republicans have been quite successful in using social issues to mobilize working-class Americans, who in turn vote culture instead of class. In his subsequent analysis of the 2004 election, Frank wrote:

> The power of the conservative rebellion is undeniable. It presents a way of talking about life in which we are all victims of a haughty overclass—"liberals"—that makes our movies, publishes our newspapers, teaches our children, and hands down judgments from the bench. These liberals generally tell us how to go about our lives, without any consideration for our values or traditions. The culture wars, in other words, are a way of framing the ever-powerful subject of social class. They are a way for Republicans to speak on behalf of the forgotten man without causing any problems for their core big-business constituency.[31]

Thus, for Frank, issues of class and culture are very much intertwined.[32] We have already demonstrated that income and class are important factors, but not necessarily dominant ones, in American politics. In this section, we offer our own interpretation of the importance of the cultural divide in the partisan assessments and vote choices that Americans make.

Defining the Cultural Divide

Like several other important concepts we have examined, there is no simple and widely accepted definition or measure of the cultural divide in American politics. Having surveyed the possibilities, we offer three potential measures of cultural polarization in American politics. The first is religious worship, which we have used in previous sections of this chapter (see Figure 3.7).[33] Much of the popular interpretation of recent election outcomes has focused on the different vote choices made by religious versus secular voters. The second candidate is attitudes on abortion.[34] Since *Roe v. Wade* in 1973, abortion has arguably received more attention than any other "cultural issue" and its polarizing and uncompromising nature has come to typify the larger culture war. Moreover, since the early 1990s, abortion became a more visible component of each party's image, as reflected in responses to open-ended party likes and dislikes survey questions.[35] The final candidate is attitude toward gays and lesbians, an area that has attracted increased attention in recent years as gays in the military and gay marriage have been taken up by parties and candidates.[36]

In Table 3.5, we examine how these various measures of the cultural divide are related to party identification and vote choice over time.[37] In the table, positive numbers indicate a greater partisan distance between holders of extreme positions. For example, in 1972, pro-life respondents were seven percentage points more likely than pro-choice respondents to vote Republican (bottom panel). In 2008, that figure increased to +56, meaning that pro-life respondents were now fifty-six percentage points (90 percent minus 34 percent) more likely than pro-choice respondents to support the Republican presidential candidate.

TABLE 3.5 The Cultural Divide, Party Identification and Vote Choice, 1972–2008 (Whites Only)

PARTY ID	Religious Commitment*	Abortion**	Attitudes toward Gays***
1972	+6	−6	
1976	+10	−4	
1980	+18	0	
1984	+12	+11	+30
1988	+9	+9	+28
1992	+18	+19	+31
1996	+25	+19	+41
2000	+22	+24	+29
2004	+19	+36	+36
2008	+30	+30	+35

* Percentage identifying as Republican among those who worship every week—percentage identifying as Republican among those who never worship.

** Percentage identifying as Republican among pro-life respondents—percentage identifying as Republican among pro-choice respondents.

*** Percentage identifying as Republican among those who put gays and lesbians below 25 degrees on the feeling thermometer—percentage identifying as Republican among those who put gays and lesbians above 75 degrees on the feeling thermometer.

VOTE	Religious Commitment*	Abortion**	Attitudes toward Gays***
1972	+19	+7	
1976	+8	+2	
1980	+17	+20	
1984	+11	+18	+45
1988	+10	+14	+45
1992	+30	+34	+42
1996	+31	+38	+50
2000	+27	+42	+45
2004	+21	+46	+47
2008	+32	+56	+49

Source: American National Election Studies.

* Percentage voting Republican among those who worship every week—percentage voting Republican among those who never worship.

** Percentage voting Republican among pro-life respondents—percentage voting Republican among pro-choice respondents.

*** Percentage voting Republican among those who put gays and lesbians below 25 degrees on the feeling thermometer—percentage voting Republican among those who put gays and lesbians above 75 degrees on the feeling thermometer.

There are two principal substantive conclusions to be drawn from this table. First, attitudes toward gays and lesbians have very consistently produced high levels of polarization with respect to vote choice (bottom panel). Citizens who express antipathy toward gays and lesbians are about forty-five to fifty percentage points more likely to vote Republican than are citizens who express more sympathy toward gays and lesbians. These were the highest degrees of polarization associated with any of our cultural divide variables until 2008, when views on abortion produced the +56 split described above. Our second conclusion is that 1992 appears to have been a watershed year with respect to cultural polarization. Both the religious commitment measure and the abortion measure show major increases in the levels of voting polarization beginning in 1992. Abortion became a far better predictor of vote choice than it had been previously and, to a lesser degree, so did religious differences. Finally, from 2000 to 2008, both pro-life voters and antigay voters were on average forty-seven to forty-eight percentage points more likely than pro-choice and pro-gay voters to support the Republican candidate.

The analysis of party identification (top panel) tells a similar tale. Again, 1992 appears as a pivotal time point when the cultural divide began to manifest itself much more clearly in patterns of party identification. Religious Americans became increasingly likely to identify as Republicans, and attitudes toward abortion became a stronger predictor of party identification beginning in 1992 and continuing to the present. A high degree of polarization in party identification based on attitudes toward gays and lesbians has been present since the question was first asked. All of these findings support the claim that cultural issues became a more important shaper of partisanship and vote choice in the 1990s than in previous decades.

Returning to the question of how best to measure the cultural divide, the figures in Table 3.5 suggest that all three of these measures do a fairly good job on this score. As one might expect, there is a significant degree of overlap among the groups defined by these three variables. For example, from 1984 to 2008 (aggregated), almost two-thirds of those who rated gays and lesbians highest on our scale (76 to 100 degrees) also believed that by law a woman should always be able to obtain an abortion. Similarly, 68 percent of those who worship every week believe that abortion should either never be allowed or allowed only in the case of rape, incest, or danger to the mother's health. In short, these divisions are reinforcing. Still, the abortion attitude and gay feeling thermometer measures produce somewhat sharper divisions, especially in recent years.

Taking all of this into account, we decided that the abortion variable is the best single measure of the cultural divide. It has a longer history with NES than the gay feeling thermometer, and has been asked in similar form since 1972. Additionally, there is good deal of evidence that attitudes toward abortion are reflective of a larger worldview, and thus this may be the best indicator of a broader cultural outlook.[38] For these reasons, we believe that taking a strong stand for or against abortion is a fairly pure indicator of cultural differences;

variations in religious observance do not capture these differences as neatly or as cleanly. It is also important to point out that respondents who embrace the polarized positions on the abortion issue constitute a significant share of the population. Since 1972, between 10 and 15 percent of respondents in the NES surveys have endorsed the pro-life position and about 35 to 40 percent have embraced the pro-choice position.

Abortion as a Measure of the Cultural Divide

As we have demonstrated, pro-life and pro-choice Americans have grown further apart in their voting behavior and party identification. These partisan differences seem to reflect the increasing clarity of the parties' relative positions and images. By 1980, the party platforms began to separate themselves on abortion and other cultural issues.[39] As we have already discussed, since the 1980s, the Democrats have become widely regarded as the party of social liberalism in contrast to the Republican Party, which is perceived as the party of traditional values. As the images and positions of the parties became increasingly distinct, it stands to reason that pro-choice and pro-life citizens would be more likely to make partisan assessments on the basis of abortion and related issues. An intriguing new wrinkle in this story, which emerges most clearly in 2004 and 2008, is the possibility that the cultural divide may also be affecting attitudes on noncultural issues.

In Table 3.6 we examine assessments of the parties on a number of different dimensions, broken down by respondents' position on abortion.[40] NES respondents were asked about the party to which they felt closer (2004 only), and the party that best represented their views. They were also asked about the competence of each party to handle the economy, the war on terrorism (2004 only) and to keep the country out of war. Given the strengthening relationship between abortion and party identification, the findings on which party respondents felt closer to and which party best represented their views are not surprising. Pro-life respondents feel a lot closer to the Republicans, and more than two-thirds of them say that the Republican Party best represents their views. However, the figures on perceptions of party competence (bottom four rows of Table 3.6) suggest that abortion has become increasingly connected to partisan assessments in areas that are unrelated to the abortion issue. For example, 19 percent of pro-choice respondents believe that the Republican Party is best able to deal with the economy, compared to 49 percent of pro-life respondents. A similar split can be observed on the question of which party is best able to deal with the country's most important problem. We find the same pattern in dealing with terrorism and war. Pro-life respondents are a lot more likely than pro-choice respondents to cite Republican competence. At least on the surface, these partisan assessments have nothing to do with social or cultural issues; yet, might they somehow be influenced by the latter?

TABLE 3.6 Abortion and Perceptions of the Parties in 2004 and 2008 (Whites Only)

(Entries are percentage selecting Republican Party)

	POSITION ON ABORTION			
	Always permitted	If need is clearly established	Only for rape, incest, health of mother	Never permitted
Which party do you feel closer to (2004)	19%	38%	34%	48%
Which party best represents your views (2008)	26	37	64	78
Party best on most important problem (2008)	19	37	39	46
Party best on economy (2008)	19	27	33	49
Party best on War on Terrorism (2004)	35	47	53	63
Party best on keeping U.S. out of war (2008)	7	17	18	47

Source: American National Election Studies.

Interestingly, we have found that that this connection extends to a wide range of nonsocial issues. In Table 3.7, we examine the correlations between abortion and positions on six other issues, none of which is obviously related to abortion. These correlation coefficients are relative and run on a scale that extends from −1 to +1. Positive numbers indicate that respondents who are conservative on the abortion issue also tend to be conservative on the other issue. On most of the issues, we can compare correlations going back to the 1970s and '80s. Our principal finding, when we compare these coefficients across time, is that the relationship between abortion and other noncultural issues appears to be strengthening. In recent elections, people who are pro-life are more likely to oppose a government role in providing jobs, they are more likely to oppose government health insurance, they are also more likely to oppose tax increases that would allow government to expand its services, and they are more likely to oppose government aid to African Americans. Even in the area of national defense, pro-lifers are more likely than they used to be to support more spending. And

TABLE 3.7 Abortion and Other Non-Cultural Issues, 1972–2008 (Whites Only)

(Entries below are Spearman rho correlation coefficients)

	Abortion and Jobs/ Standard of Living	Abortion and Health Insurance	Abortion and Government Services	Abortion and Aid to Blacks	Abortion and Defense	Abortion and the Environment
1972	.01	.07*		.14**		
1976	−.01	.05		.09**		
1980	−.01			.07**	.08*	
1984	−.02	.06	.06*	.03	.13**	
1988	−.01	.03	.06	.02	.09**	
1992	.06*	.09**	.12**	.07**	.19**	
1996	.13*	.17**	.13**	.10**	.20**	.17**
2000	.06	.15**	.14**	.09*	.17**	.21**
2004	.17*	.14**	.17**	.12**	.20**	
2008	.16**	.21**	.17**	.19**	.31**	.29**

(Entries below are percent placing themselves on the conservative side of the issue scale)

2004	Pro-Choice Respondents	Pro-Life Respondents
Government jobs	44%	71%
Government aid to blacks	51	68
Government services	20	41
Government health insurance	32	48
Defense spending	47	75

Source: American National Election Studies.
* $p < .05$
** $p < .01$

although the question about the environment was not asked before 1996, our findings indicate that there is a fairly strong connection between opposition to abortion and opposition to environmental regulation.

The pattern from these correlation coefficients is fairly clear and consistent across issues: a strengthening relationship beginning in the late 1980s or '90s. Indeed by 2004–2008, the correlations between abortion and other issues are strongest on all of the issues for which we have comparisons over time, signifying that the cultural divide is alive and well in contemporary America. In the bottom panel of Table 3.7, we illustrate these strengthening connections by providing some examples of the relationship between abortion and other issues in 2004 using simple percentages. The figures in the table contrast the proportions of pro-life and pro-choice respondents who took conservative positions on various issues. As is apparent, the gaps run from sixteen percentage points (health insurance) to twenty-eight points (defense spending). These differences are large and suggest a high and generalized degree of polarization between pro-life and pro-choice Americans. To be clear, we are not arguing that attitudes toward abortion are causal antecedents to attitudes on nonsocial issues. Rather, we are arguing that distinct attitudes toward abortion are reflective of a cultural divide among Americans, and that this divide now extends beyond cultural issues to other issues associated with the parties' images.[41]

On this latter point, we take issue with Fiorina et al., who suggest that in the 2000–2004 period the degree of polarization among Americans was overstated. These authors compare aggregate levels of support for various policies between respondents in "blue states" and respondents in "red states." They find, for example, residents of blue states are "only" eight percentage points more likely to support gay marriage than residents of red states. The comparable gaps in pro-choice opinion and support for gay adoption are twelve and sixteen points, respectively.[42] But comparing and contrasting aggregate measures of attitudes between residents of blue states and residents of red states both obscures and understates the differences between key groups (Democrats versus Republicans, pro-choice versus pro-life) *within* these states, and in the country as a whole. In Table 3.7, we presented data from 2004 that show *very* large gaps on various nonsocial issues between supporters and opponents of abortion rights nationwide. On social issues, the gaps are even bigger, as can be seen in Table 3.8. Thus while Fiorina et al. found that there was only an eight-point gap between red state and blue state citizens in support of gay marriage in 2004, we find that if polarization is measured not geographically but "culturally," then the gap between pro-life and pro-choice citizens on this same issue is fifty-five percentage points! Even within blue states and within red states, differences rooted in attitudes toward abortion are very large.[43] With the exception of the death penalty, all of the issues displayed in Table 3.8 show large differences, which attests to the presence of a significant cultural divide, Fiorina et al. notwithstanding.

Conclusion

In this chapter, we have taken a detailed look at the foundations of partisanship in the United States. The abundant data we have presented point to one central conclusion: that the major political parties in the United States attract decidedly different followings. In our view, the combination of evidence showing widespread recognition of party images (Chapter 2) and the distinctive coalitions of citizens comprising the parties (this chapter) suggests that the choices most Americans make about the parties and their candidates are rational calculations based on what the parties stand for. African Americans and women are drawn to

TABLE 3.8 Abortion and Other Cultural Issues, 2004 (Whites Only)

	Pro-Choice Respondents	Pro-Life Respondents
Supports death penalty	71%	71%
Stricter gun control	63%	41%
Supports gay marriage	59%	4%
Supports school vouchers	21%	46%
Supports gays in military	91%	53%
Prays at least once a day	32%	90%
Feeling thermometer rating of Christian Fundamentalists (mean)	42 degrees	74 degrees

Source: American National Election Studies.

the Democrats because of the stands the party has taken on certain issues; likewise for white, male Southerners and the Republicans. Many of these calculations are self-interested in the traditional sense—wealthy Americans prefer Republicans, and poor Americans prefer Democrats. Others reflect choices made on the basis of ideology, or especially strongly held views on certain issues (abortion). The key point, however, is that the main patterns in party identification and vote choice in relation to demographic variables such as region, race, gender, age, and others are readily understandable in terms of the prevailing images of what Democrats and Republicans represent.

Our intensive analysis of the effect of class and culture on partisanship and voting suggest that both of these factors can play an important role in shaping the partisan choices that Americans make. For example, we have shown that income and class interact with other factors to produce a stronger effect on partisan choice both in the South and among men than is the case among women and non-Southerners. We have also established that the abortion issue, which we use to characterize a larger cultural divide, has become a reliable predictor of partisanship and the vote, especially since 1992. Furthermore, individuals who hold polarized views on this issue are quite different, not only in the partisan assessments they make, but also in the positions they take on an array of issues—both cultural and noncultural. The evidence we have presented also indicates that the impact of issues related to class and culture vary from one election to the next, depending on the particular circumstances at play.

Most of the relationships we have examined in this chapter are bivariate in nature (the exception being those displayed in Table 3.1) and, therefore, do not measure the effects of factors such as income and views on abortion while controlling for others. For example, how much does ideology (liberal versus conservative) affect vote choice independently of income? Or, does the region of the country one lives in affect how much impact extreme views on abortion have on voting? In order to assess the independent effect of the various factors we have examined in this chapter, we have constructed a multivariate model that uses key demographic variables (gender, education, region, income, and race), and selected nondemographic variables (ideology, attitudes on abortion, and party identification) as possible explanations (independent variables) for the vote choices (dependent variable) that citizens make.[44] The main findings are displayed in Figure 3.10, where the relative effects of four variables (party identification, ideology, abortion, and income) are displayed over time (the full model is displayed in Appendix B.8).

In Figure 3.10, we graph each variable's standardized coefficient over time. The advantage of standardization is that it enables us to compare the relative sizes of the coefficients, which reflect the magnitude of the impact of each variable on vote.[45] The clear and overriding conclusion of such a comparison is that the independent effect of party identification on vote choice is much larger than the effect of the other factors in every presidential election since 1972. We can also see that from 1976 through 1984, the impact of party identification on the vote grew substantially, and that from 1984 through 2000, it continued to grow, albeit at a more modest level. The upshot is that in spite of all the recent talk about economic populism and cultural backlashes, party identification is still (and by far) the most important influence on vote choice.[46] Other important political influences, such as where one lives (region), or how much money one has (income), exert their influence on voting mainly through choices Americans make about the parties. Democratic identifiers (strong, weak, and leaning) tend to vote for the presidential candidate of their party; the same holds true for Republicans (see Appendix B.1). As we argued in Chapter 2, parties represent a central point of political reference for most Americans. The evidence we present here adds additional support to the idea that for most Americans parties matter a great deal.

Figure 3.10 also shows that ideology is the second most powerful influencer of vote choice. Conservative voters (regardless of partisan affiliation) tend to support Republican candidates; liberal voters (even a few liberal Republicans) tend to support Democrats. To be certain, the effect of ideology is smaller than that of party identification, but like party identification, it is statistically significant in every election year. Interestingly, from 1972 to 1984, as the effect of party identification grew, the impact of ideology diminished somewhat. This makes sense in that parties were less salient during these years, relatively few voters perceived important differences between the parties, and hence the ability to make ideologically driven choices was somewhat muted. But beginning in 1984, and continuing through the 1990s, we find a modest growth in the influence of both party identification and ideology on vote choice. As we have already argued, it is during these years that public awareness of differences between the

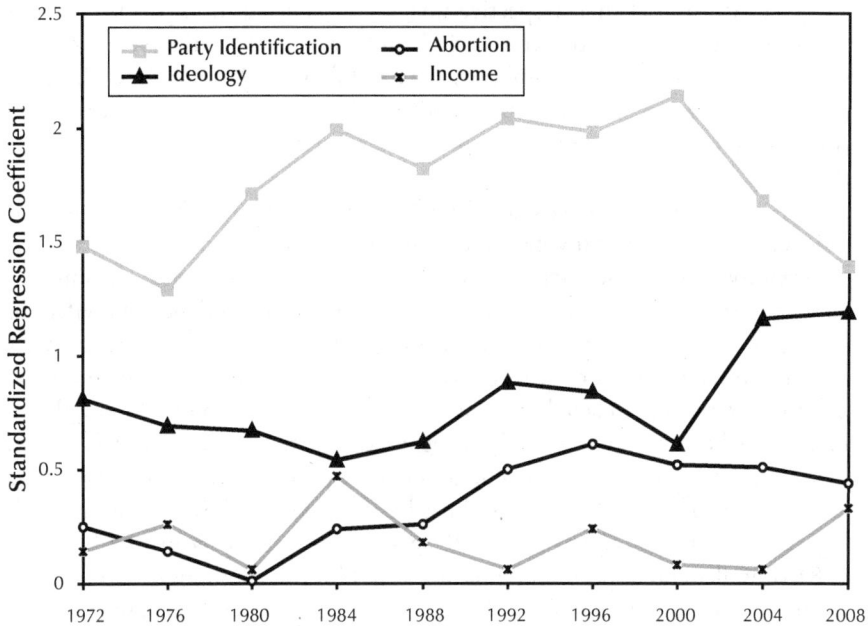

Figure 3.10 Influences on Vote Choice, 1972–2008

Source: American National Election Studies.

parties heightened. What all of this suggests is that increasing elite-level party differentiation puts a larger portion of the electorate in a position to make ideologically driven choices. The sharp rise in the impact of ideology during the 2004 and 2008 campaigns is a case in point. More than 75 percent of Americans perceived important differences between the parties in these two elections (see Table 2.5), the highest figure since that question was first asked in 1952. This context induced liberal-leaning voters to vote for Kerry and Obama, and conservative-leaning voters to vote for Bush and McCain.

The only other consistently significant independent relationship is between race and vote choice (see Appendix B.8). As we have demonstrated in numerous ways up to this point, African Americans, regardless of their income, ideology, where they live, views on abortion, or anything else, vote consistently for Democratic presidential candidates. Exit polls revealed that Kerry won a whopping 88 percent of the African American vote in the 2004 election, and that was the lowest Democratic total in the past three elections (Gore won 90 percent in 2000 and Obama won 95 percent in 2008).

Some of the other factors featured in Figure 3.10 come into play at different points in time and under different circumstances. Attitudes on abortion have had a significant independent effect on voting since 1984, and this effect became stronger during the 1990s. As we discussed earlier, in the 1990s each party's platform and their respective images, as reflected in respondents' open-ended likes and dislikes, began to include more references to the Democrats as a pro-choice party and the Republicans as a pro-life party. As more voters began to associate the parties with these polarized positions, abortion (and other cultural issues) emerged as a more important dividing line in shaping voters' choices at the polls.

In recent years, social class, as defined by income, has not been a significant independent influence on vote choice. Although there are important differences between the political preferences of the bottom and top third of the income distribution, these differences have not exerted a significant independent effect on voting in recent elections. Thus the income effect appears to run through partisanship on its way to voting. In the earlier years, there were instances in which income differences impacted vote choice directly. The most notable example was in 1984, when the policies of the Reagan administration were on trial after a major recession in 1981–1983. The result was a presidential vote strongly influenced by income and class—those hurt by the recession (lower-income, working-class Americans) voted against Reagan; those helped by his tax breaks of 1981 (middle- and upper-middle classes) voted for him. Although income-based voting rose a bit in 2008, our analysis suggests that in recent years, the independent influence of cultural issues on voting has been stronger than that of income and social class.

Culture, class, race, and ideology are all important factors in the American political environment, but their importance is quite simply dwarfed by partisanship. This finding echoes that of the authors of the seminal work on the American electorate, *The American Voter*, who also placed parties at the center of Americans' political universe. However, these authors expressed several concerns about the centrality of partisanship in voting behavior. What their exhaustive study had uncovered was a citizenry that made its choices about party affiliation too early in life, and held on to them, even though some of the political beliefs they had acquired later in life might have steered them in another direction. This is the New Deal–driven, partisanship-as-loyalty phenomenon we discussed in Chapter 2. The electorate of the 1950s also showed high levels of political ignorance and apathy, and low levels of ideological sophistication. Although our examination of the twenty-first-century American electorate also places the parties at the center of America's political universe, it is a very different universe. Voters are better informed, have more strongly held political beliefs, and can, for the most part, navigate the political world intelligently and choose between two parties that represent distinct ideological positions. Their choices about parties and presidential candidates, by and large, reflect their issue beliefs and their ideological persuasion. One might go so far as to say that the quality of our electoral democracy in the United States has improved.

Appendix B

Appendix B.1 Income and Party Identification, 1952–2008

Republican Partisan Advantage*

	Income Percentile			
	0%–33%	34%–67%	68%–100%	All respondents
1952	–30	–28	–16	–23
1956	–20	–20	–4	–13
1960	–20	–22	–14	–18
1964	–42	–41	–13	–31
1968	–32	–21	–13	–23
1972	–26	–23	–4	–18
1976	–33	–24	0	–18
1980	–37	–18	–2	–20
1984	–28	–8	+10	–9
1988	–23	–5	+10	–6
1992	–28	–17	+7	–12
1996	–37	–19	+13	–14
2000	–27	–8	0	–12
2004	–25	–7	+2	–9
2008	–35	–13	+14	–14

Percentage Identifying as Independent

	Income Percentile			
	0%–33%	34%–67%	68%–100%	All respondents
1952	6%	5%	6%	6%
1956	9	10	9	9
1960	9	6	6	9
1964	9	8	6	8
1968	12	11	10	11
1972	12	15	11	13
1976	12	15	16	14
1980	11	16	11	13
1984	13	10	9	11
1988	12	11	9	11
1992	14	12	9	12
1996	9	10	7	9
2000	13	12	8	12
2004	14	7	6	10
2008	9	10	6	8

Source: American National Election Studies.

*Republican Partisan Advantage = Percent of group identifying as Republican—percent of group identifying as Democrat. Positive numbers indicate Republican advantage; negative numbers indicate Democratic advantage.

Appendix B.2 Region and Party Identification, 1952–2008

Republican Partisan Advantage*

	Non-South	South	Southern Whites	All respondents
1952	−11	−68	−70	−23
1956	−2	−49	−50	−13
1960	−9	−47	−50	−18
1964	−24	−56	−50	−31
1968	−15	−47	−36	−23
1972	−13	−33	−26	−18
1976	−12	−36	−22	−18
1980	−15	−31	−20	−20
1984	−3	−21	−2	−9
1988	+1	−22	−2	−6
1992	−10	−18	+1	−12
1996	−13	−17	+4	−14
2000	−13	−9	+11	−12
2004	−10	−7	+20	−9
2008	−22	−3	+16	−14

Percentage Identifying as Independent

	Non-South	South	Southern Whites	All respondents
1952	7%	2%	2%	6%
1956	10	6	6	9
1960	10	9	9	9
1964	8	8	8	8
1968	10	11	14	11
1972	13	15	14	13
1976	14	14	16	14
1980	13	13	14	13
1984	10	15	14	11
1988	11	10	11	11
1992	11	14	13	12
1996	9	9	8	9
2000	11	13	13	12
2004	10	9	7	10
2008	8	9	9	8

Source: American National Election Studies.

*Republican Partisan Advantage = Percent of group identifying as Republican—percent of group identifying as Democrat. Positive numbers indicate Republican advantage; negative numbers indicate Democratic advantage.

Appendix B.3 Gender and Party Identification, 1952–2008

Republican Partisan Advantage*

	Men	Women	All respondents
1952	−26	−21	−23
1956	−20	−7	−13
1960	−20	−16	−18
1964	−31	−31	−31
1968	−18	−26	−23
1972	−13	−21	−18
1976	−16	−19	−18
1980	−15	−24	−20
1984	−4	−12	−9
1988	+2	−13	−6
1992	−3	−21	−12
1996	−1	−25	−14
2000	−2	−19	−12
2004	0	−17	−9
2008	−7	−21	−14

Percentage Identifying as Independent

	Men	Women	All respondents
1952	7%	5	6%
1956	10	9	9
1960	10	9	9
1964	8	8	8
1968	11	11	11
1972	15	12	13
1976	16	13	14
1980	15	12	13
1984	12	11	11
1988	11	10	11
1992	13	11	12
1996	9	9	9
2000	11	12	12
2004	10	9	10
2008	−11	−6	−8

Source: American National Election Studies.

*Republican Partisan Advantage = Percent of group identifying as Republican—percent of group identifying as Democrat. Positive numbers indicate Republican advantage; negative numbers indicate Democratic advantage.

Appendix B.4 Race and Party Identification, 1952–2008

Republican Partisan Advantage*

	White	Black	All respondents
1952	−20	−56	−23
1956	−11	−45	−13
1960	−16	−36	−18
1964	−26	−78	−31
1968	−15	−92	−23
1972	−12	−66	−18
1976	−8	−80	−18
1980	−12	−76	−20
1984	+2	−66	−9
1988	+9	−71	−6
1992	−1	−71	−12
1996	−3	−72	−14
2000	0	−77	−12
2004	+5	−76	−9
2008	+1	−81	−14

Percentage Identifying as Independent

	White	Black	All respondents
1952	6%	4%	6%
1956	9	8	9
1960	9	13	9
1964	8	6	8
1968	12	3	11
1972	13	12	13
1976	15	8	14
1980	14	7	13
1984	10	11	11
1988	11	6	11
1992	12	13	12
1996	8	11	9
2000	12	10	12
2004	9	11	10
2008	8	7	8

Source: American National Election Studies.

*Republican Partisan Advantage = Percent of group identifying as Republican—percent of group identifying as Democrat. Positive numbers indicate Republican advantage; negative numbers indicate Democratic advantage.

Appendix B.5 Age and Party Identification, 1952–2008

Republican Partisan Advantage*

	18–24	25–34	35–44	45–54	55–64	65 or older	All respondents
1952	−39	−27	−34	−22	−7	−11	−23
1956	−26	−16	−23	−10	+5	−4	−13
1960	−42	−24	−24	−21	−9	−6	−18
1964	−45	−37	−30	−36	−37	−6	−31
1968	−32	−16	−30	−21	−20	−22	−23
1972	−31	−13	−16	−23	−17	−10	−18
1976	−20	−21	−15	−18	−18	−14	−18
1980	−13	−23	−17	−12	−31	−23	−20
1984	−11	−4	−3	−17	−19	−4	−9
1988	+3	−4	−4	−17	−3	−11	−6
1992	−9	−6	−13	−10	−18	−19	−12
1996	−19	−15	−15	−12	−8	−17	−14
2000	−24	−3	−9	−15	−17	−14	−12
2004	−29	−16	−1	−6	−2	−9	−9
2008	−28	−25	−13	−5	−20	−5	−14

Percentage Identifying as Independent

	18–24	25–34	35–44	45–54	55–64	65 or older	All respondents
1952	7%	6%	6%	6%	7%	6%	6%
1956	13	9	9	8	11	6	9
1960	5	12	10	13	5	6	9
1964	11	9	9	7	6	6	8
1968	18	13	11	10	10	7	11
1972	18	18	16	10	8	8	13
1976	20	19	18	10	9	9	14
1980	21	17	12	9	10	9	13
1984	15	12	13	8	10	9	11
1988	15	13	13	7	7	8	11
1992	17	14	11	11	10	9	12
1996	10	10	9	9	8	7	9
2000	22	16	11	9	9	9	12
2004	12	7	11	10	9	11	10
2008	12	11	9	7	6	6	8

Source: American National Election Studies.

*Republican Partisan Advantage = Percent of group identifying as Republican—percent of group identifying as Democrat. Positive numbers indicate Republican advantage; negative numbers indicate Democratic advantage.

Appendix B.6 Education and Party Identification, 1952–2008

Republican Partisan Advantage*

	Less than high school	High school diploma	Some college	College degree	All respondents
1952	-33	-24	0	+9	-23
1956	-12	-19	-4	+7	-13
1960	-25	-25	+2	+14	-18
1964	-51	-33	-13	+2	-31
1968	-47	-27	-4	+12	-23
1972	-28	-21	-13	+4	-18
1976	-38	-23	-7	+10	-18
1980	-43	-24	-12	-2	-20
1984	-30	-13	0	+4	-9
1988	-31	-13	+5	+10	-6
1992	-43	-21	-5	+3	-12
1996	-51	-24	-10	+1	-14
2000	-36	-25	-9	+3	-12
2004	-25	-15	-4	-6	-9
2008	-40	-24	-10	-4	-14

Percentage Identifying as Independent

	Less than high school	High school diploma	Some college	College degree	All respondents
1952	7%	6%	4%	3%	6%
1956	8	11	6	6	9
1960	8	10	11	6	9
1964	8	8	9	6	8
1968	9	12	11	8	11
1972	13	15	12	9	13
1976	12	17	14	10	14
1980	13	17	9	8	13
1984	20	12	8	8	11
1988	14	13	8	7	11
1992	11	13	13	9	12
1996	16	11	7	6	9
2000	12	15	11	8	12
2004	25	13	9	5	10
2008	6	11	10	3	8

Source: American National Election Studies.

*Republican Partisan Advantage = Percent of group identifying as Republican—percent of group identifying as Democrat. Positive numbers indicate Republican advantage; negative numbers indicate Democratic advantage.

Appendix B.7 Religious Worship and Party Identification, 1952–2008

Republican Partisan Advantage*

	Every week[a]	Almost every week[b]	1–2 times per month	Few times per year[c]	Never	All respondents
1952	−26	−14		−23	−27	−23
1956	−15	−8		−13	−7	−13
1960	−19	−12		−25	−2	−18
1964	−27	−26		−36	−42	−31
1968	−22	−27		−20	−28	−23
1972	−19	−8	−24	−14	−24	−18
1976	−15	−7	−27	−15	−22	−18
1980	−10	−11	−27	−21	−29	−20
1984	−3	+5	−23	−9	−13	−9
1988	−6	+3	−14	−4	−9	−6
1992	+1	−2	−17	−16	−23	−12
1996	+6	−7	−24	−19	−28	−14
2000	+3	−3	−17	−24	−19	−12
2004	+1	−6	−31	−24	−13	−9
2008	+14	+1	−31	−30	−24	−14

Percentage Identifying as Independent

	Every week[a]	Almost every week[b]	1–2 times per month	Few times per year[c]	Never	All respondents
1952	5%	6%		6%	13%	6%
1956	8	8		11	9	9
1960	8	10		10	13	9
1964	6	11		7	10	8
1968	10	7		10	15	11
1972	11	10	13%	16	15	13
1976	12	10	11	16	20	14
1980	11	10	10	13	20	13
1984	11	6	13	11	13	11
1988	9	6	8	12	16	11
1992	10	9	11	13	14	12
1996	7	5	7	8	12	9
2000	8	11	13	12	14	12
2004	8	10	10	10	10	10
2008	5	7	9	9	10	8

Source: American National Election Studies.

*Republican Partisan Advantage = Percent of group identifying as Republican—percent of group identifying as Democrat. Positive numbers indicate Republican advantage; negative numbers indicate Democratic advantage.

[a] Category was "Regularly" before 1972.

[b] Category was "Often" before 1972.

[c] Category was "Seldom" before 1972.

Appendix B.8 Predicting Vote Choice, 1972–2008

(Cell entries are unstandardized logistic regression coefficients)

	1972	1976	1980	1984	1988	1992	1996	2000	2004	2008
Party ID	.75**	.66**	.86**	.96**	.87**	1.00**	.94**	1.04**	.81**	.66**
Ideology	.64**	.51**	.48**	.39**	.45**	.62**	.62**	.42*	.82**	.77**
Abortion	.25**	.14	.01	.22*	.24*	.46**	.56**	.47*	.47**	.40*
Gender	.19	-.12	.27	-.11	.03	-.14	-.07	-.18	-.14	-.80*
Education	-.20*	.13	-.21	-.24	-.07	.17	.20	-.62*	-.01	-.40
Region	1.09**	-.12	.20	.61*	.74**	.46	.49	.38	.17	1.20**
Income	.12	.23*	.05	.42**	.16	.05	.21	.07	.05	.28
Race	-2.67**	-1.18*	-2.01**	-1.64**	-2.43**	-2.51**	-4.10**	-1.32	-1.60**	-5.31*
Constant	-3.60	-4.30	-2.70	-4.43	-4.34	-6.19	-5.58	-4.12	-5.74	-0.96

Source: American National Election Studies.

* $p < .05$.

** $p < .01$.

Dependent variable. Vote: 0 = Democratic candidate; 1 = Republican candidate.

Independent variables. Party ID: 1 = Strong Democrat; 2 = Weak Democrat; 3 = Independent-Democrat; 4 = Independent; 5 = Independent-Republican; 6 = Weak Republican; 7 = Strong Republican.

Ideology: 1 = Extremely liberal; 2 = Liberal; 3 = Slightly liberal; 4 = Moderate; 5 = Slightly conservative; 6 = Conservative; 7 = Extremely conservative.

Abortion: 1972 and 1976: 1 = Abortion should never be forbidden, since one should not require a woman to have a child she doesn't want; 2 = Abortion should be permitted if, due to personal reasons, the woman would have difficulty in caring for the child; 3 = Abortion should be permitted only if the life and health of the woman is in danger; 4 = Abortion should never be permitted.

1980 to 2008: 1 = By law, a woman should always be able to obtain an abortion as a matter of personal choice; 2 = The law should permit abortion for reasons other than rape, incest, or danger to the woman's life, but only after the need for the abortion has been clearly established; 3 = The law should permit abortion only in case of rape, incest, or when the woman's life is in danger; 4 = By law, abortion should never be permitted.

Gender: 1 = Female; 2 = Male.

Education: 1 = Less than high school; 2 = High school diploma; 3 = Some college; 4 = College degree.

Region: 1 = Non-South; 2 = South.

Income: 1 = 0–16 percentile; 2 = 17–33 percentile; 3 = 34–67 percentile; 4 = 68 to 95 percentile; 5 = 96–100 percentile.

Race: 1 = White; 2 = Black.

CHAPTER 4

The Midterm Elections of 1994 and 2006

The congressional midterm elections of 1994 and 2006 share many common elements. The most obvious and important point of commonality was the dramatic outcomes; in both cases long-standing majorities of the president's party in Congress were overturned by the party out of power. And, in both cases, the outcome was largely an expression of dissatisfaction with the policies and performance of the president and Congress. Another noteworthy aspect of these two midterm elections is that parties, and party labels, were front and center in both of them. These were not typical congressional elections where what matters most is the candidates, especially incumbents, who almost always win over relatively weak challengers, and where state and local issues trump national issues in determining the results. In both of these elections, the parties, as national entities, helped to focus the attention of voters on the deficiencies of the president and his allies in Congress. There was a call for change in national direction, which the voters heard loudly and clearly, and the parties played a central role in shaping and articulating that call. In this chapter, we examine congressional elections in general, and the 1994 and 2006 elections in particular, with the goal of extending our description of the resurgence of partisanship

The Election of 1994:
Gingrich Leads the Charge Against Clinton

The 1994 congressional election was as close as this country is ever likely to get to a party-based election of the "strong" or "responsible" party mode, particularly on the House side. Newt Gingrich put together a strategy whereby Republican House candidates, both incumbents and challengers, would sign a document called "The Contract with America," which listed a number of specific legislative steps Republicans would take if they secured a majority in the chamber.[1] The contract was the product of several months of work by Gingrich and future Majority Leader Richard Armey (R-TX). They were successful in getting some 367 Republican candidates to sign it, and later assembled more than three hundred of them in front of the Capitol for a major unveiling ceremony on September 27, 1994.² Most Republican House candidates around the country designed their campaigns around all or most of the items in the contract, and Gingrich and Armey promised to have the House vote (and pass) each item within one hundred days of the 104th Congress. Gingrich pitched the contract right out of the responsible party playbook; the idea was to tell the American public what a Republican majority would do, and then do it. Shortly after the election, the soon-to-be Speaker of the House Gingrich said, "At the end of the first one hundred days, the American people, at Easter, will be able to say they saw a group of people who actually said what they were going to do and then kept their word."³

Of course, the 1994 congressional elections were about a lot more than the Contract with America. Public dissatisfaction with President Clinton, with politics in Washington, and with the overall conditions and trends in the country led large numbers of citizens to vote for change. Clinton's troubles stemmed in part from a perception that he was politically inept. The high visibility failure of his (and his wife's) health care reform proposal to attract support in a Congress controlled by Democrats made a huge contribution to this perception. But even his successful legislative efforts did not necessarily make him popular with the public. His breakthrough budget bill in 1993 included tax increases, his anti-crime bill had gun control components, and the North American Free Trade Agreement (NAFTA) was strongly opposed by blue collar workers and many other Democrats. Couple this with the stands he took on cultural issues, such as gays in the military ("don't ask, don't tell") and abortion (pro-choice), not to mention the "Whitewater" scandal that would not go away, and you had a recipe for low public approval. In the fall leading up to the 1994 midterm election, Clinton's job approval rating averaged around 45 percent, and 57 percent of Americans thought the country was heading down the wrong track.⁴ Congress's approval rating was even lower at 23 percent.⁵

The unpopularity of Clinton and Congress in 1994 should be considered, or reflected upon, by taking into account the larger political context in which it occurred. The early 1990s was a time of considerable political unrest. George H. W. Bush had been voted out of office two years earlier—even though he was enormously popular following the first Gulf War (in 1991)—because of a bad economy and the fact that he had two formidable opponents (Clinton and Ross Perot), both of whom promised change. Clinton only received 43 percent of the popular vote, while Perot got a whopping 19 percent—the most by a third-party candidate since Teddy Roosevelt in 1912. Perot's campaign was all about changing "business as usual" in Washington, DC, especially partisan gridlock. As described above, the record of Clinton and the Democratic Congress in 1993–1994 did nothing to quell the calls for a shakeup in Washington.

And quite apart from Clinton, congressional scandals were an important element of the public's view of Washington. In 1992, public cynicism about Congress escalated when it was revealed that House members regularly borrowed money from the House bank, with no interest being charged. In 1994, powerful

Democratic Ways and Means Committee Chairman Dan Rostenkowski was indicted on various financial abuse charges, for which he was later convicted and sent to jail.[6] The media lavished quite a bit of attention on both of these episodes. The 1994 election year mixture of scandal, limited legislative accomplishments, widespread dissatisfaction with the economy, and the widely held belief that the country was on the "wrong track" certainly did not bode well for the party in power.

Still, very few pundits and scholars predicted the partisan landslide that occurred. The Republicans gained fifty-three seats and a 230 to 205 majority in the House. They picked up seven seats for a 53 to 47 majority in the Senate. As noted in Chapter 1, this was the first time the Republicans enjoyed a majority in the House since 1954. The recent electoral history of Republicans in the Senate was only slightly better, having secured a majority in that chamber in 1980 for the first time since 1954, but losing it in 1986. The 1994 Republican gains in the House came from defeating 34 Democratic incumbents (out of 225 who ran for reelection) and winning 39 of 52 elections for open seats. Not a single Republican incumbent lost, and they took away 22 of the 31 open seats previously occupied by Democrats. In the Senate, the Republicans won 21 of the 35 races held that year. All the Republican incumbents won, they retained all the open seats they had previously held, took six open seats away from Democrats, but they defeated only two Democratic incumbents. All told, there were 87 new members of the House, including 74 Republicans, and 11 new senators.[7]

The mood in the two chambers immediately following the election was somewhat different. Gingrich and House Republicans were on a mission. One Republican leader put it this way, "We are going to be revolutionary. This is not patty cake, this is not pickup sticks. This is serious. We're going at their throats."[8] Senate Majority Leader Robert Dole set a contrasting tone, distancing himself from House antigovernment radicals by saying, "There are a lot of people who consider themselves conservative who still understand the government has some responsibility and . . . does a lot of good things."[9]

A bit of context is again important in interpreting the 1994 election results. The 1992 congressional elections were also unusual in producing high turnover (110 new House members and 11 new Senators); 43 House incumbents lost their bids for reelection.[10] Indeed, the House incumbent reelection rate in 1992, at 88 percent, was slightly lower than the comparable rate in 1994 of 90 percent. The average House incumbent reelection rate for the five congressional elections immediately preceding and following 1992 and 1994 was 95 percent.[11] Thus both of these elections reflected unusual voter dissatisfaction with the economy, congressional behavior, and presidential performance.

The key difference in the two elections, of course, was that there was no real partisan slant to the 1992 voting patterns—Democrats lost ten seats in the House and none in the Senate.[12] Thus, the 1994 election was much more significant than its immediate predecessor for at least two reasons. First, it changed the power structure in Washington from Democratic to Republican. Second, it had to be read as conveying a national mandate for a change in policy. Even President Clinton acknowledged the latter point shortly after the election as he offered his interpretation of what voters were saying in 1994: "We [the voters]don't think government can solve all the problems, and we don't want the Democrats telling us from Washington that they know what is right about everything."[13]

While there can be no doubt about the partisan effects of the 1994 elections on the composition of Congress, the national mandate aspect is questioned by many scholars. Preelection polls indicated that most (71 percent) potential voters claimed to have never heard of the Contract for America; only 7 percent of those polled said the contract made them more likely to vote Republican, while 5 percent said knowledge of it made them less likely to vote Republican.[14] However, most analysts agree that the contract did make a difference. Some Republican candidates embraced it as a whole, while others used it selectively, emphasizing issues that played best in their districts. Republicans running in the South and parts of the West made great use of the contract, whereas candidates in the Northeast tended to avoid associating themselves with it.[15]

Enid Waldholtz, who won a House seat in Utah, explained how the contract helped her to better promote her position on issues such as a balanced budget amendment and welfare reform: "I sought to explain that my support for this legislation was part of a national movement. The contract bolstered my argument that these themes were national. And people could see that everyone was concerned with the same issues they were. . . . The contract showed everyone that I was not a lone voice. I was part of a team."[16] Gary Jacobson, a leading political science expert on congressional elections, while skeptical about the direct effect of the contract on voters, did acknowledge its effect on Republican candidates: "Fed a constant stream of advice and encouragement by Gingrich and his allies, Republican candidates around the country followed a common script designed to squeeze the most advantage from the public's discontents." He went on to conclude that the Republicans (candidates and party leadership) succeeded in making the 1994 midterm elections a national plebiscite on Clinton, Democrats, and business as usual in Washington, a rarity among modern congressional elections.[17]

While the contract and Republican Party organizations at all levels were at the forefront of the campaigns around the country, they were very ably assisted by a variety of conservative groups and forces. The Christian Coalition mounted a massive voter education drive, which steered many of its members toward Republican candidates. They were joined by the National Rifle Association (NRA) and those seeking congressional term limits (part of the contract), a movement that had enjoyed a good deal of success around the country in several prior elections. Rush Limbaugh and other conservative talk show hosts were also given credit for helping the Republican revolution to succeed in 1994.[18] The culture war that Republicans tried to accentuate in 1994 was apparent in voting. Beginning in the 1990s, there is a noticeable gap between pro-life and pro-choice

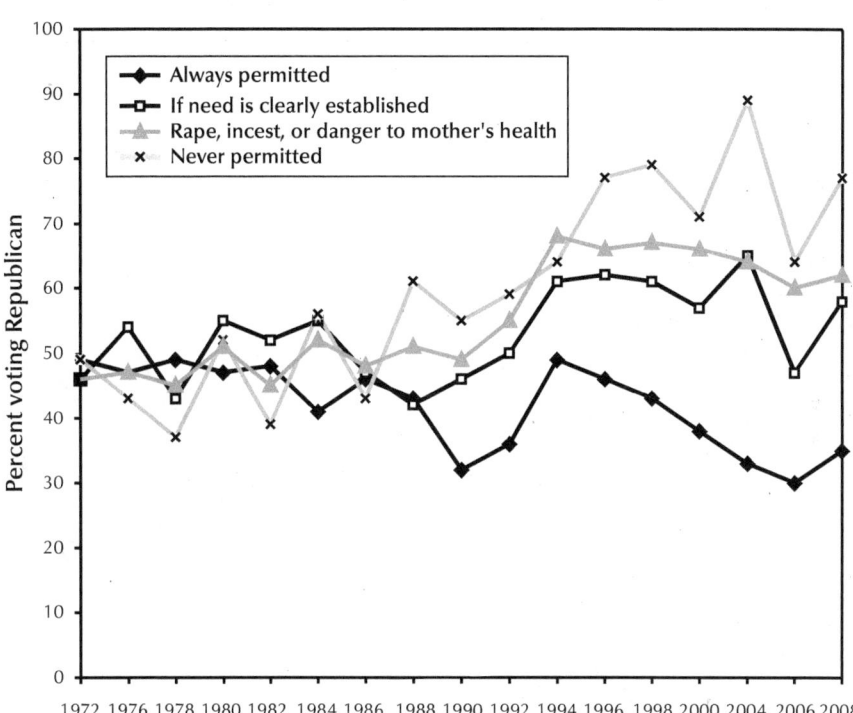

Figure 4.1 Abortion and Voting in House Elections, 1972–2008 (Whites Only)

Source: American National Election Studies.

voters (see Figures 4.1 for House and 4.2 for Senate). Perhaps more importantly, in all the congressional elections since 1994 this gap has persisted, in some cases even widened.

In previous chapters we have described the evolution of the contemporary Republican Party coalition, placing considerable emphasis on the movement of white Southern voters to the party. This movement was certainly on display in 1994, as Republicans realized a net gain of 19 House seats and 4 Senate seats (two in Tennessee—Bill Frist and Fred Thompson) across the South to finally (for the first time since Reconstruction in the late 1800s) achieve a majority of Southern congressional seats (73 to 64 in the House, and 16 to 10 in the Senate). Eight of the 34 House Democratic incumbents who lost were from the South, and 11 of the 39 open House seats the Republicans won were in the South.[19] As shown in Figures 4.3 and 4.4, support for House and Senate Republican candidates among white Southerners reached new heights in 1994 and remained high until 2006, when it dipped a bit, only to return high levels in 2008.

Figure 4.2 Abortion and Voting in Senate Elections, 1972–2008 (Whites Only)

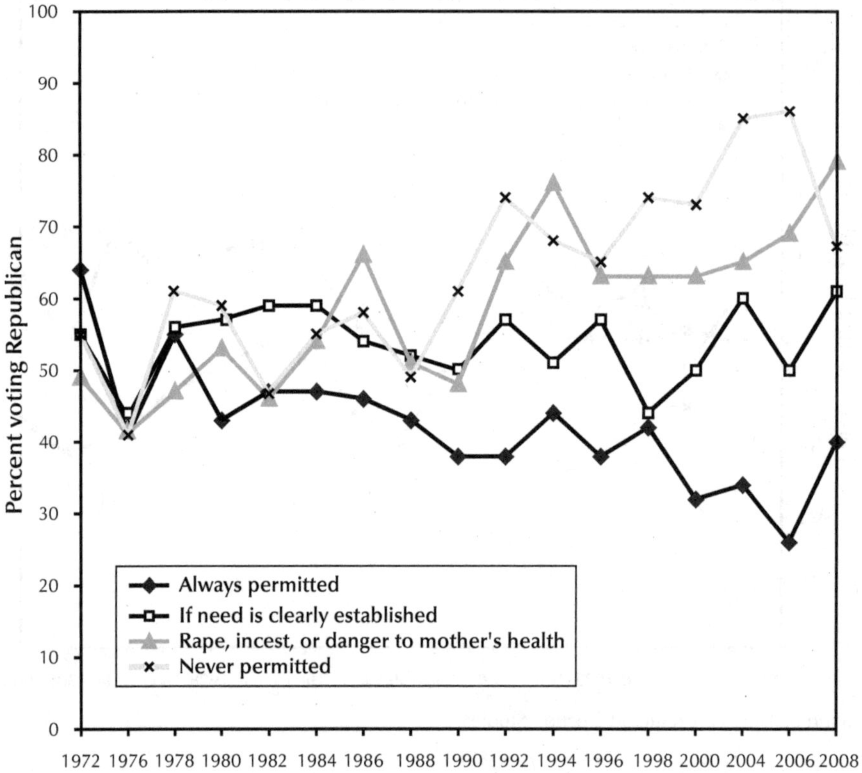

[Line graph showing percent voting Republican from 1972 to 2008, with four lines: Always permitted; If need is clearly established; Rape, incest, or danger to mother's health; Never permitted.]

Source: American National Election Studies.

It was not just white Southerners, but whites in general, both men and women, who played a key role in the Republican success in 1994. African Americans did not make a large vote contribution to Republican candidates running for the House or the Senate that year. As shown in Table 4.1, African American voting for Republican House and Senate candidates actually declined a bit in 1994 relative to 1992, and quite a bit compared to 1990. However, whites did change their voting preference substantially in 1994. White women went from favoring Democrats by a small margin (51 percent to 49 percent in the House, and 53 percent to 47 percent in the Senate) in 1992, to preferring Republicans by 53 percent to 47 percent in both House and Senate races in 1994. White men also upped their percentage of votes for Republican congressional candidates quite significantly in 1994. They went from favoring House and Senate Republican candidates by a small margin (51 percent to 49 percent) in 1992, to

Figure 4.3 Region and Voting in House Elections, 1952–2008

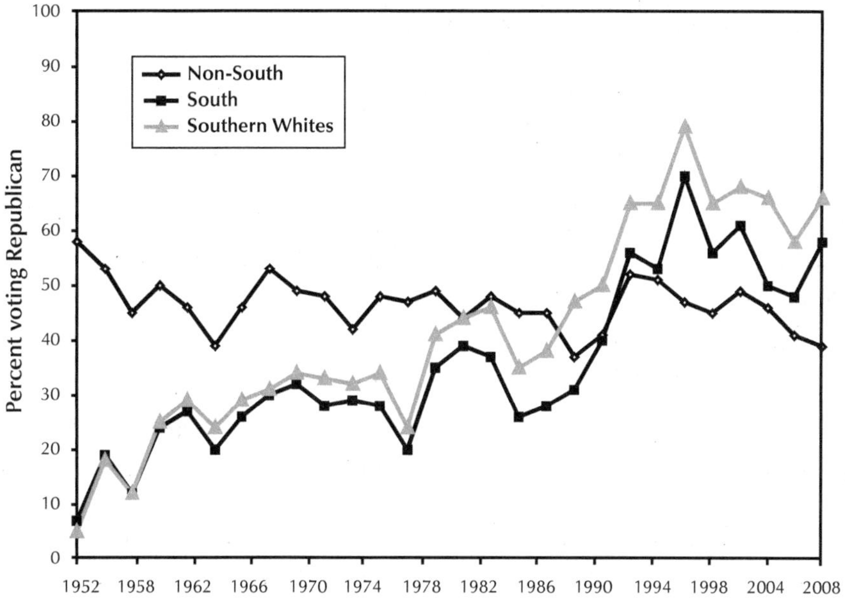

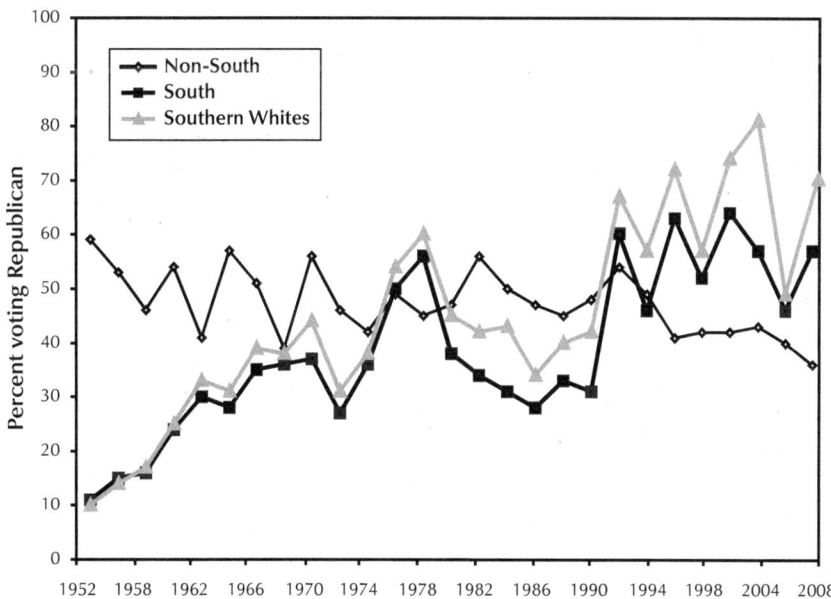

Source: American National Election Studies.

Figure 4.4 Region and Voting in Senate Elections, 1952–2008

Source: American National Election Studies.

TABLE 4.1 Gender, Race, Independents, and Congressional Voting, 1990–1994

(Cell entries are percentage voting Republican)

House Election

	1990	1992	1994
Whites	48	50	58
Blacks	20	11	8
White men	50	51	63
White women	47	49	53
Independents*	47	45	59

Senate Election

	1990	1992	1994
Whites	52	49	56
Blacks	23	13	12
White men	54	51	60
White women	49	47	53
Independents*	50	45	58

Source: Exit Polls.
* All Independents

favoring Republicans by large margins (63 percent to 37 percent for House candidates, and 60 percent to 40 percent for Senate candidates) in 1994.[20]

As would be expected, Independents voted for Republicans for the House at a rate that was 14 percentage points higher than in 1992; they went from favoring Democrats by a 55 percent to 45 percent margin in 1992 to favoring Republicans by a 59 percent to 41 percent margin in 1994. In the Senate, the increased Republican support among Independents between 1992 and 1994 was 13 percentage points (see Table 4.1).

The Election of 2006: Voters Turn Against the Republicans

It is hard to say exactly when the electoral tide turned definitively against President George W. Bush and congressional Republicans in 2006. They began the year with a host of liabilities, and things only got worse as the year progressed. The deteriorating situation in Iraq was the number one problem and, in the end, it was the most important factor in the electoral results. But the president's handling of the aftermath of Hurricane Katrina in New Orleans added new and compelling evidence of insensitivity and incompetence to the public's negative assessment of the Bush administration. There was also Jack Abramoff, the super lobbyist who pleaded guilty to a variety of influence-peddling violations, and whose client list seemed to include mostly Republicans; the abrupt arrest of the pitiful Representative Randy "Duke" Cunningham, who had accepted old-style bribes; and the indictment and eventual resignation of Majority Leader Tom DeLay, probably the most powerful person on Capitol Hill and certainly the man Democrats most loved to hate. All of this gave Democrats a powerful battlefield message: Republicans had to go because of the president's bad judgment on Iraq, the incompetence of his administration (Brownie's "heckuva job" notwithstanding), and the corruption of congressional Republicans.[21]

Still, the Republican electoral machine had a long-standing record of success, and a mystique of invincibility. President Bush, and his political guru Karl Rove, had won two important and hotly contested presidential elections (2000 and 2004), and had helped to guide the successful 2002 midterm election, in which the Republicans gained seven seats in the House and two in the Senate, thus restoring their majority in the latter chamber. The party was having no trouble raising money in the post McCain-Feingold era of campaign finance, so Republican candidates in 2006 could expect lots of help from party committees. And judging from the results of the 2002 and 2004 congressional elections, it looked to many experts, journalists, and politicians as if aggressive partisan redistricting following the 2000 census had made most Republican House seats "safe" from Democratic competitors.[22]

Indeed, in the spring of 2006 most prognosticators were predicting that the Republicans would suffer some losses in November, but would retain their majorities in both houses of Congress. For example, an April projection by the *Congressional Quarterly* political staff had the Republicans losing only one seat in the Senate (leaving them with 54) and seven in the House (leaving them with 224).[23] In May, political science soothsayer, Larry Sabato, was projecting a six- to eight-seat Democratic gain in the House and two to three additional Senate seats for the Democrats.[24] Nevertheless, all of the pundits were noting some key similarities to 1994: Congress's approval rating matched its 1994 low at 23 percent, and President Bush's job approval ratings, which ranged from 33 percent to 39 percent during the spring, were ten to fifteen points lower than those of President Clinton in spring of 1994.[25]

During the summer, the news from Iraq kept getting worse, as sectarian violence escalated, and public pessimism about our ability to succeed in our Middle East endeavors was strengthened by the outbreak of a new war in Lebanon in July. To almost everyone's surprise, Israel's mighty military machine had difficulty silencing the rockets being launched out of southern Lebanon by the militant Islamic group Hezbollah, and Israel received much international criticism (from almost everyone but the United States) for its counterattacks that resulted in many civilian casualties. A July 27, 2006, *New York Times/CBS News* poll found that 62 percent of Americans disapproved of President Bush's handling of the Iraq War, 56 percent thought the United States should set a timetable for withdrawal from Iraq, and only 25 percent thought the Iraq War was worth the lives and funding that was being put into it.[26] By the end of the summer, one trend was clear: more and more congressional seats that had once been considered solidly Republican were now in play. By August, the *Congressional Quarterly* political staff was projecting a Republican majority of between 220 and 227 in the House, and of 52 in the Senate.[27] They listed 76 House races as competitive, which was 21 more than they had listed this way at the beginning of the year (20 of the 21 were seats held by Republicans).[28] They predicted Republicans winners in only 5 of the 17 competitive Senate races; in the end, Republicans won only two.

The final nail in the GOP coffin in 2006 was probably the revelations about Congressman Mark Foley (R-FL) and his dealings with congressional pages, which broke in the national media in late September. What followed Foley's quick resignation was a series of clumsy attempts to suggest that the Republican leadership, particularly Speaker Dennis Hastert, was not aware of the nature and extent of Foley's flirtatious behavior until they heard about it from the media, and that the leadership staff had dealt with the matter, as they understood it, by cautioning Foley months earlier to be careful about how he interacted with the pages. The specter of a gay Congressman preying on teenage boys while the leadership looked the other way was too much for some cultural conservatives and others. More than half the public thought the Republican leadership had handled the matter badly, and many in the party worried about the potential impact on turnout in November.[29] Just before the Foley story broke, a *New York Times* poll showed that 77 percent of the public thought it was time to put "new people" in Congress, which was the highest percentage to express this view since 1994.[30]

By October, the once unthinkable had become common wisdom: more and more of the experts were predicting that Democrats would take the House and possibly the Senate. The *Congressional Quarterly* political staff had expanded its list of competitive House seats from 76 in August to 93 by October, with 72 of the 93 seats in play held by Republicans. They were now predicting a House Democratic majority of 219 (net gain of 16 seats), and a likely 50–50 split in the Senate.[31] Sabato was projecting that the Democrats would gain 21 to 26 seats in the House and 3 to 6 seats in the Senate.[32] The dean of congressional election forecasters, Charles Cook, may have been the first to put a thirty-seat House swing on the table, when on October 13 he commented that a thirty-seat gain for the Democrats was "more likely" than a fifteen-seat gain.[33] A *New York Times* poll taken a week before the election delivered more bad news for Republicans. The main issue on voters' minds was the war in Iraq, and 61 percent of the public thought the United States should change its war strategy, 69 percent did not think President Bush had a clear plan for dealing with Iraq, and 76 percent thought a Democratic Congress would bring the troops back more quickly than a Republican one.[34]

As election day approached, the attention of both parties and all candidates was on turnout. Democrats worked hard to convince their base, especially African Americans, that their votes mattered. Many such voters were discouraged by both the results and the procedures they had experienced in 2000 and 2004, and some of them had concluded that American elections were rigged in favor of Republicans. Repeated stories and Internet blogs about voting machine malfunctions and vulnerabilities (to hackers) did nothing to quell these fears.[35] President Bush and Republicans latched on to a late October New Jersey Supreme Court ruling that gay couples should have the same rights as heterosexual couples to rally cultural conservatives, especially in states with gay marriage bans on the ballot. Democrats tried to counter by reaching out to religious voters with messages about the importance of Christian values.[36] There were a few apparent dirty tricks down the stretch, including a telemarketing spin-off that asked respondents a series of loaded questions then ended with advice to either vote against a Democrat, or for a Republican.[37] In the end, the turnout efforts by both sides were modestly successful; the national turnout rate was 41.2 percent, as compared to 40.5 percent in 2002 midterm election, and key groups in each party's constituency showed up at the polls more or less as expected.[38] Still, on election day 2006 it is fair to say that no one was quite sure what to expect, although most of the signs pointed to a Democratic success.

The national party organizations were high-profile players in the 2006 midterm elections from beginning to end. The Democratic congressional campaign committees actively selected, encouraged, trained, and supported well-qualified candidates around the country to run against vulnerable Republican incumbents and to compete in open races. The House's Democratic Congressional Campaign Committee (DCCC) chair, Rahm Emanuel (Ill.), and the Democratic Senate Campaign Committee chair, Charles Schumer (NY), were given a lot of credit for recruiting mainly centrist candidates who were able to compete effectively against their Republican opponents in several states and districts carried by President Bush in 2004.[39] The Republican national party committees raised $511 million and the Democratic committees $392 million in the 2005–2006 election cycle.[40] These amounts were very similar to what the parties had raised in the last midterm election (2002), but this time it all had to be raised in limited donation "hard money" because large donation "soft money" contributions had been outlawed by the McCain-Feingold Act.[41]

The most prominent new wrinkle in campaign spending involved so-called independent expenditures by party organizations. The right of parties to spend as much money as they wanted for activities that were independent of both candidates, and the party's own coordinated spending on behalf of candidates, was established in a 1996 Supreme Court case and clarified in a subsequent 2001 case.[42] This resulted in bizarre organizational arrangements in which the part of a party committee (DNC or RNC) that was involved in developing independent campaign ads could not communicate with either the candidate for whom the ad would be aired, or top party committee officials about the content of the ads. In several instances in 2006 this resulted in candidates and party officials repudiating inflammatory ads produced by their own party's independent spending wings. The most celebrated such situation occurred in the Tennessee Senate race between Republican Bob Corker and Democrat Harold E. Ford, Jr. The ad played off of an invitation Ford had received several years prior to attend an event sponsored by the Playboy Company, and depicted a young, attractive white woman extending a flirtatious invitation to Ford to come see her (sometime). The racial and other implications were explosive, and both Corker and RNC Chairman Ken Mehlman quickly and publicly repudiated the ad. Mehlman, however, had to admit that his organization had paid for the ad, even as he maintained (no doubt honestly) that he had no prior knowledge of its content.[43]

National Republican Party and campaign committees spent a total of $117 million independently in 2006; the comparable figure for Democrats was $106 million.[44] A large majority (more than 80 percent) of this money went to the production and display of negative ads. Democrats were typically pilloried for being soft on defense, welcoming to illegal aliens, and approving of gay marriage. Republicans were skewered for being cozy with lobbyists, in the back pocket of big corporations, and, most importantly, for their mindless support of the policies of George Bush.[45] Indeed, a *New York Times* headline in late September read, "In Campaign Ads for Democrats, Bush Is the Star."[46] Independent spending enabled both parties to support their candidates in tight House races to the tune of $1 million or more (combining direct contributions, coordinated expenditures, and independent spending); in key Senate races Democrats averaged $5.2 million in party support, while the Republican average was $3.7 million. Clearly, party money was a big factor in all the competitive congressional elections of 2006.[47]

Spending enough money to get a candidate's name registered with the public is a necessary, but not sufficient, condition for winning a congressional election. When all the voting dust had settled in 2006, what mattered most, particularly among Independents, was the Iraq War, followed by corruption and scandals in Congress, the economy, and the general course of the country under President Bush's leadership. Exit polls showed that two-thirds of Independents were unhappy with Republicans; a similar percentage of all voters were motivated more by national issues than local issues in deciding how to vote.[48] Partisan voting remained strong, with 92 percent of Republicans and 93 percent of Democrats supporting the candidates of their respective parties. The key to the election was Independents, who split 59 percent to 41 percent in favor of Democrats (see Table 4.2). Nationwide, the vote split was 54 percent Democratic and 46 percent Republican, but this was good enough to give the Democrats a majority in both houses of Congress.[49]

One of the reasons that many experts were reluctant to predict a Democratic victory in the Senate in 2006 was that going into the election there were seventeen competitive Senate races, and the Democrats needed to win fifteen

TABLE 4.2 Gender, Marital Status, Independents, and Congressional Voting, 2002–2006

(Cell entries are percentage voting Republican)

House Election

	2002	2004	2006
Men	56	54	48
Women	50	47	44
Married men	59	59	52
Married women	55	55	51
Single men	46	45	37
Single women	39	36	33
Independents*	52	48	41

Senate Election

	2002	2004**	2006
Men	55		45
Women	48		40
Married men	57		47
Married women	53		46
Single men	45		35
Single women	39		31
Independents*	46		38

Source: Exit Polls.
* All Independents
**2004 National Exit Poll did not ask respondents to indicate their Senate vote choice.

of these in order to get to fifty-one seats (counting Joe Lieberman of Connecticut as a Democrat, even through he ran as an Independent, not as a Democrat).[50] Remarkably, they succeeded in taking fifteen of the seventeen seats, with only John Kyl of Arizona and Bob Corker of Tennessee winning on the Republican side. The closest races were in Virginia and Montana, where well-known Republican incumbents George Allen and Conrad Burns were defeated by Democratic challengers Jim Webb and Jon Tester. In all, six Republican incumbents were defeated to account for the net change of six seats in the direction of Democrats. In both the Senate and the House, Democrats did not lose a single seat they held before the election—all of their incumbents who ran won, and they won all the open races for seats they held previously. In the House, their net gain of thirty seats was composed of eight wins of open seats previously occupied by a Republican, and the defeat of twenty-two Republican incumbents. It was a Cinderella outcome for the Democrats, to be sure.

Figure 4.5 Income and Voting in House Elections, 1952–2008 (Whites Only)

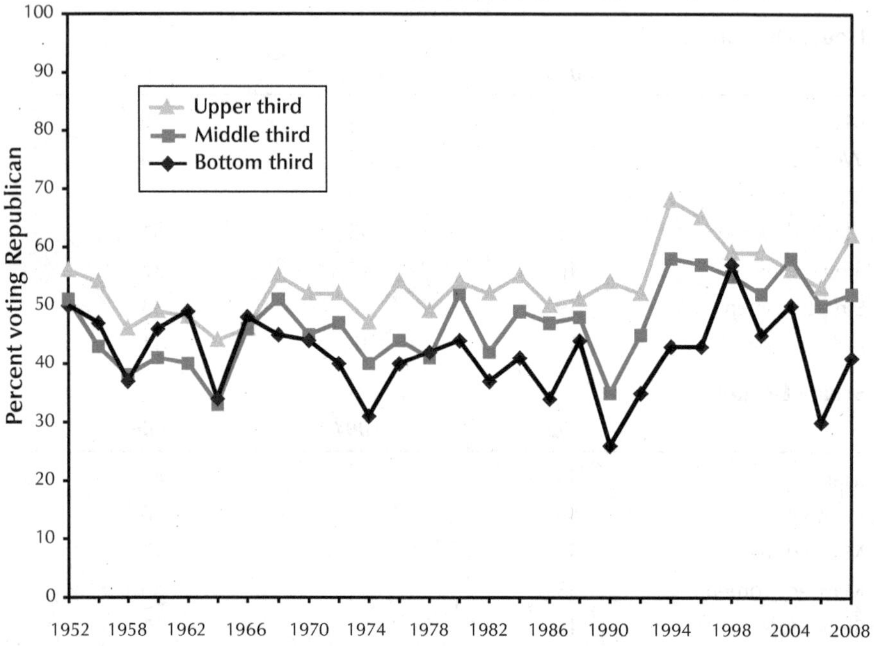

Source: American National Election Studies.

Big states for Democrats were Pennsylvania and New York, where they picked up four seats in each state; Ohio, Indiana, and Florida, where they picked up three; and Arizona, Connecticut, Minnesota, and New Hampshire, where they netted two.[51] (Several of these states would figure prominently in the 2008 presidential election.)

Although a big story in the election was the movement of Independents away from Republicans, several other voting trends and patterns were worthy of note. One involved women, who provided the margin of victory for Democrats in many races, both because they outnumbered men among voters and because they were more inclined to vote for Democrats. The level of Republican support among women decreased from 50 percent in the House and 48 percent in the Senate in the 2002 midterm to 44 percent in the House and 40 percent in the Senate in 2006 (see Table 4.2). But the interesting wrinkle here was that this pattern had more to do with marital status than gender. In the 2006 House elections, single women voted for Democrats by a margin greater than 2 to 1, whereas married women actually preferred Republicans by a small margin (51 percent to 49 percent in the House). The same pattern could be found among men: single men supported Democrats in the House (63 percent to 37 percent),

Figure 4.6 Income and Voting in Senate Elections, 1952–2008 (Whites Only)

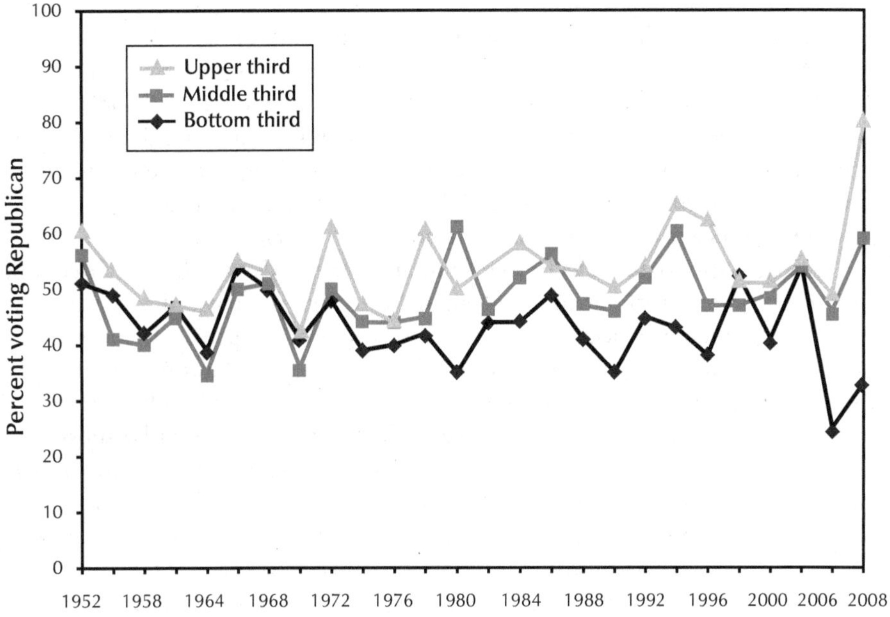

Source: American National Election Studies.

while married men favored Republicans (52 percent to 48 percent).[52] As far as other demographic groups go, Southerners remained the top supporters of the GOP, even though, as noted earlier, the percentage of the Southern vote going Republican declined in 2006 relative to both 2004 and 2002 (see Figures 4.3 and 4.4). Finally, low-income voters emphatically rejected Republicans, lowering their percentage of support for House and Senate Republicans from 50 percent (see Figure 4.5) and 54 percent (see Figure 4.6) in 2004 to 30 percent and 25 percent in 2006.[53]

Explaining Congressional Elections

Virtually all scholars who study congressional elections, as well as nearly all political consultants and campaign operatives, view these elections through a framework that emphasizes "strategic choices" made by candidates, potential candidates, and donors. Developed most fully by political scientists Gary Jacobson and Samuel Kernell, this model pulls together the work of numerous other scholars and practitioners and thus has considerable theoretical and practical appeal.[54] What is the dominant aspect of modern congressional elections? The high incumbent, especially House incumbent, reelection rates. Why are these rates so high? Because the strategic choices made by political actors at various levels conspire to make them so. Incumbents pay a lot of time, money (much of it supplied by taxpayers in the form of congressional mailing privileges, travel allowances, etc.), and attention to matters in their districts, and thus build a formidable presence (name recognition and popularity) backed by tangible benefits conveyed to constituents through legislation for which incumbents take credit. Over time, the record and presence of an incumbent discourages well-qualified and well-known opposition politicians from running against them (strategic choices of politicians), a tendency that is exacerbated by incumbents' recognized ability to raise large sums of money for reelection campaigns if needed (strategic choices of donors).

Voters respond to the choices they are presented with by first deciding whether to vote (turnout in congressional elections is almost always below 50 percent; in midterm elections it is usually very near 40 percent), and then, in part, by whether they recognize the names of the candidates on the congressional ballots. Too often House incumbents, who are recognized by virtually all the voters, are pitted against challengers who are not recognized by substantial numbers of voters, which leads to a highly predictable result: the incumbent wins. In many other cases, incumbents elicit a variety of favorable responses from voters, while their challengers elicit very few, leading to the same predictable result. There are many other important elements in this framework, including candidates' campaign strategies, the salience of national issues, presidential popularity, and others. Thus it is also applicable to Senate races, where candidate recognition is less of a factor.[55]

Parties and partisanship are by no means absent from the strategic choice model. In fact, Jacobson was one of the first to emphasize the increasingly important role parties could, and did, play in congressional elections going back to the 1980s. National and state party organizations, especially the congressional campaign committees, were affecting elections by grooming promising candidates, supplying them with all-important startup funds, and providing technical support and expertise for their campaigns. Most of these efforts were directed at open races and races where the incumbents were considered vulnerable. By the 1990s, this arsenal of party support was being augmented by increasing amounts of soft money and independent spending by party organizations. Thus Jacobson and others recognized party leaders as increasingly important strategic actors; nevertheless, the parties were portrayed mainly as the supporting cast. The lead actors were the candidates—in particular, incumbents.

Our point in reviewing the strategic choice model is not so much to dispute its accuracy or explanatory power as it is to draw attention to the preceding point. By emphasizing the candidate-centered nature of congressional elections, the strategic choice framework relegates parties and partisanship to a secondary role, which we think can be a bit misleading. Some elections are mostly about parties and partisanship, usually in the form of widespread and strongly felt rejection of the policies and personalities of the party in power. Although strategic choice theorists acknowledge this and can fit such elections within their framework, sometimes their explanations seem to us to miss the forest for the trees. In the midterm elections of 1994 and 2006, the forces associated with parties and partisanship were more important than factors pertaining to incumbency and localism in determining the outcome. Many voters, in particular Independents in 2006, went to the polls knowing that they had something important to do. They wanted to change the course of national policy and power, and they voted accordingly. They voted for the candidates of the party out of power in a purposeful way.

Midterm Madness: Recapping the Elections 1994 and 2006

Congressional midterm elections have a long history of producing big changes in the partisan composition of Congress. Successful presidential candidates often carry a number of marginal congressional candidates of their party into office with them, and it is not uncommon for many such candidates to be defeated in the midterm election that follows. This pattern is especially likely if the new president's performance has been widely criticized, and/or the country is experiencing troubles (especially economic hardships). In the 1890 midterm, when Republican Benjamin Harrison occupied the White House, the Republicans lost a whopping 78 House seats, going from a majority of 166 to a minority of 88 (the House included 325 members at the time).[56] The Democrats lost 70 House seats and 7 Senate seats in the 1938 midterm during Franklin Roosevelt's second term as president (depression-induced unemployment remained high).

In the modern era (post World War II) the big-swing midterms occurred in 1946, when the Republicans gained 55 House seats while Harry Truman was president; in 1958, when the Democrats gained 50 House seats and 15 Senate seats while Dwight Eisenhower was president; and in 1974, when Democrats gained 52 House seats during the Gerald Ford (post-Watergate) presidency. Judged by historical midterm standards, the 1994 Republican pickup of 53 House seats and 7 Senate seats ranks right up there with some of the other big-swing elections, whereas the 30-seat House gain by Democrats in 2006 was only a medium-size shift (the 7-seat Senate gain in 2006 was impressively large). (In the 2008 elections, the Democrats picked up 21 more seats in the House and 8 more Senate seats, bringing their majorities to 257 in the House and 59 in the Senate.)

Political scientists have developed the "surge and decline" theory to explain these occurrences. The gist of the theory is that the combination of high turnout among partisans of the winning presidential candidate and large numbers of Independents voting for the winning president sets up a situation in the subsequent midterm where neither of these two things is likely to be present, which gives the opposition party a very good chance of gaining a considerable number of congressional seats.[57] However, during the 1970s and 1980s, there were fewer surges and declines. The Democrats seemed to have a firm hold on the House, even though three Republicans (Nixon, Reagan, and Bush) were elected president. The strategic choice model explained all of this by focusing on the power of Democratic incumbents to serve their constituents well and thereby maintain their advantage over challengers, also noting the decline in presidential "coattails."[58]

Amid the apparent stability in congressional electoral outcomes in the 1980s was a wildcard element: congressional redistricting. Following the 1990 census, redistricting around the country (seats were being added to states in the South and West, and being subtracted from states in the Northeast and Midwest) was widely considered to have advantaged Republicans. Thus the fact that Republicans gained ten seats in the House, even though Clinton won the presidency in 1992, may have not have been a signal of Clinton's lack of coattails as much as it was a mask for larger Republican House gains that were already in the works.[59] The 1994 results were, in part, the culmination of changes put in motion by redistricting.

In Chapter 2, we examined partisan loyalty in presidential elections in some detail. Recall that Republicans were, on average, somewhat more loyal in voting for candidates of their party than Democrats, at least until recently. When one looks at House and Senate congressional voting, a different pattern is apparent. Beginning in 1972 and extending until 1992, Republican partisans of all varieties (strong, weak, and leaners) were less loyal in voting for House and Senate candidates than were Democrats; they were also less loyal than Republican voters in years prior to (1952 to 1970) and after (1994 to the present) this period (see Appendices C.1 and C.2). As displayed in Figure 4.7, Republican loyalty in House elections dipped below 80 percent in 1972 and stayed there until 1994, when it rose quite dramatically. Democratic loyalty during this period varied from a low of just under 80 percent in 1980 (Reagan won the presidency in a landslide) to a high of close to 90 percent in 1990. The pattern in Senate elections is similar (see Figure 4.8). The level of Republican voting for Democratic congressional candidates during this period (1972 to 1994) is a very concrete manifestation of the advantage of incumbency that Democrats exploited very adeptly (as explained by strategic choice theorists).[60] Although Gingrich and the Contract for America may only have been salient to a limited number of voters, the dramatic change in Republican voting in congressional elections in 1994 shows that something very significant went on among rank and file voters during this election cycle.

The change in congressional voting since 1994 shows some expected, and some unexpected, patterns from the standpoint of the strategic choice model. Since the Republicans had a majority of members in the House from 1994 to 2006, one would expect their larger number of incumbents to attract votes from some Democrats and many Independents. As shown in Figure 4.7 (see also Appendix C.1), this did occur between 1994 and 1998. But, beginning in 2000, and continuing through 2006, Democratic loyalty in House elections increased very substantially and, in fact, exceeded that of Republicans. Once again, the pattern in Senate elections is very similar (see Figure 4.8 and Appendix C.2). As

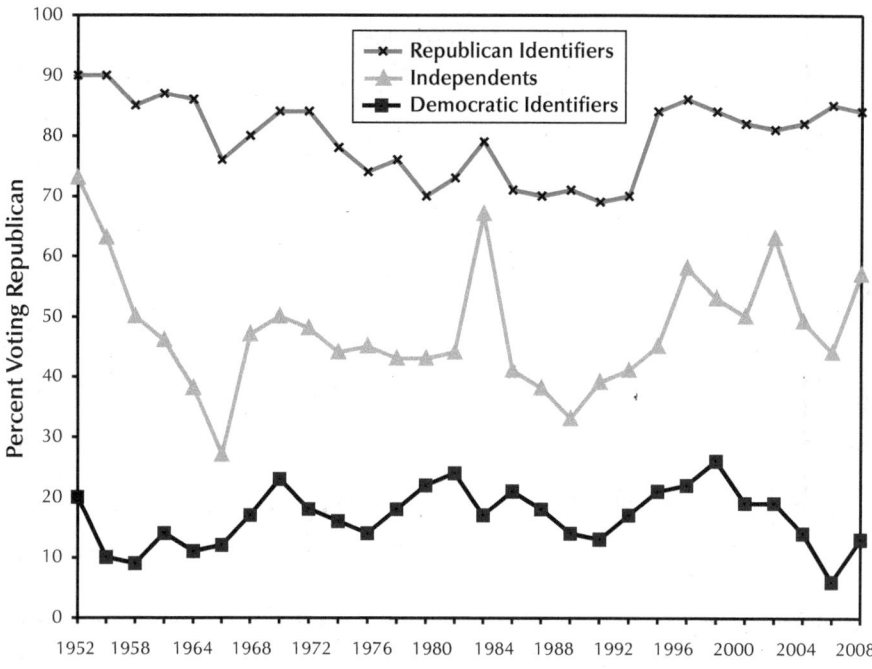

Figure 4.7 Party Identification and Voting in House Elections, 1952–2008

Source: American National Election Studies.

displayed in Figure 4.9, loyalty among all partisans in House and Senate voting has been quite high by historical standards since 2000, reaching levels that have not been seen since the 1950s and '60s (although it did fall a bit in 2008).[61] In fact, from 2000 through 2006 voting in House and Senate elections closely resembles that of voting in presidential elections in terms of the loyalty of different types of partisans (compare figures in Appendices A.1, C.1, and C.2).

The high level of partisan loyalty in congressional elections since 2000 seems somewhat at odds with the strategic choice model in that the presence of incumbents does not appear to be leading many voters away from their partisan inclinations.[62] One direct way of illustrating this point is by examining the effect of voters' partisanship in elections with incumbents running. In Figure, 4.10, we track the percentage of partisans who voted for their party in House elections, separating open seats from races with incumbents. It should come as no surprise that in most years, partisan loyalty is stronger in races without an incumbent. But what is noteworthy in recent years is the steady rise in partisan loyalty in both types of races. In 2006, 93 percent of partisans voting in districts with open seats supported the candidate of their party, the highest this figure has been

Figure 4.8 Party Identification and Voting in Senate Elections, 1952–2008

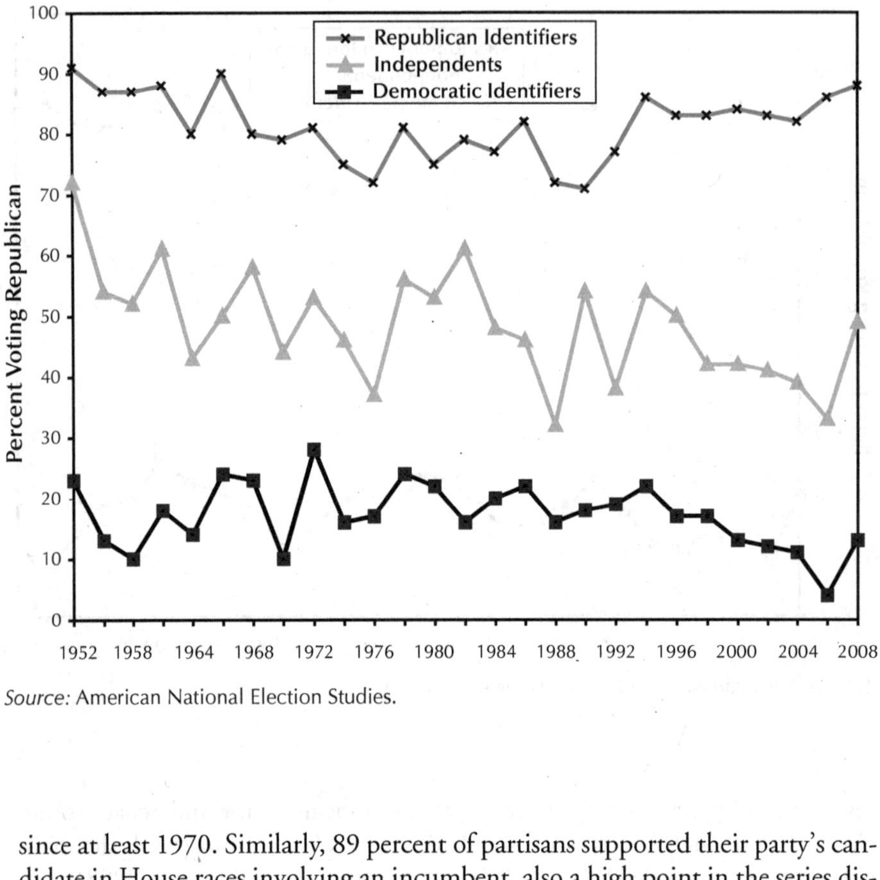

Source: American National Election Studies.

since at least 1970. Similarly, 89 percent of partisans supported their party's candidate in House races involving an incumbent, also a high point in the series displayed in Figure 4.10. In 2006, partisan loyalty was about ten percentage points higher than its average since 1970, for races both with and without an incumbent. The level of partisan voting in House elections declined somewhat in 2008 but still remained high by historical standards.

Our sense is that heightened partisanship in voting may now be trumping incumbency as the most important factor in congressional elections. We offer one final piece of evidence in support of this claim. In Table 4.3, we classify congressional districts into four categories of partisanship (strong Democrat, marginal Democrat, marginal Republican, strong Republican) for the last four midterm elections. This classification scheme is based upon the performance of each party in that district in the previous presidential election.[63] A district in which the Democratic (or Republican) presidential candidate won at least 60 percent of the vote would be considered a strong Democratic (or Republican) district. If the party's candidate won between 50 percent and 55 percent of the vote, then

Figure 4.9 Partisan Loyalty in Congressional Elections, 1952–2008

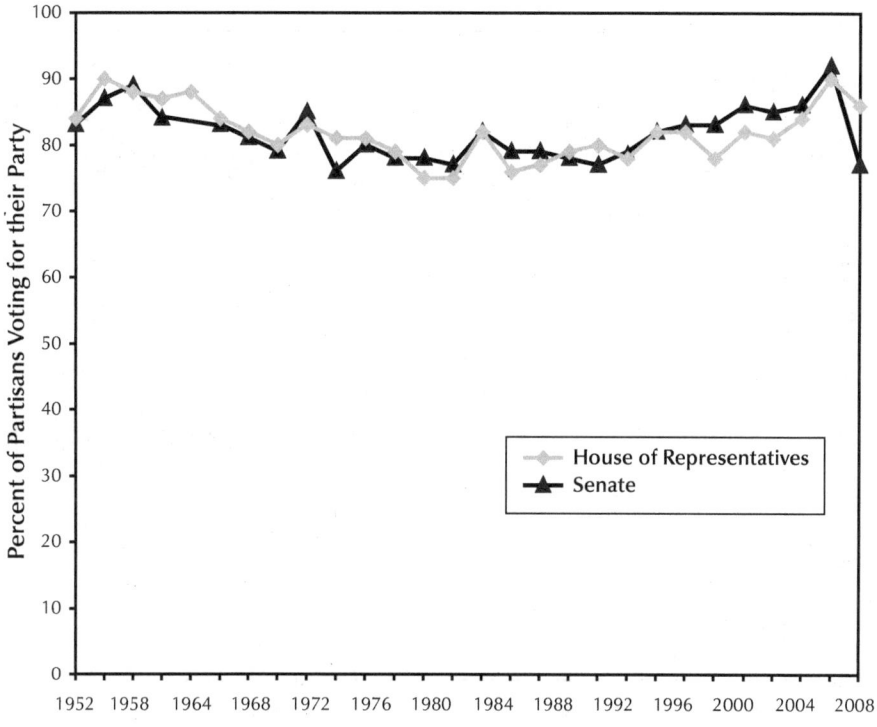

Source: American National Election Studies.

the district is classified as marginal. We then proceed to examine the proportion of House seats won by the district's majority party in each category over time.

There are a number of noteworthy findings in Table 4.3. As expected, districts that are strongly partisan are very likely to elect House candidates from the majority party. Since 1994, strong Democratic districts have elected Democrats to the House more than 90 percent of the time, reaching 100 percent in 2006. The Republican success rate in their strong districts exceeds 90 percent in 1994 and 1998, but drops to 86 percent in 2006, when the Democrats took back the House.

Changes in the behavior of marginal districts also support the resurgence of partisanship claim that we are advancing. In 1994, marginal Democratic districts abandoned many House Democratic candidates—only 44 percent of them elected Democrats. These districts continued to be prime territory for Republicans in 1998 (the advantages of incumbency were no doubt at work here). But beginning in 2002 and continuing through 2006, marginally Democratic districts became increasingly likely to elect Democratic candidates, with the percentage of Democratic winners rising from 37 percent in 1998 to a whopping

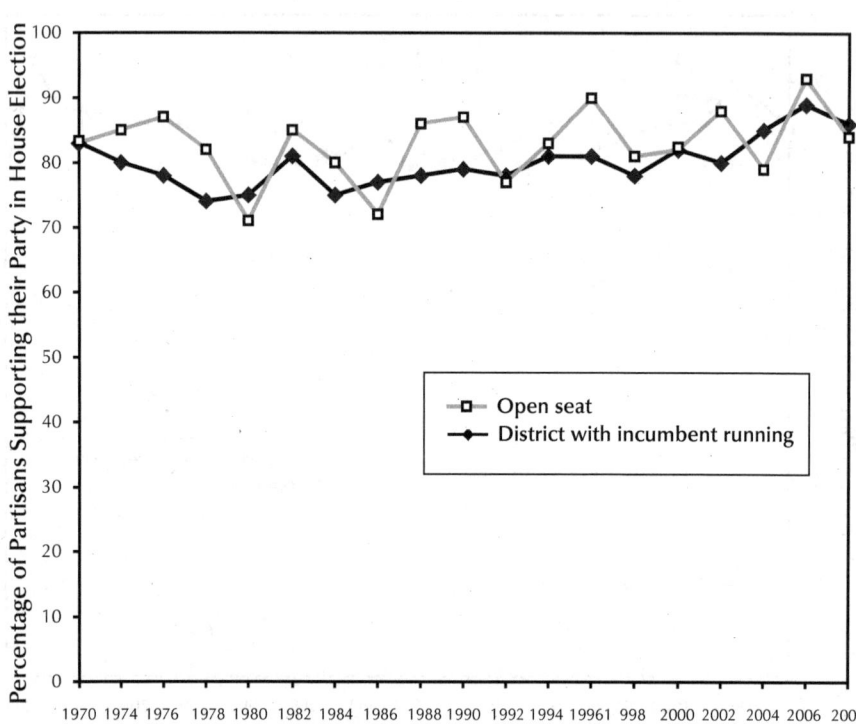

Figure 4.10 Partisan Loyalty in House Elections, Incumbents versus Open Seats, 1970–2008

Source: American National Election Studies.

80 percent in 2006. In marginal Republican districts, we see parallel patterns. Republicans enjoyed a high level of success in such districts in 1994 and 1998. Republicans continued to do well in their marginal districts through 2002, but in 2006 the bottom fell out and they barely won a majority of such districts.

Republican losses in 2006 (and 2008) were motivated by a strong anti-Republican sentiment, as many voters cast a ballot against the party in power. In 2009–2010, Democrats face a "live by the sword, die by the sword" situation. They succeeded in convincing a majority of the 2006 and 2008 voters that the Republicans could not solve the country's problems, and promised that they (Democrats) could do better. It will be very interesting to see whether they can they maintain their advantage among the electorate as the party in power during the 2010 midterm. The first midterm of the last Democratic president (Clinton) was a disaster, but President Bush did pretty well in his first midterm (2002). This is one area where President Obama would obviously prefer to be more like Bush than Clinton.

TABLE 4.3 Percentage of Congressional Districts Won by Majority Party in District, 1994–2006

	Strong Democratic district	Marginal Democratic district	Marginal Republican district	Strong Republican district
1994	94	44	78	94
1998	94	37	76	94
2002	94	53	67	87
2006	100	80	52	86

Source: See note 63 on page 209.

Appendix C

See Appendix Tables C.1 and C.2 on pages 116 and 117.

Appendix C.1 Republican Voting in House Elections Broken Down by Party Identification, 1952–2008

	SD	WD	ID	IND	IR	WR	SR
1952	10%	22%	36%	73%	81%	90%	95%
1956	6	14	17	63	83	88	95
1958	4	12	23	50	77	78	93
1960	8	18	18	46	79	83	94
1962	3	16	25	38	73	84	94
1964	7	16	21	27	72	64	92
1966	8	18	39	47	67	78	87
1968	12	27	37	50	82	78	92
1970	11	23	24	48	65	83	96
1972	8	19	21	44	73	76	85
1974	8	20	14	45	62	68	88
1976	11	22	21	43	68	72	86
1978	14	20	38	43	63	66	80
1980	15	31	30	44	68	74	78
1982	10	25	17	67	63	80	88
1984	11	30	22	41	62	66	85
1986	8	25	27	38	64	66	79
1988	12	19	13	33	63	70	77
1990	7	20	17	39	66	61	82
1992	11	18	23	41	65	65	81
1994	12	26	31	45	74	79	93
1996	12	29	31	58	79	79	97
1998	18	35	33	53	78	77	95
2000	10	26	27	50	75	82	88
2002	5	28	27	63	71	75	92
2004	9	14	20	49	68	82	90
2006	4	8	11	44	78	78	90
2008	8	16	17	57	78	78	93

Source: American National Election Studies.

SD = Strong Democrat; WD = Weak Democrat; ID = Independent who leans Democrat; I = Independent; IR = Independent who leans Republican; WR = Weak Republican; SR = Strong Republican

Appendix C.2 Republican Voting in Senate Elections Broken Down by Party Identification, 1952–2008

	SD	WD	ID	IND	IR	WR	SR
1952	12%	25%	43%	72	87	93	91
1956	9	15	22	54	77	83	96
1958	4	16	17	52	69	83	97
1960	11	23	25	61	83	82	96
1962							
1964	10	17	21	43	68	73	93
1966	8	32	39	50	83	91	93
1968	11	25	45	58	68	79	91
1970	2	16	16	44	61	77	92
1972	19	31	37	53	78	77	87
1974	10	18	24	46	65	67	93
1976	8	22	23	37	62	68	87
1978	17	25	34	56	81	69	93
1980	13	23	34	53	67	69	92
1982	4	23	28	61	85	69	85
1984	11	26	26	48	70	76	85
1986	8	35	25	46	79	73	90
1988	12	18	19	32	64	66	83
1990	12	25	25	54	66	64	83
1992	13	22	24	38	75	69	86
1994	11	31	28	54	80	75	96
1996	11	15	33	50	73	79	92
1998	13	19	22	42	82	74	92
2000	6	15	21	43	77	82	90
2002	4	18	17	41	71	83	91
2004	6	17	12	39	71	77	91
2006	2	11	2	33	83	78	92
2008	6	25	17	49	81	88	94

Source: American National Election Studies.

SD = Strong Democrat; WD = Weak Democrat; ID = Independent who leans Democrat;
I = Independent; IR = Independent who leans Republican; WR = Weak Republican;
SR = Strong Republican

CHAPTER 5

Parties in Power: Congress, Presidents, Partisanship, and Gridlock

The previous chapter chronicled two dramatic changes in the partisan composition of Congress. In both cases voters and politicians were motivated, at least in part, by a desire to change existing policies. The purpose of this chapter is to illustrate what happens when electoral results confront policymaking institutions in the United States, with a special focus on the role that partisanship plays in determining legislative outcomes. There are, of course, three main institutions to consider: the House of Representatives, the Senate, and the presidency. All have evolved in distinctive ways and have developed different policymaking processes and powers, which are described below. Common goals, based on partisanship, have at times produced a meshing of these institutional operations, which has resulted in profound changes in national policy. However, the more common condition has been a grinding of institutional gears that has frustrated ambitious attempts at policy change.

The 1995 and 2007 legislative sessions are excellent examples of the latter. House Speaker Newt Gingrich fulfilled his promise to bring all items in the Republican Contract with America to a vote in the first one hundred days of the 1995 legislative session.[1] And all but two contract items (balanced budget and congressional term limit amendments) passed the House. After that, however, the institutional grinding began. As mentioned in the previous chapter, the Senate had a limited commitment to enacting the contract, even though it had a Republican majority. Majority Leader Robert Dole made an effort to move some of the items, but he had to deal with a moderate faction within his own party that sought to soften many elements of the contract. He also had to contend with Democrats, who enjoyed a number of legislative privileges in the upper chamber (the filibuster being the most significant) and were united in opposition to most aspects of the contract. Thus many important contract items, such as welfare reform and crime legislation, were delayed and/or significantly altered in the Senate.[2]

Then, of course, there was President Clinton who vetoed several bills that included contract items, most notably budget legislation that called for tax cuts and reduced spending in key domestic programs. Republicans tried to force the president to agree to their budget priorities by withholding funding for government operations, leading to a brief government shutdown, but in the end they backed off. Clinton was widely perceived as having won this political showdown, paving the way for his reelection in 1996.[3]

Republicans did enjoy some successes in 1995. Contract (and other) items calling for legal reforms, penalties for child pornography, government paperwork reductions, and limits on federal unfunded mandates were enacted.[4] The one part of the contract President Clinton *did* favor—a bill granting line-item veto power to the president—was also enacted in 1996 but later declared unconstitutional by the Supreme Court (another institutional actor).[5]

Taking Gingrich's 1994 contract strategy to a new level, one of the first things new Speaker of the House, Nancy Pelosi (CA), announced when Democrats took over the House in 2007 was that they would pass a series of bills, addressing the key issues Democrats had emphasized in the election (so-called New Directions for America), within one hundred hours of the opening of the 110th Congress (before the president's 2007 State of the Union Address).[6] The "one hundred hours" strategy worked, as Democrats first passed internal resolutions to reform lobbying rules, to regulate the "earmarking" of legislation by members, and to enforce fiscal discipline by reinstating "pay as you go" budget rules.[7] They then passed six bills that dealt with national security and key domestic policy concerns. The first called for implementation of several September 11 Commission recommendations regarding national security. The second would raise the minimum wage from $5.15 per hour to $7.25 per hour. The third would free federal stem cell research from restraints imposed by the Bush administration. The fourth would empower the government to negotiate with drug companies for lower prescription drug prices for Medicare recipients. The fifth called for lower interest rates on federal higher education student loans. And the sixth sought to cut federal subsidies to oil producers and shift the subsidies to those producing renewable energy sources.[8]

Despite this promising start, the first session of the 110th Congress ended up being a disappointment for Democrats. President Bush, with loyal support from congressional Republicans, staved off most of the Democratic attempts to make major changes in government policy. The legislative dynamic was very similar to the one that played out in 1995. Once again, the House was able to pass a good deal of partisan legislation, but most of it either got bogged down or substantially altered in the Senate, or vetoed by the president.[9]

The highest visibility clashes in 2007 were over efforts by Democrats to steer the Iraq war in a different direction, all of which failed. The first big showdown occurred in late spring, when the supplemental appropriations bill that funded the war through 2007 cleared Congress in April with a stated goal of withdrawing troops within six months. President Bush vetoed this bill without hesitation on May 1, and an attempt to override the veto in the House failed.[10] Before the end of the month, Congress passed a supplemental with no war instructions, and the president signed it. A similar episode occurred at the end of the year over a supplemental appropriations bill to fund the war in 2008. The House passed a bill that called for troop withdrawals within thirty days of its enactment, but Senate Republicans successfully blocked any attempt to include troop withdrawal language in the supplemental.[11] Eventually, on the very last day of the session (December 20), Congress cleared a $70 billion supplemental, with no strings attached, that would fund the wars in Iraq and Afghanistan for part of 2008. (Bush had sought $196 billion for the full year, but signed this bill.)[12]

Other notable successes for President Bush in 2007 included vetoes of bills that called for increased funding for stem cell research and for an expansion of the State Children's Health Insurance Program (SCHIP). Congressional Democrats had high hopes for the SCHIP expansion, believing they could parlay public support for this popular program into enough pressure to either convince Bush not to veto it, or to override his veto. They failed on both counts. Bush vetoed the SCHIP expansion on October 3, and an override vote in the House fell thirteen votes short.[13]

Democrats did not emerge from the 2007 session empty handed. Their first big success was the minimum wage increase they had promised, which included some tax breaks for small businesses, and was signed by President Bush on May 25.[14] Democrats also delivered on their promise to pass a major overhaul of lobbying rules and ethical practices (The Honest Leadership and Open Government Act of 2007), and to reform and expand student loans for college students (signed September 27).[15] At the end of the session, they also succeeded in enacting a major energy bill that would impose higher fuel economy standards on automakers and require greater use of renewable fuels, a bill to postpone the effects of the Alternative Minimum Tax for another year, and a bill to provide relief for those suffering from the subprime mortgage crisis.[16] Final bits of bad news for congressional Democrats, however, were October polls showing Congress's approval rating at 23 percent—the same as in 1994 and 2006.[17]

The Evolving Role of Partisanship in Congress

The kind of party-directed policymaking that was on display in the House during the 104th and 110th Congresses, is the product of years of institutional evolution that has seen the power of partisan majorities ebb and flow. The inability of party majorities in the Senate to pass highly partisan policies in 1995 and 2007, on the other hand, reflects a condition that has been common in that institution since its inception.

When the first Congress convened in New York in April of 1789, there were officially sixty-five members of the House of Representatives and twenty-six Senators, although some of them hadn't been elected yet, and a number of others had not arrived.[18] Even though these numbers seem small and manageable, the early Congresses struggled with questions of leadership and organization. Who should their leaders be, and what powers should they have? How should the assemblies organize themselves to conduct business? The Constitution specified that there would be a Speaker of the House, which helped to answer the first question in that chamber. Frederick Muhlenburg of Pennsylvania was elected the first Speaker. In the Senate, the leadership situation was more amorphous (a condition that persists to the present). The vice president was the constitutionally designated presiding officer, but he wasn't really a member. Furthermore, Vice President John Adams didn't show up until two weeks after the Senate convened, so they elected a president pro tempore to serve as presiding officer in his absence. While the Speaker of the House has evolved into a very important and powerful leadership position, the same cannot be said of the vice president or the president pro tempore in the Senate. Their powers have become largely, but not entirely, ceremonial. In terms of organization, the first Congress, and every one since, has employed committees to draft legislation.

The first major organizational development in the U.S. Congress was the gradual change from heavy reliance on ad-hoc or select committees to the establishment of permanent (or "standing") legislative committees. Prior to the 1820s, literally hundreds of temporary committees were formed each session to prepare legislation for consideration on the floor. (In those days the House generally acted first on important bills.) From the 1820s forward, both houses moved to reliance on permanent, specialized committees to formulate legislation that the rest of the chamber would consider. The present committee system is a direct descendant of these early standing committees, which were created by leaders such as Henry Clay, who held the speakership three times between 1811 and 1825.[19]

During the first half of the nineteenth century, the party organizations within each chamber were quite weak and undeveloped. Thus party groups did not provide the organizational muscle they would assert in later Congresses. In the House, the principal power of the Speaker was to assign representatives to committees. Aspiring Speakers would promise plum committee assignments to members in an effort to assemble a coalition large enough to elect the candidate making the promises. Once elected, however, Speakers had trouble maintaining order and getting things done. House standing committees were the leading players in the legislative process. They had recognized policy jurisdictions, and the passage of a rule in 1822 that required amendments to committee-proposed legislation to be "germane" helped committees protect their policy turf.[20] But floor debates could be something of a free for all because early Speakers did not have the exclusive power to recognize members wishing to speak on the floor. Final proceedings on legislation were often very disorderly and unpleasant; in some cases, members even brought weapons into the chamber and/or challenged each other to duels after nasty exchanges on the floor.[21]

In the pre–Civil War Senate, things were even more loosely organized. The only elected leader, the president pro tempore, sometimes held the committee assignment responsibility, but at other times the parties took on this function.[22] Furthermore, committees were less central to the legislative process, as their jurisdictions were not well defined and there was no germaneness rule. Senate procedures were highly informal, and leaders were often difficult to identify (Daniel Webster and John C. Calhoun being the exceptions). As in the House, floor proceedings could be raucous at times. Perhaps the most famous incident was the nearly fatal clubbing of Massachusetts Senator Charles Sumner by one of his colleagues in 1856.[23]

Way back in 1806 the Senate took the seemingly unimportant step of abolishing a rule that allowed the majority to shut off a floor debate.[24] This established the precedent of unlimited debate and filibusters, which enabled individual members and/or minority coalitions to tie up Senate business at their will. Although Senate rules regarding filibusters have changed over the years, the right of minorities to engage in unlimited debate remains the most distinctive, and important, feature of that institution, particularly as it affects the ability of party majorities in recent years to pass legislation they prefer (more on this later).

The parties became much more prominent players in the post–Civil War Congress. In the immediate aftermath of the war, Republicans enjoyed huge majorities in both houses of Congress and had little trouble pushing a large amount of party-supported legislation through each chamber, much of which focused on the Reconstruction of Southern states and civil rights for former slaves.[25] But by the 1870s Democrats again became competitive as a national party, and many of the messy features of the pre–Civil War Congress returned.

Both parties came to recognize the disadvantages of this, and a series of changes were made over the next thirty years that conferred new and extensive powers on the Speaker of the House. The first of these was a change in 1876 that gave the Speaker the power (not subject to appeal) to recognize members wishing to speak on the floor.[26] However, this proved insufficient as representatives (often of the minority party) continued to engage in an array of delaying, or "dilatory" tactics. One of their favorites was the "disappearing quorum" whereby members would refuse to vote on bills before the chamber, even though they were physically present on the floor, thus preventing the bill's sponsors from achieving the quorum necessary for a binding vote for passage. These problems were addressed emphatically in 1890, when the House voted in "Reed's Rules" named after their author Thomas B. Reed (Maine)—who assumed the speakership in 1889. Reed, and who became known as "Czar" Reed—was instructed by his own rules to refuse to entertain any dilatory motions, and to achieve quorums by simply counting those present on the floor during legislative debates. He also made extensive and strategic use of the House Rules Committee, which he chaired, to set the timing and conditions of debate on important bills before the House.[27]

Reed's Speakership (1889–1891 and 1895–1899) and that of Joseph ("Uncle Joe") Cannon of Illinois (1903–1911) represent a high water mark in terms of centralized control over the House; and, in both cases, the Speaker was acting as an agent of the majority party (Republican). The combination of power over committee appointments and control over the floor proceedings allowed the

Speaker, and his cooperative party majority, to shape the legislative process to serve their interests. It also provided a model that would reappear, with various elaborations and modifications, almost exactly one hundred years later, as the House again moved decidedly in the direction of majority party control.

In the late 1800s and early 1900s, there was also a consolidation of power in the Senate by a leadership group headed by Republican Nelson Aldrich of Rhode Island. However, Aldrich and his allies exercised their power much more informally, as the prerogatives of individual senators, and the minority party, were preserved.[28] Thus the House-Senate relationship at the turn of the twentieth century paralleled that of the House and Senate at the turn of the twenty-first century. In both time periods, the House was pretty much controlled by the majority party leadership, but the Senate was run in a more bipartisan fashion because the threat of filibusters, and other obstructionist tactics available to Senators, required negotiation between party leaders in order for the chamber to conduct its business in an orderly and productive manner.

As indicated above, Reed's reign over the House was interrupted after two years. The Democrats regained the majority in the election of 1890, and their first order of business was to deliver on one of their campaign slogans to abolish most of Reed's rules. However, in the four years that followed they readopted many of these rules as they realized that fairly strict control over floor proceedings was necessary if the House was to function in a reasonably effective manner.[29] What we see here is the House struggling with a set of legislative trade-offs of great significance. On the one hand, elected representatives like to have the freedom to pursue their own policy (and pork) interests. This not only makes legislative life more interesting and fulfilling; it is also an important way of bolstering one's popularity with constituents. On the other hand, if everyone is pursuing their own narrow interests, and the major issues of the day are not being dealt with because minorities can easily block the legislative process, the whole Congress looks bad, which can lead to the electoral defeat of large numbers of members. Therefore, even though most elected officials are not fond of the idea of having their legislative activities dictated by a powerful leader, the members of the majority party may, at times, decide that such leadership is in their collective interest.

The era of strong, party-based leadership under Speakers Reed and Cannon ended in 1910, when the Democrats regained the majority and voted to strip the Speaker of most of his powers (to make committee assignments, to chair the Rules Committee and others). Over time the changes they made would result in a new and enduring power structure in the House: a decentralized system of legislative power based on standing committees. By the 1920s, the most important currency of power became seniority, as most committee leadership positions were based on it. Party leadership positions did not disappear after 1910; indeed, some existing ones were strengthened and new ones were created. Both parties had recognized floor leaders (majority leader and minority leader), who had deputies called "whips" and party "committees on committees" to carry out the committee assignment process. Thus senior members, who chaired committees, together with party leaders (who were more inclined toward accommodation than issuing directives) formed a legislative oligarchy that managed most of the business of the House. A similar setup existed in the Senate, although the Senate remained a much more quirky and individualistic institution.[30]

The revolt against Cannon was not so much a rejection of party rule as autocratic rule, at least in the short term (1911–1917). Rank and file members wanted to be more involved, and the House Democratic Caucus (all Democratic members meeting as a group) became a powerful force, especially after Woodrow Wilson was elected president in 1912 with an enlarged majority. The result was something new and very significant: Congress was called upon to enact a legislative program developed and led by a president.[31] Throughout the nineteenth century, an article of faith for nearly all members of Congress, regardless of party, was legislative supremacy. Congress was the lawmaking branch under the Constitution, and it was not to be led in this endeavor by any outside party, including the president, except perhaps in times of war. During his first term Wilson, with the organized support of the Democratic caucus and congressional party leaders, was able to propose and enact a series of policies known as the "New Freedom." The main elements of the New Freedom program were the elimination of certain protective tariffs, banking reform (the Federal Reserve Act of 1913), and new regulations on corporate behavior that included the creation of the Federal Trade Commission.[32]

Although Congress continued its path toward decentralization in the 1920s, Franklin Roosevelt, with his "New Deal," would build upon Wilson's model of legislative leadership to join with Democrats in Congress in his first term (1932–1936) to enact a much larger and more significant program of policies (see Chapter 1). From Roosevelt's administration forward, legislative leadership from presidents became an expectation rather than an aberration. Thus the question for Congress in most of the second half of the twentieth century was whether they were willing and/or able to organize themselves is such a way to provide effective support for, or opposition to, the legislative initiatives of presidents.

The Modern Congress

One of the first careful, empirical studies of Congress was written by none other than Woodrow Wilson and published in 1885.[33] However, the systematic study and analysis of congressional behavior began at more or less the same time as the NES studies of the electorate—in the late 1940s and early 1950s. Those who studied the Congress of the 1940s and 1950s described what some have called the "Textbook Congress."[34] The textbook view of Congress featured the power of committees and committee chairmen, especially in the House, with many of the most powerful chairmen being conservative Southern Democrats. The Senate's governing group, dubbed the "Inner Club," was less grounded in committees and more bipartisan, but also had a decidedly conservative bent.[35]

As described above, the textbook Congress evolved in fits and starts going back to the 1920s. A good way of demarcating the emergence of what might be described as the "modern" Congress, the one covered in most of the textbooks of the 1950s, is to take note of the passage of the Legislative Reorganization Act of 1946. This act reduced the number of standing committees from forty-eight to nineteen in the House, and from thirty-three to fifteen in the Senate. In so doing it created a much better correspondence between congressional committees and major departments and agencies in the executive branch. It also provided for ample staffing for congressional committees in an effort to help them keep up with executive branch agencies.[36] The reduced number of committees and the addition of substantial numbers of professional staff cemented the power of committee chairs.

The Legislative Reorganization Act was the product of studies and discussions undertaken by the Joint Committee on the Organization of Congress, known as the LaFollette-Monroney Committee.[37] The main purpose of the group was to develop recommendations for enabling Congress to respond to the growing dominance of the executive branch. Interestingly enough, the committee's report endorsed many of the principles of the responsible party model of governance (Chapter 1) and made some recommendations accordingly; however, very few of the responsible party elements of the report found their way into the final version of the Reorganization Act. The Senate did act on one of the party-strengthening recommendations by creating party "policy committees" in 1947.[38] The original idea behind such committees was that they would help party leaders to develop policy agendas, reflecting the wishes of their party delegations in Congress, for which the congressional party could be held publicly accountable. In practice, the party policy committees of the 1950s never came close to performing the role envisioned by reform advocates, but they did add a new piece to the parties' organizational apparatus that would become more significant over time.

Party Machinery in Congress

The preceding discussion has identified the core elements of congressional party organizations (most of which go back to the 1950s and continue to the present). The first element is the party caucus or conference, which consists of all of the party members (Democrats separately from Republicans) in each chamber (House and Senate).[39] Caucus/conference meetings are held at the beginning of each session and periodically throughout the session. In these meetings party leaders are elected, committee assignments are approved, and various issues are discussed.

The conferences/caucus have great potential power, however, it is fairly rare to see it exercised. In 1975, after having been subdued for years by powerful committee chairmen, the House Democratic Caucus voted out three longtime Southern committee chairmen as part of a revolt against Southern conservatives that Northern liberals had started several years earlier.[40] In recent years the key to caucus/conference power is the ability of these party groups to achieve consensus on policy matters. With a cohesive caucus/conference the majority party can pretty much control the legislative process in the House. Conference cohesion is also vital in the Senate because the majority and minority leaders need to be sure they have the support of their colleagues in order to bargain with each other effectively. Caucus/conference meetings (they also have retreats) give large numbers of members a chance to participate in, and feel a part of, the legislative agenda-setting process.[41]

At the other end of the party organization chart lies a second key element in the party apparatus: the leaders. In the House, the majority party elects three main leaders: the Speaker (also voted upon by the whole chamber), a majority leader, and a minority whip. The minority party elects a minority leader and a whip. In recent years two other important leadership positions are the chairs of the Democratic Caucus and the Republican Conference. On the Senate side, the key leaders are the majority and minority leaders and whips. All of these leadership teams try to establish a legislative agenda for their party in their chamber and oversee the committee assignments of their party members. The majority parties also attempt to orchestrate the legislative process to achieve their (and possibly the president's) policy goals, while the minority parties try to frustrate these efforts. The ability of leaders to succeed in these endeavors depends mainly on the powers they possess (which have changed over time) and their ability to wield them effectively.

The third and fourth components of the party structures in each chamber are policy committees and steering committees. The policy committees help the leadership to set legislative priorities and establish a policy agenda for each congressional session. The steering committees work with the leaders to develop a slate of committee assignments for each party's members at the beginning of each Congress. House Democrats have usually combined the policy and steering functions in a single committee, in the other three cases (House and Senate Republicans and Senate Democrats) there are separate committees for each task. The autonomy of these groups varies, but in recent years they have tended to act as loyal arms of the leadership.

A final set of party committees that should be noted are the campaign committees. As described in Chapters 1 and 4, these groups have become key actors in congressional elections, targeting money and other forms of support on promising candidates around the country. Successful leaders of these organizations often move on to other leadership positions in Congress. Rahm Emanuel, who headed the DCCC in 2005–2006 was elected chairman of the Democratic Caucus in 2007 (he left Congress in 2009 to become President Obama's chief of staff); and Charles Schumer, Emanuel's Senate counterpart, was appointed to the number-three position in the Senate leadership by being made vice chair of the majority caucus.[42]

Another group that has to be covered in this overview is the House Rules Committee. Although it is technically a standing committee, since the 1970s (and at times before that) it has operated more like a party committee. Its basic job is to decide when, and in what form, legislation will be debated and voted upon on the floor of the House of Representatives. For example, the committee can issue a "closed rule" for a bill it schedules for consideration, which means that no amendments can be offered when that bill is on the floor for debate and a final vote. And, this is just the tip of the iceberg; modern Rules Committees have developed many kinds of specialized rules. The arsenal of specialized rules at the disposal of the Rules Committee are vital weapons the Speaker and the majority leader can use in carrying out the legislative scheduling function so as to achieve their policy goals. The members of the Rules Committee are hand-picked by the leaders, and the majority party gives itself a supermajority (more than 2 to 1) on this committee. In the Senate, the legislative scheduling, and the terms and conditions of floor debate are worked out by the majority and minority leaders.

The purpose of this outline of party structures in Congress is to suggest that the congressional parties possess the organizational tools they need to direct much of the business of each chamber. How much power is actually exercised by the parties and party leaders is ultimately a product of the wishes and preferences of the members, the size of the majority party, and to some extent the skills of the leaders. A cohesive majority caucus/conference in the House that wants to control the legislative process through its leadership can do so. In the Senate, because of the filibuster, it would take a cohesive majority of sixty or more to achieve the same result. In both cases, the main cost of disciplined, party-based legislative leadership is the suppression of policy entrepreneurship and policy and pork credit claiming opportunities for individual members, most of which stem from their service on committees.[43] Losing such opportunities is a high price to pay for public officials who are looking to make a career in the Congress, and who are subject to periodic elections in which constituents are always asking, "What have you done for me lately?"

Therefore, a useful way of thinking about and analyzing how the U.S. Congress works is to view committees/subcommittees and their leaders as competing with party organizations/leaders for power over policy (and process). Committee power leads to a decentralized and fragmented legislative process, and party power leads to a more centralized and integrated one.[44]

Party Resurgence in Congress

Earlier reference was made to a revolt staged by liberal House Democrats in the early 1970s aimed at breaking the power of the Southern committee chairman. What did these rebels do? They worked on two main fronts. First, they empowered the Democratic Caucus and ordinary members relative to the standing committees. Second, they bestowed additional powers on the Speaker and the majority party leadership. The result was a somewhat paradoxical combination of increased decentralization and greater centralization.

On the first front, the Caucus enacted a series of rule changes that were called "the subcommittee bill of rights." These gave the Democratic members of standing committees, rather than the committee chairs, the authority to appoint subcommittee chairs, and guaranteed each subcommittee staffing that was controlled by the subcommittee chair (Democrat) and ranking member (Republican). As noted earlier, the Caucus also asserted its right to vote for committee chairs, rather than having these positions determined solely on the basis of seniority. (Nevertheless, the norm of seniority continued as the principal qualification for committee leadership positions.) The main effect of the subcommittee bill of rights and related reforms was to spread influence much more widely around the chamber. With nineteen standing committees and close to 140 subcommittees in the House, and new rules preventing members from chairing more than one committee and/or subcommittee, the leadership positions now reached more than half of all Democratic (and Republican) members. A similar spreading of committee leadership positions in the Senate guaranteed all members a committee power base (as a subcommittee chair or the status of a ranking member).[45]

With these changes, the old textbook Congress had clearly evolved into a new form characterized in the House by further decentralization of power from committees to subcommittees, widespread policy entrepreneurship on the part members interested in making a name for themselves, and leadership that sought to accommodate rather than direct. In the Senate, the longstanding tradition of "individualism" was being taken to new extremes.[46] All of this is captured succinctly and elegantly by political scientist David Mayhew in his seminal book *Congress: The Electoral Connection*.[47] The second half of Mayhew's book is organized around this question: If members of Congress were single-minded seekers of reelection, how would they organize their chamber to conduct policy business? His answer is that they would set up a committee system much like the one they had in order to provide themselves with ample opportunities for "advertising," "credit claiming" (especially for constituency-based benefits, or "pork") and "position taking."[48] The high rates of incumbent reelection in the 1970s suggested that the system was working more or less as planned. (For the decade of the 1970s, the House incumbent reelection rate averaged 93 percent; for the Senate, the comparable figure is 72 percent.[49])

The second set of House Democratic reforms of the early 1970s—those strengthening the leadership—received less attention at the time but proved later to be at least as important as those directed at committee power. Reformers ended a practice, which had been in place for many years, of having the Democratic members of the Ways and Means Committee perform the committee assignment function by reassigning this task to a new party Policy and Steering Committee, which included the elected party leaders, eight members appointed directly by the Speaker, and regional representatives.[50] As mentioned earlier, the Speaker also gained the ability to appoint the majority party members of the Rules Committee—another potentially powerful tool.

In addition, the Speaker was given the power to refer bills to more than one committee if he thought it necessary or appropriate. This may not seem like much on the face of it, but defined and exclusive jurisdiction is one of the foundations of a strong committee system. Although nearly everyone recognized that major legislation for things such as comprehensive health and energy bills cut across numerous committees' jurisdictions, giving the party leadership the power to decide which committees would and would not be involved in processing such legislation was an important step toward empowering the leadership to direct the committee process. By the late 1970s, the leadership began using its new powers by creating special "task forces" to manage major legislation of special importance to the party, thus further diminishing the role of standing committees in the passage of such legislation.[51]

According to Barbara Sinclair, the leading expert on House party leadership in the 1970s and 1980s, the Democratic leadership learned gradually how to use the new powers they had acquired to achieve more and more control over the legislative process in the House.[52] They worked with the Caucus to develop policy agendas, and then made an effort to communicate with the public about the importance of the main issues on the agendas. They built an elaborate whip system that involved as many as eighty members in intelligence gathering and persuasion efforts designed to achieve the passage of key legislation on the leadership's agenda. The Whip, working with the Speaker and the majority leader, and his many lieutenants (deputy and regional whips) could be very persuasive when it came to convincing fence-sitting members to support the leadership's policy goals. The Speaker and majority leader began issuing specific instructions to standing committees as to when, and in what form, legislation should be reported. Finally, the Speaker frequently prevailed upon the Rules Committee to grant special rules that maximized the chances that key legislation would be passed.[53]

Through an adept combination of accommodating members' main concerns and objectives, including large numbers of members in the legislative process, and structuring floor choices to encourage cohesive, party-based voting on the floor, Speaker Jim Wright (D-TX) used all the tools just described to achieve remarkable success in enacting his legislative agenda in the 100th Congress.[54]

Wright's skills notwithstanding, one might ask why Democrats, who had controlled the House since 1955, would move away from the committee/subcommittee-based system that had served them so well. One answer is that they didn't entirely; there was still a lot of fragmentation and constituency-oriented policymaking going on in the Democratic Congresses of the late 1980s and early 1990s. Certainly, President Clinton did not encounter a unified Democratic Congress eager to enact his key legislative priorities in 1993–1994, as the failure of his health care plan demonstrates.[55] Nevertheless, there was a good deal more policy agreement among Democrats in the late 1980s and early 1990s than in earlier eras, as the Southern conservative wing of the party became smaller and smaller. Also of great importance was the fact that the amount of new policy and pork to be extracted from the legislative process diminished during the Reagan administration as chronic federal deficits (stemming in large part from Reagan's success with tax cut and defense spending legislation in 1981) stared legislators in the face year after year. Fighting Reagan's budget proposals focused more of the Democrats' attention on how they could preserve popular domestic programs (by being unified), rather than on what they wanted to give away in new policy and pork. Awareness of limited resources was further stimulated by the passage of the Budget and Enforcement Act of 1990.[56]

Stepping back from the details, and returning to the theme of centralization versus decentralization, the advantages and disadvantages of, and the circumstances associated with, each type of legislative organization should be fairly clear.

Decentralized legislative bodies give primary policy responsibility to semi-autonomous subgroups (standing committees and subcommittees), which develop policies that reflect the preferences of the members of these groups (but not necessarily the wishes of the larger body). Legislators join the groups that will best help them achieve their policy and electoral goals, and the policy jurisdiction of subgroups is protected by institutional rules. We would expect legislatures organized in this way to favor policies that confer tangible benefits on identifiable constituencies, and to operate under a norm of reciprocity whereby the work of each subgroup is supported (voted upon favorably) by the others. When they are forced to face major substantive issues, such legislatures would be expected to produce policies riddled with compromise and ambiguity, reflecting the complex bargaining process that would be needed to come to agreement. This type of legislative process is likely to occur when there is no cohesive majority that favors a clear course of major policy action, which was true for most of the Democratic majorities in Congress from the 1950s through the 1970s (Lyndon Johnson's Great Society being the notable exception). Under these circumstances, we expect institutional leadership (presumably party-based) to be weak. The decentralized, fragmented Congress that has typified much of the modern era (1950–1980) has been described by many as "Responsive, but not Responsible."[57]

A centralized, well-integrated legislative body has more or less the opposite characteristics. Policy objectives are developed by centralized bodies—party conferences or caucuses in concert with party leaders. Any legislative subgroups, such as standing committees, would take their marching orders from these central sources, and the membership, jurisdiction, and leadership of such groups would also be determined centrally. Party leaders would direct most aspects of the legislative process, with the assistance of whip organizations and rules crafted to promote favorable floor votes on bills embodying the majority party's policy agenda. This model of legislative organization and functioning fits pretty well with the House as it operated under Czar Reed and Joe Cannon, and with the House since the late 1980s, particularly during the period of Republican control from 1995–2007.

In reality, of course, the U.S. Congress is far too complex an organization to follow a straightforward or one-dimensional pattern of collective behavior. Thus it is neither a wholly centralized nor a wholly decentralized institution. Still, it seems fair to say that the trend since the mid-1980s has been in the direction of more centralized, party-based legislative activity.

As we have noted, this is seen most clearly in the House. When Newt Gingrich became Speaker in 1995, his pledge to take action on the items in the Contract with America within one hundred days (described earlier) led him to make a number of dramatic changes in the way the House was organized and run. He struck at the heart of the committee system (seniority) by announcing that committee chairs would serve limited (six-year) terms. He then decided who the chairs would be, replacing seniority with loyalty to him and the contract as the primary criterion for appointment. These loyal committee chairs were then given complete authority over the subcommittees, determining their leadership, jurisdiction, and staffing.[58] Finally, the standing committees were given timetables for reporting and specific instructions about how to process legislation related to the contract and other bills important to the Republican Conference and the leadership.

Gingrich also continued Wright's practices of using an elaborate whip system to keep members in line, while using the Rules Committee to structure floor votes so as to produce the desired outcomes. He went farther than any other congressional leader in the modern era in presenting himself to the public as the spokesperson not just for the Republicans, but for Congress as a whole. He was determined to compete with President Clinton for the attention and support of the public. In short, he used the party organizational apparatus to full effect and achieved extraordinary central control over his chamber. As Gingrich's star fell (1997–1999), some of the committees pushed back a bit, but most of the House party leadership system he established remained intact.[59] Thus Speaker Dennis Hastert (1999–2007) operated much like Gingrich and, most recently, Speaker Nancy Pelosi has also retained many of Gingrich's methods. Although Pelosi and the Democrats have returned to using seniority as the norm for determining committee chairmanships, like Gingrich, she has imposed a six-year term limit on committee chairs.[60]

While the House moved decidedly toward party-based policymaking from the 1990s to the present, the Senate did not exactly follow suit. Senate Democrats under majority leaders George Mitchell (1989–1995) and Tom Daschle (2001–2003) did try to bring more policy unity to their conferences by creating policy agendas and encouraging members to support them, as they (the leaders) attempted to communicate a Democratic message to the public. In one of the more significant policy showdowns in the Bush administration, Mitchell appeared to out-maneuver the president in a debate over how to move to a balanced budget when Bush agreed to certain "revenue enhancers," thus breaking his famous "no new taxes" campaign pledge.[61]

Republican majority leaders Robert Dole (1994–1997), Trent Lott (1997–2001), and Bill Frist (2005–2007), followed some of the leads of their House counterparts, moving to six-year terms for committee chairs and using the Republican Conference to establish policy agendas the committees were expected to follow in each session.[62] The current majority leader, Harry Reid (D-NV), has also attempted to achieve more centralized control by working closely with his conference, but Senate Democrats have not placed term limits on their committee chairs.[63] Party unity in Senate floor voting has increased steadily since the 1980s (see the next section), but increased partisan unity has not led to a smoothly functioning legislative process. Indeed, much the opposite has occurred as the filibuster (actual or threatened) has been employed as a partisan tool with great frequency, and neither party has had majorities large enough to break filibusters. Thus as the House has evolved into a well-oiled partisan policymaking machine, the Senate has been forced to rely on prolonged and often painful bipartisan negotiation to make policy headway.[64]

Congress and Presidents

As the preceding discussion has made clear, another difficulty in trying to accurately, yet parsimoniously, portray the national policymaking process is the fact that it is a three-ring circus. Not only are there important differences in the ways the House and Senate have operated over time, but there is also the president and his legislative initiatives to consider. All U.S. presidents since Franklin Roosevelt have attempted to influence, if not control, the national policy process. In periods of unified government, the president and the Congress have tried, with varying degrees of success, to cooperate. Lyndon Johnson's Great Society (1965–1966) was the most successful example of presidential-congressional policymaking cooperation since Roosevelt's New Deal (see Chapter 1). Jimmy Carter (1977–1981) was never able to get his fellow Democrats in Congress to work with him in a similar fashion, nor was Bill Clinton in his two years of unified government (1993–1995).

A much more common condition in the modern era has been divided government, in which one or both houses of Congress have a majority of the party that is not occupying the White House. This situation was in effect for thirty-eight of the sixty years between 1947 and 2007. Indeed, the movement toward more party-based organization and activity in Congress was stimulated in large part by the desire of congressional majorities to assert themselves against presidents. Wright sensed weakness in the White House during Reagan's last two years and thought the Democrats could make a statement for the 1988 presidential election through policy action. In 1990, Senator George Mitchell knew that existing laws governing budget deficits could force President Bush to seek a compromise with Congress, and he exploited this opening to achieve a major and long-lasting agreement on spending and taxes.[65] As described in this and the previous chapter, Gingrich's contract was very much about taking the national policy agenda away from President Clinton; similarly for Speaker Pelosi and President Bush in 2007. Although the overall effect of divided government is an increase in deadlock and indecision (see below), it can also result in some real and important policy breakthroughs, such as the welfare reform law passed in 1996, and budget deals made during Clinton's second term that paved the way for the first budget surpluses since the 1960s.[66]

Unified government under President George W. Bush from 2003 to 2007 deserves a somewhat more extended treatment, since we have not covered it much up to this point. Bush was able to team with Speaker Dennis Hastert and Majority Leader Tom DeLay to move many of his preferred policies through the House without much difficulty. Hastert and DeLay used the tools Gingrich had assembled, as well as some new ones of their own making, to pass bills that reflected the wishes of the president and loyal Republican followers with virtually no input from Democrats. The main problem Bush and House leaders faced, of course, was the Senate, where many, though certainly not all, of their preferred policies got bogged down because negotiation with Democrats was necessary.[67] The Bush administrations also pursued many of their policy preferences without congressional action, by aggressively asserting executive power, especially with regard to military and national security policy. Most of these actions went unchallenged by Congress until Democrats won the 2006 midterm election.

President Bush scored early in 2001 with the passage of a ground-breaking education law (No Child Left Behind) and major tax cut legislation. In the case of No Child Left Behind, his legislative success was marked by extensive cooperation between the White House and Democratic Senator Edward Kennedy—an episode of bipartisan cooperation that suggested the new president might live up to his campaign pledge to be a "uniter, not a divider."[68] But any hopes for continued bipartisan cooperation were soon dashed when the president's tax cut plan ($1.35 trillion over ten years) was rammed through Congress with much less of an inclination toward compromise displayed.[69] Indeed, the lack of consultation and compromise exhibited by the Bush administration during the tax cut debate led Republican Senator James Jeffords of Vermont to renounce his party (in May), which gave the Democrats a slim Senate majority (51 to 49) until 2002.

The events of September 11, 2001, shook up everyone, even hardened political leaders in the House and Senate. One memorable scene was President Bush embracing Senate Majority Leader Tom Daschle just after delivering a speech to the nation on September 20.[70] Bush parlayed the post-9/11 consensus on the need to fight terrorism into a number of legislative victories in 2001–2002, including increased military spending, enactment of the USA Patriot Act, passage of a Joint Resolution to authorize the use of force against Iraq, and the creation of the Department of Homeland Security.[71] Bush campaigned hard for a Senate majority in 2002 and succeeded in this endeavor as well.

As the 108th Congress commenced in 2003, bipartisanship was unraveling, but the president had a majority of 229 Republicans in the House and 51 Republicans in the Senate. The approach he took was highly partisan: lean on the House to pass the legislation he proposed with few modifications, try to get something through the Senate, then rely on Republican leaders to get the most they could out of House-Senate conferences. Part of the grease House Republican leaders used to secure loyalty to the president's agenda was a liberal sprinkling of earmarks around the chamber, which enabled members to secure pet projects for their constituents and took some of the sting out of following orders. Between 1998 and 2005, the number of earmarks in transportation bills increased from 1,850 to 6,371.[72]

Bush's biggest win in 2003 was the enactment of a Medicare Prescription Drug bill in November. The final passage of this bill in the House has already gained legendary status, as Republican leaders Hastert and DeLay ignored House rules that required floor votes to be completed within fifteen minutes and kept the floor open for nearly three hours (from 3 a.m. to almost 6 a.m. on November 22), while they cajoled (some say threatened) members opposed to the bill into changing their votes. The final vote was 220 to 215.[73] The president also got most of what he asked for in tax cuts and war funding. Senate Democrats did thwart him on several federal appeals court nominations, on important energy legislation, and on class-action litigation reforms.[74]

The 109th Congress started out very well for President Bush. His narrow victory over John Kerrey in the 2004 election was accompanied by an expansion in his House and Senate Republican majorities (three seats in the House and four in the Senate). They went to work in 2005 and passed the energy and class action litigation bills that had failed in 2003, and a new bankruptcy law.[75] Then, the president was also able to get his choice for a new chief justice of the Supreme Court, John Roberts, through the Senate. This was accompanied by a good deal of partisan drama because Senate Democrats had enjoyed a lot of success from 2001 to 2004 in filibustering Bush's court nominees who they considered extremely conservative. Going into the 109th Congress, Senate Republicans were threatening a so-called "nuclear option" that would have used a simple majority vote to declare filibusters out of order for floor consideration of judicial nominations (with the help of the vice president as presiding officer). Democrats declared their intention to revolt in numerous ways if Majority Leader Bill Frist pursued this approach, but the matter was resolved when a group of fourteen senators (seven Democrats and seven Republicans), dubbed the "Gang of 14," took it upon themselves to decide which nominees would be subject to filibusters and which ones would not.[76]

In 2006, the Republicans succeeded in passing legislation to extend the USA Patriot Act and to enact new rules for the detention and treatment of enemy combatants, with limited input from Democrats.[77] The president also succeeded in getting his second new Supreme Court justice, Samuel Alito, approved by the

Senate. However, the 109th Congress was far from an unequivocal success for Bush and the Republicans. His Social Security reform plan, which called for the creation of optional personal investment accounts, never got off the ground. His "Clear Skies" initiative failed, as did the effort to drill for oil in the Alaskan National Wildlife Refuge. The House and Senate were unable to agree on how to revise immigration policy, and how to reauthorize welfare and education laws.[78] By the summer and fall of 2006, Bush's declining popularity was evident as members of Congress, including some Republicans, began to reassert themselves. Still, what is most noteworthy about the 2002–2006 period is the extent to which the president (and vice president) were able to push Congress into a subservient role by invoking party loyalty and executive authority. This era of unified government is unlikely to be accorded a policy breakthrough legacy that matches those of the New Deal or the Great Society, but the Bush administration will likely be recognized as having exercised more unchecked (by Congress) executive power than any administration in American history, save perhaps the Lincoln administration.

Voting Trends in Congress

There is virtual unanimity among congressional scholars, and others who observe Capitol Hill, that Congress became more sharply divided along party lines beginning in the 1980s and continuing to the present. Increasing congressional polarization can be demonstrated through various measures of partisan/ideological differences among senators and representatives. For example, various interest groups have for some time assigned scores to members of Congress based on their voting records on bills about which the groups are especially interested. *The Almanac of American Politics* includes the ratings of ten different groups in its profiles of each members of Congress.[79] A shortcoming of these measures is that each of them is based on a limited number of roll call votes.

In the early 1970s, political scientist Aage Clausen developed a statistical scaling technique that identified different "policy dimensions" from an analysis of all non-unanimous roll call votes, and then assigned scores to members of Congress on each dimension. His goal was to explain congressional voting by showing that members tended to have stable (and thus predictable) positions within each of his dimensions (government management, social welfare, international involvement, civil liberties and agricultural assistance).[80]

In recent years, the analysis of congressional roll call voting, and the assignment of liberal versus conservative scores to members of Congress based on their voting records, has been dominated by political scientists Keith Poole and Howard Rosenthal.[81] Beginning in the early 1980s, they developed, and then refined, a mathematical estimating procedure for identifying the ideological positions of every member of Congress going back to 1789. Their most recently developed set of scores (DW-NOMINATE) involves two dimensions. The first dimension is a liberal-conservative measure that revolves around the role of

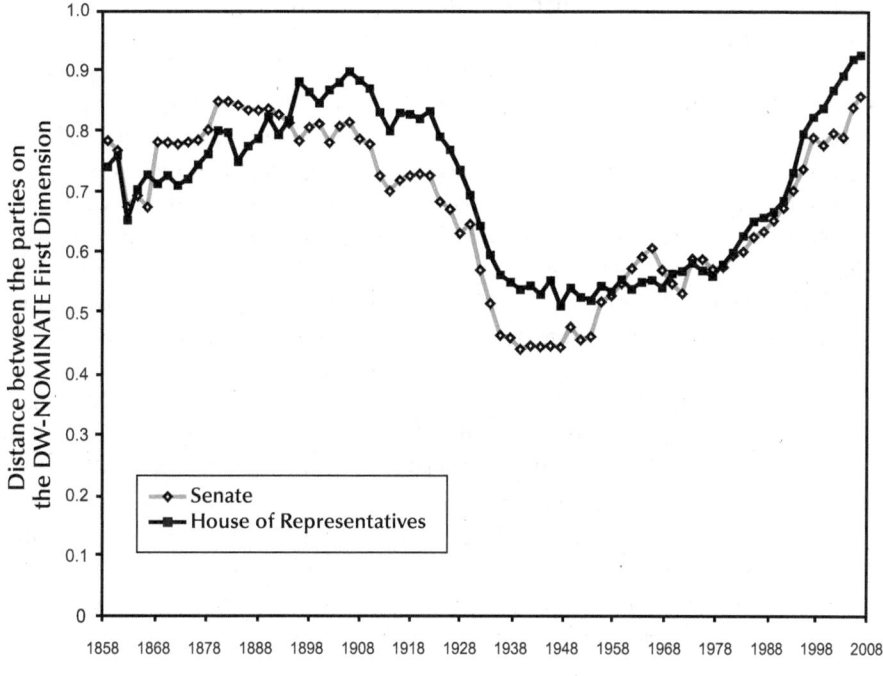

Figure 5.1 Party Polarization in Congress, 1858–2008

Source: voteview.com.

government in the economy/society, and members are assigned scores from 1.0 (most conservative) to -1.0 (most liberal). The second dimension focuses on race issues (especially slavery in early Congresses) and shows a decidedly regional (North versus South) pattern of voting on these issues. However, by the 1970s the second dimension had more or less disappeared, according to Poole and Rosenthal, as congressional voting on issues such as civil rights and affirmative action began to fit very well into the first (liberal/conservative) dimension. Thus Figure 5.1 is based on DW-Nominate scores from Poole and Rosenthal's first dimension only.

What Figure 5.1 displays are the numerical distances (expressed in absolute values) between the DW-Nominate first dimension mean score for each party delegation (House and Senate) going back to the 35th Congress (1857–1858) and continuing to the 110th Congress (2007–2008). Thus if the mean score for all House Democrats in the 100th Congress was -.313 and the corresponding mean for House Republicans was .343, then the distance between them would be .656, which appears in Figure 5.1. What is striking here is not only the recent (since 1980) surge in partisan/ideological voting in Congress, but also the high level of such voting in past Congresses (of the late nineteenth and early twentieth centuries). In fact, over the 150 years of voting history depicted, the period of relatively low partisan/ideological voting (1930–1980) is considerably shorter in duration than the combination of the two periods of high partisan/ideological voting (1868–1920 and 1980–2008).

Figures 5.2a and 5.2b add another set of scores to the DW-NOMINATE series as a further point of comparison. These are the *Congressional Quarterly's* (CQ) "Party Unity" scores.[82] One of their measures of partisan voting is what they call "party unity votes," which includes those votes in which a majority of one party votes in opposition to a majority of the other party. Since 1970 the percentage of party unity votes relative to all roll calls has ranged from as low as 30 percent to as high as 70 percent. Party unity scores for individual members are calculated by counting the number of times a member voted with his/her party on party unity votes, and converting this into a percentage. Using these percentages, an average for all members of each party in both chambers can be determined.

In Figures 5.2a and 5.2b both the distances between the party DW-Nominate means and the average party unity scores for Democrats and Republicans in both the House and Senate from the 87th (1961–1962) to the 110th (2007–2008) Congresses are displayed.[83] The trend lines speak for themselves: there has been a steady increase in the level of partisan voting in both chambers over the last forty years. As the parties have become more internally unified, they have also become more ideologically polarized. Having established that party polarization is real, we now turn to the question of how it has affected national policy output.

Polarization and Public Policy

How does increasing partisan polarization affect the performance of Congress as a legislative institution? The responsible party school always thought that more unified, disciplined parties would make the legislative process function more smoothly and effectively. However, as we have discussed, the American legislature operates in an environment that includes a number of features that confound and frustrate such an expectation. One of the most important is bicameralism, especially as it pertains to the peculiar qualities of the U.S. Senate. A disciplined legislative party in the Senate would have to include at least sixty members to function as efficiently as a simple majority in the House, and neither party had sixty senators for the twenty years between 1979 and 2009. (With the defection of Arlen Specter and the seating of Al Franken, the Democrats reached the sixty-seat level in mid-2009, which they retained when Paul Kirk replaced the recently deceased Ted Kennedy in October.) Of course, it is also possible to have majorities of different parties in the two houses of Congress; indeed, this has occurred in four of the last fifteen Congresses. Add to this mix the separation of powers, with the very real possibility of divided government (see above), and the question of what to expect from the national policy-making process in an era of heightened partisanship becomes especially perplexing. Nevertheless, it is an important question to pursue.

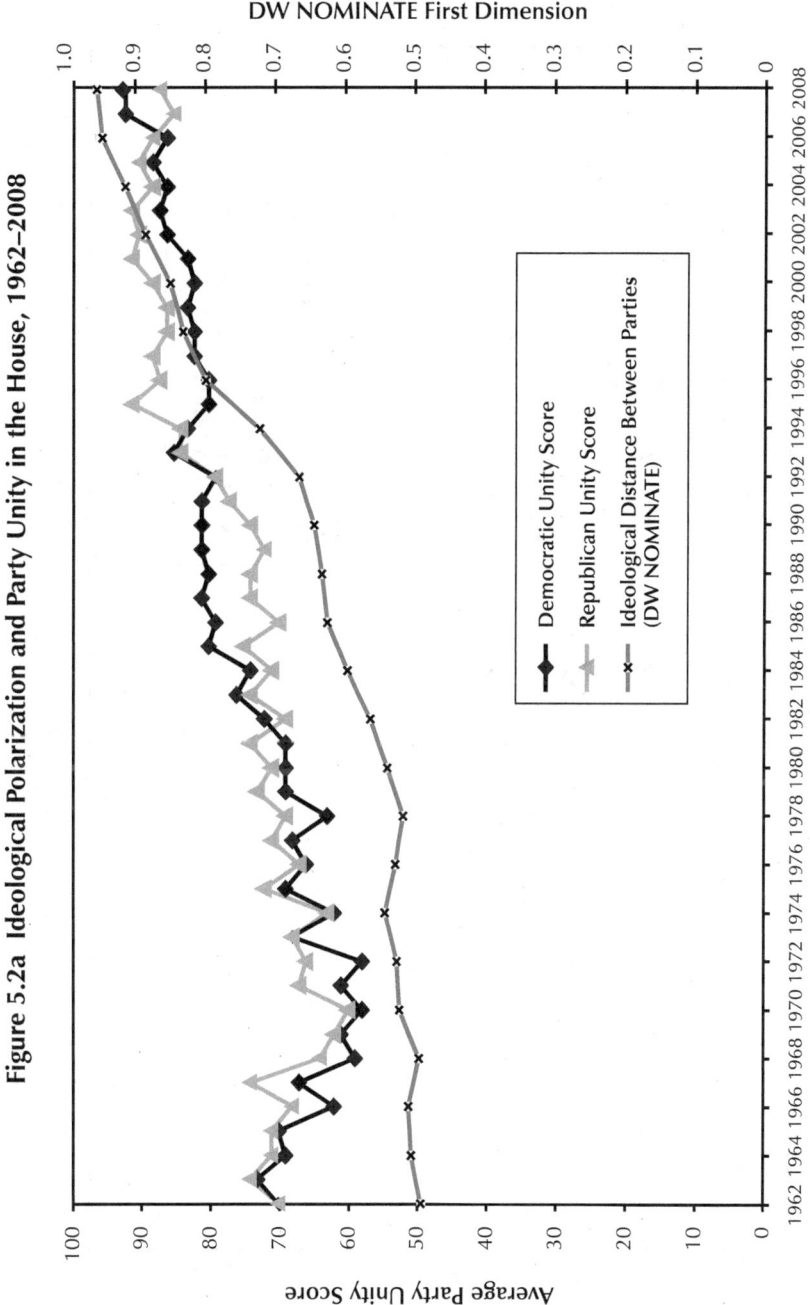

Figure 5.2a Ideological Polarization and Party Unity in the House, 1962–2008

Source: Congressional Quarterly; and voteview.com.

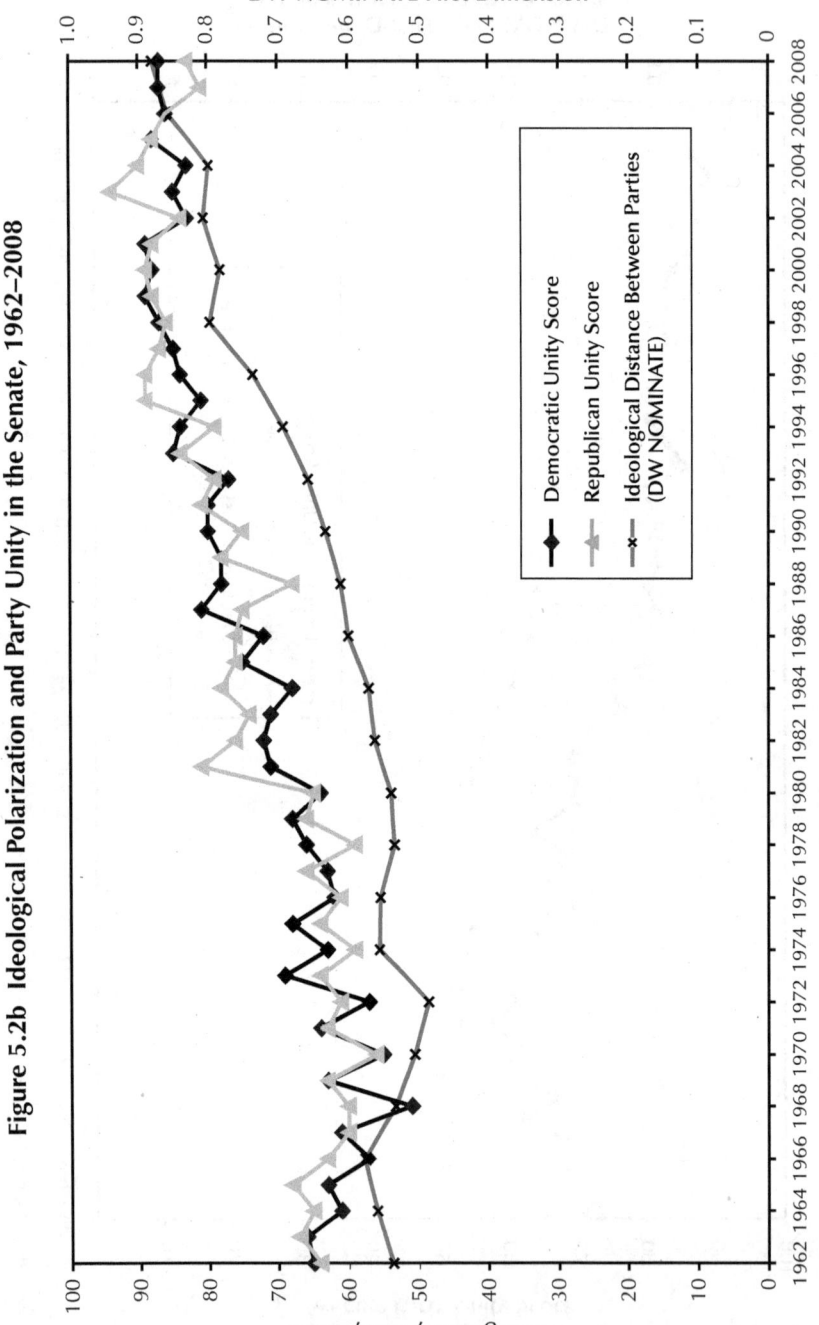

Figure 5.2b Ideological Polarization and Party Unity in the Senate, 1962–2008

Source: Congressional Quarterly; and voteview.com.

The most common observation about the national governmental process since the 1970s is that it tends toward gridlock or stalemate. At first, many of those concerned about gridlock pointed their fingers at interest groups. They argued that the proliferation and diversification of the interest group world by the 1970s had created a situation in which any important change in government policy would almost certainly affect one or more interest group(s) negatively, and usually the groups potentially affected would be powerful enough to head off such a change (using their influence in committees and/or by mobilizing public opinion).[84] However, there were numerous examples of powerful interests being negatively affected by policy changes in the 1970s and 1980s, and by the 1980s, gridlock was increasingly being associated with partisanship.[85]

In 1991, David Mayhew came out with a new and important study of divided government and gridlock.[86] Using a combination of major newspaper (*New York Times* and *Washington Post*) assessments of the productivity of congressional sessions and expert opinion on the significance of legislation passed in each session, he developed a list of some 267 "landmark laws" passed between 1946 and 1990. He then analyzed the relationship between the Congress that passed relatively large numbers of landmark laws and the presence or absence of divided government, and found that it was insignificant. During periods of divided government Congresses passed an average of 11.7 landmark laws, while during periods of unified government the average was 12.8 landmarks.[87] In other words, the presence or absence of divided government is not a very good predictor of legislative productivity in the United States.

Several prominent political scientists took issue with various aspects of Mayhew's analysis, with the most compelling criticism being that Mayhew did not take into account the size of the policy agenda for each of the sessions of Congress included in his study. The point here is that passing fifteen landmark laws in a given session of Congress may look pretty good compared to output of other sessions, but if the number of actions the public thought Congress needed to take during that session was especially large, the legislature's performance might be considered disappointing.[88]

So, Sarah Binder undertook an even more comprehensive analysis, which measured gridlock as the percentage of laws passed relative to the overall number of laws being demanded, and found that there was, in fact, a significant relationship between gridlock and divided government.[89] Her analysis further revealed that partisan polarization (using the same measures that were presented in the previous section) and House-Senate policy differences were also major contributors to deadlock. That is, higher levels of polarization among members of Congress increased the probability of gridlock, as did pronounced differences in the policy views of House members compared to Senate members.[90] She tested for the effects of several other variables, including changes in the public mood and the presence or absence of large deficits, but the consistent finding was that three (and only three) factors had a significant independent effect on gridlock: divided government, partisan polarization, and House-Senate policy differences.

Binder and others have used these findings to make the point that more cohesive and disciplined parties cannot be expected to break policy gridlock in a legislative system with as many pluralistic elements as that of the contemporary United States government. What is needed, the argument goes, is an inclination toward compromise, not an eagerness to emphasize partisan differences.[91] Thus, strong parties, which help to clarify choices for voters, may also make it more difficult for the national government to act, especially during periods of divided government. But it may also be that what is truly needed to break gridlock in Washington is unified government with sixty votes in the Senate and a large majority in the House.

Because Congress is such a complex institution, making judgments about the effectiveness of a given legislative session is very difficult. One reason for this is that the American Congress does a lot more than just legislate. It frequently undertakes investigations and other fact-finding efforts, many of which are part of its oversight function *vis-à-vis* the executive branch.[92] There may be circumstances in which these investigative and oversight duties are more important than any new legislation Congress might pass. And both the presence and absence of investigations and oversight can be important. Many believe that the lack of oversight of the Bush administration by the Republican Congresses of 2002–2006 was a major failing, one that contributed greatly to Democratic success in 2006. In 2007, Democrats flexed their legislative muscles by conducting a number of high visibility investigations that involved not only the war in Iraq, but also domestic matters such as firings (of federal prosecutors) in the Justice Department.[93] Shining light on issues is sometimes more important than enacting legislation.

A second aspect of the complexity of the American legislative process is that a lot of what is done is as much about symbolism and communication as substance. In 2005, the Republican leaders of the House went out of their way to get involved in a decision about continuing life support for Terri Schiavo, who had been in a coma for several years. Their attempt to force Florida courts to reconsider a decision to end life support for Schiavo failed, but it seems clear their real goal was make a symbolic statement to their followers about the importance (sanctity) of human life.[94] As described earlier, Democrats in 2007 insisted on passing supplemental appropriations bills to fund the Iraq War that included timetables for withdrawing American troops from Iraq, even though it was clear that President Bush would veto the bills. Their purpose was to take a stand against the president as a way of showing antiwar supporters that congressional Democrats understood how badly they wanted the war to end. Taking public stands on important issues is an important part of what legislators do, and can have significance beyond the symbolic.[95]

These examples just scratch the surface of the nuance and complexity of American legislative activity. Often the most consequential decisions and actions take place behind the scenes, as legislators make deals about what will be included and excluded from a bill, or the precise language to be incorporated into legislation. It can be very difficult for citizens to comprehend what is at issue when votes are taken on legislation because of the way some bills are packaged. These nuances also make it difficult for scholars who rely on analyses of floor voting patterns and outcomes to capture the totality of the legislative process. Thus all efforts to make definitive evaluations of the performance of Congress will have their flaws and inadequacies. Nuance notwithstanding, we feel confident in stating that over the last twenty years, whether it is roll call voting patterns, minority party opposition tactics, presidential assertions of power, legislative oversight and investigations, or symbolic actions designed to elicit popular support, parties and partisanship have motivated and inspired most of the major debates and controversies in Washington.

CHAPTER 6

Political Parties in Anglo-America

In Chapter 2, we described the decline and resurgence of political parties in the United States. But there is plenty of evidence to suggest that changing perceptions of political parties are not a uniquely American phenomenon. In some industrialized democracies across the globe, there is evidence that factors such as increasing education, proliferation of media, and the emergence of new issues have contributed to a decline of partisan salience. On the other hand, there are also some indications that, in recent years, parties have become more relevant. In this chapter, we explore party decline, resurgence, and polarization in a comparative context in order to highlight both the similarities and the differences between the American experience and that of other democracies.

Going back several decades, comparative studies of political parties have emphasized the relative weakness of American parties compared to their counterparts in Great Britain and other European countries. European parties were ideologically cohesive, occupied a narrow place on the ideological spectrum, and were distinct from each other. American parties, it was said, were "brokerage" parties that housed within them diverse and at times contrasting points of view, and that were not always distinguishable from each other. As third-party candidate George Wallace famously put it in the 1968 campaign, there was "not a dime's worth of difference" between the Democratic and Republican parties.[1] However, over the last thirty years, as we have shown in several chapters, the parties in the United States have become stronger and more salient. During this same period, European parties have begun to show some of the weaknesses traditionally associated with American parties—volatility in voting behavior and shifting coalitions. Indeed, at this point the two major parties in the United States may well occupy a more prominent and enduring place in the political system than their counterparts in many other advanced industrial democracies.

As we noted in Chapter 2, early studies of party identification in the United States (from the 1950s and 1960s) emphasized its psychological component. For many, it was a deep-seated loyalty, a kind of prepolitical orientation that shaped political attitudes and behaviors. However, by the 1970s, this type of party identification became less common, partisanship was more about issues and competence than simple loyalty. Comparative party scholars have found a similar role for parties in other countries—large numbers of citizens identify with them, but this identification is not necessarily regarded as a long-term loyalty or orientation.² The likelihood of shifting affiliations among citizens is further increased in countries where new parties emerge with some regularity. In recent years, new parties have achieved considerable and ongoing success at the polls in many countries (for example, the National Front in France and the Liberal Democrats in Great Britain), but not so much in the United States. A shifting multiparty system, therefore, encourages a more fleeting conception of party identification.

Yet despite these changes in the nature of party identification, there is a great deal of evidence to suggest that party affiliation continues to be more stable than other political attitudes.³ Studies conducted in France, Germany, and Great Britain have all pointed to similar conclusions: that citizens' party identification tends to be quite stable; and that the stability of party identification exceeds that of vote choice. It is worth pointing out, however, that the connections between party identification and vote choice have been strongest in the United States.⁴

In Chapter 2, we presented considerable evidence to document a decline of partisanship in the American electorate, during the late 1960s or early 1970s (depending on the indicator). This development was not limited to the United States. Dalton assembles party identification data from nineteen countries (including the United States) and demonstrates that in seventeen of the nineteen countries, the percentage of individuals identifying as partisans has undergone a steady decline over time (the time period varies, depending on the availability of survey data for each country). Moreover, in all nineteen countries, the percentage of strong identifiers also declined over time.⁵

Other indicators point to a similar conclusion. In recent years, more individuals have reported changing their vote from one election to the next, producing larger aggregate swings between consecutive elections in many countries. This increased electoral volatility is rooted in a decline in partisan salience—voters have become more likely to take their cues from a variety of different sources. In addition, there is more evidence of split-ticket voting and of individuals delaying their vote decision until close to the election—suggesting that short-term forces instead of a longer-term partisan anchor are influencing vote choice. Survey data from various countries suggest that the public is less confident in, and/or satisfied with, the major parties. And, perhaps as a consequence of this diminished confidence, new parties have sprung up all over the globe, in places such as Canada, New Zealand, Italy, Austria, and France, to name a few. In some instances, these new parties have attracted not only a significant share of the national vote, but they have also gained a critical mass of representatives in the national legislature.

What accounts for this secular decline of parties across national boundaries? Dalton offers two possible explanations.⁶ The first has to do with important sociodemographic changes over time. As in the United States, citizens of industrialized democracies all over the world have become more educated and thus can more easily access relevant political information, without needing to rely upon the cues provided by political parties. This has been supported by the proliferation of media outlets that provide alternative sources of information, thereby working to undermine the influence of parties.

A second explanation for cross-national dealignment rests with rising dissatisfaction with political parties. In the American context, the Vietnam War, Watergate, and economic downturn all contributed to a loss of confidence in institutions, political parties among them. There is also plenty of evidence to support the contention that British citizens have turned negative toward their parties. In the *British General Election Study, 2001*, large majorities of respondents stated that parties make idle promises, that they are more interested in winning than governing, that they spend too much time bickering with each other, that they fail to find qualified candidates, and that they ignore the nation's most pressing problems.[7] Dalton suggests that the decline of Britain's status in the world along with greater partisan conflict after World War II, have contributed to this growing partisan disaffection. The emergence of new "post-materialist" issues such as environmental protection and gender equality have also undermined traditional class and religious cleavages that were associated with party systems in industrialized democracies across the globe.[8]

Traditional class and religious cleavages were at the heart of party systems in virtually every industrialized democracy. As we saw in Chapter 3, social class, no matter how it is defined, has played an important role in shaping the two parties' respective coalitions in the United States. Once again, this phenomenon is not limited to the United States. In many European countries, the major parties have traditionally been identified with specific social classes. In Great Britain, for example, Labour has long been viewed as the party of labor unions and of workers more generally, while business and more affluent voters have tended to support the Conservatives. Similarly in France, parties of the left (Socialists and Communists) have been closely identified with working-class voters, while the major party of the right (Union for a Popular Movement) is rooted in business and the middle class. As Seymour Martin Lipset wrote in 1981, "On a world scale, the principal generalization which can be made is that parties are primarily based on either the lower classes or the middle and upper classes."[9]

At the same time, it is important to note that in recent years, the influence of social class on voting has declined. The "Alford Class Voting Index" measures the salience of class voting by subtracting the percentage of the middle class that supported the leftist party from the percentage of the working class that supported the leftist party.[10] Thus higher numbers indicate a stronger class basis to voting. Dalton applies the Alford Index to the United States, Great Britain, Germany, and France, and finds that from the 1940s through the early 2000s, there has been a sharp decline in class voting in all four countries. In France, for example, the Alford Index stood at around twenty-five points in the 1950s, and dropped to less than ten points in the 2000s.[11] Other scholars, using other measures of social class, have come to similar conclusions: its influence has declined.[12]

Our analysis in Chapter 3 showed that religious worship has become an increasingly important predictor of party identification and voting. In many

European systems, religion traditionally served as an important dividing line between political parties. As a rule, Catholics tended to support conservative parties, and Protestants tended to support liberal parties. But this pattern has not been as consistent as the social class divide; country-specific circumstances have in some instances led to deviations from this pattern. In Great Britain, for example, Catholics have traditionally supported Labour, in part because of the issue of Irish independence. Most Anglicans supported the Conservatives, because of historical ties between the Anglican Church and the political establishment.[13] And, as in the United States, there is plenty of evidence that, as issues such as abortion, lifestyles, and other moral questions have gained in importance, religiosity has emerged as a decisive influence on the vote. Dalton presents evidence showing strong correlations in recent years between church attendance and vote choice all over Europe (Austria and the Netherlands show the strongest correlations followed by Belgium, Finland, Norway, and Switzerland). In fact, in recent years, the correlations between religious worship and the vote have been stronger in Europe than in the United States.[14]

An Overview of the Party Systems in Anglo-American Democracies

In order to analyze partisanship and polarization in the United States alongside the experiences of comparable democracies, we undertake a detailed analysis of the place of partisanship in the four Anglo-American democracies: the United States, Australia, Canada, and Great Britain.

The party systems in these four countries share many common features. First, in each of these countries, political power has alternated between two contending parties: one that is generally a center-left party, and the other which is generally a center-right party. These major parties can be characterized as "catch-all" in ideological terms. They tend to be fairly broad and cover a lot of space on the ideological spectrum. So, in the United States, for example, defenders of segregation and supporters of civil rights both could identify as Democrats in the 1960s. Similarly, in Canada, the contending right-wing party for many decades was called the Progressive Conservatives, housing small government conservatives alongside so-called Red Tories who were more willing to use government to achieve social reform. By contrast, in many non–Anglo European countries, the contending parties tend to be more numerous, more ideologically cohesive, and/or rooted in religious alliances. For example, in France, there are two important parties on the right and two on the left. In both Germany and Italy, the religiously rooted Christian-Democratic party has been the major right-wing party.

In three of our four Anglo-American countries (the United States is the exception), minor parties have met with some success in legislative elections. Yet in none of these countries has a far right or far left minor party achieved any sort of major electoral breakthrough. This stands in contrast to several other European states where extremist parties have met with considerable success. In both France and Italy, Communist parties have won many votes and at times participated in governing coalitions. In Austria and France, extremist right-wing parties have also achieved considerable electoral success, both in legislative and even in presidential elections. By contrast, in the four Anglo-American democracies, far left and far right parties have operated at the margins of the political system. This may be the product of the "catch all" nature of the major parties. It may also reflect a common British political heritage rooted in "liberalism, individualism, and a pragmatic nonideological sense of compromise."[15]

To provide some context for the analysis of partisanship in Anglo-American democracies, we begin by providing thumbnail sketches of the party systems in Australia, Canada, and Great Britain. There is one point of commonality among these three countries that is worth emphasizing. Unlike the United States, these other Anglo-American countries operate under a fusion of power system—the executive is not elected separately from the legislature. In fact, the members of the executive (the Prime Minister and members of the cabinet) are elected members of the legislature and represent individual constituencies. In other words, in contrast to the United States where separate elections can produce divided government (executive from one party and majority in the legislature from the other party), in these other countries, the majority party in the legislature is by necessity the party that forms the executive and therefore the government.

Australia

One of the hallmarks of the party systems in the Anglo-American democracies is the stability of two-party systems. In this respect, Australia is no exception. Modern Australia was founded in 1901. The party system as we know it today has been in place (with some minor changes) since 1910. As we see in Table 6.1, the two contending parties are the Australian Labor Party (ALP) and the Liberal Party.[16] The ALP is Australia's oldest party, founded in 1901, activist in its policies and closely aligned with labor unions; the Liberals are a pro-business party that draws support from the middle class. The Liberals were founded in 1910, and changed into the Nationalist Party (1917–1931) and the United Australian Party (1931–1944) before being reborn as Liberals in 1944. Although the Liberal Party has won more elections than the ALP in the post–World War II period, the ALP was the dominant party in Australian politics in the 1980s and 1990s.[17]

One of the distinguishing features of the Australian party system is the ongoing presence of an important third party in the legislature. The National Party (originally known as the Country Party) emerged in the 1920s in response to a growing economic discontent in rural Australia and formed a governing coalition with the Nationalists (see above) in 1923.[18] Since that time, the National Party and the Liberals have constituted a right-wing bloc largely known as the

TABLE 6.1 Overview of Anglo-American Party Systems

	Major Party of Left	Major Party of Right	Leading Minor Parties with Legislative Representation
Australia	Labor (9)*	Liberals (16)*	Nationals
Canada	Liberals (13)*	Conservatives (8)*	Bloc Quebecois, New Democrats
Great Britain	Labour (9)*	Conservatives (8)*	Liberal Democrats, SNP, Plaid Cymru
United States	Democrats (24)*	Republicans (8)*	None

Sources: See note 16 on page 217.
*Number of legislative elections won since 1945

anti-Labor bloc. This coalition has remained in place, with the exception of two short periods (1973–1974 and 1987), and has formed a governing majority in the House of Representatives more often than not.[19]

Other minor parties have met with occasional success. The One Nation Party emerged on the electoral scene with a bang. This anti-immigrant, anti-Aborigines, and pro-gun party won 8.4 percent of the popular vote in the election of 1998, making it the third largest party in terms of popular vote at that time (although it did not win any seats in Parliament). In subsequent elections, the party never replicated its initial success. In addition, the Australian Greens—born out of environmental concerns in the 1980s—did fairly well in some state Parliaments and emerged as the leading third party in terms of popular vote in both the 2004 and 2007 federal elections.

There are certain institutional features that distinguish the Australian electoral system from its counterparts elsewhere and greatly affect the nature of the party system. First, since 1924 (and earlier in some of the states), Australia has had a compulsory voting system in place. As a consequence, turnout in federal elections has averaged more than 95 percent. There is evidence that compulsory voting has produced a small advantage for the ALP since those who would be most likely to abstain—the young and the less educated—are more likely to support the ALP.[20] But there is also an advantage that accrues to all parties. Because voting is compulsory, parties need not devote any resources to voter mobilization. This stands in sharp contrast to the millions of dollars that American political parties spend to turn out their base. (In 2008, the national party committees, Democrat and Republican, raised and spent nearly $1 billion.)[21]

Another feature that has maintained the dominance of the two major parties is the system of preferential voting that is used in elections for the House of Representatives (the lower house). The House has 150 single-member districts.

Unlike most parliamentary systems and voting for the U.S. Congress, where first-past-the-post methods of voting are used, Australia uses a mode of preferential voting.[22] Voters must rank their candidates from most to least favored. If voters' primary choices (i.e., most preferred candidates) produce an absolute majority for any candidate, then s/he wins the constituency. If not, then the votes of the candidate who has received the fewest primary votes are redistributed according to the second choice of that candidate's supporters. This continues until a candidate has received an absolute majority of the vote in the district. There are at least three consequences of this system of preferential voting. The first is that voters are more willing (than those in a first-past-the-post system) to give their primary support to a minor party candidate, since that voter can still rank his/her preferences for the other candidates. In other words, voters need not worry about wasting their vote on a candidate who has little chance of winning. The second consequence is, ironically, the persistence of major party dominance in the legislature. Although voters may be more willing to vote for a minor party candidate as their first choice, these minor party candidates almost always fail to win an absolute majority of the primary vote, and therefore candidates from the major parties, who are often ranked second when a minor party candidate is ranked first, usually emerge victorious. And third, this system can produce very large distortions between popular vote (primary choices) and legislative representation. Another wrinkle of preferential voting is that it increases the likelihood that a party winning a minority of the popular vote (primary choices) may win a majority in the House (because it wins the second spot on many voters' ballots). This last happened in 1989 when the ALP won a majority of seats with less than 40 percent of the popular (primary) vote.[23] It is important to point out that the upper chamber, the Senate, is elected under a system of proportional representation. As a result, minor parties in the Senate have often held the balance of power and have stymied the program of the majority party in the House of Representatives.[24]

Great Britain

Like Australia, British politics has long been dominated by two major parties alongside some minor parties that have met with occasional success in legislative elections (see Table 6.1). The current alignment, which pits the right-wing Conservative Party (also known as the Tories) against the left-wing Labour party—dates to the beginning of the twentieth century. The modern Conservative Party took form after the Reform Act of 1867, which significantly expanded the eligible electorate and generated the need for highly organized political parties.[25] Its major rival, Labour, formed at the beginning of the twentieth century to represent the interests of working-class voters and eventually supplanted the Liberals as the major party of the left.

Like conservative parties elsewhere, the British Conservatives were traditionally defenders of the status quo and institutions associated with the ruling order (the Crown and the Church, mainly). They have long held a deep and abiding faith in private property as a bulwark against government tyranny.[26] Like the Republicans in the United States, the British Conservatives are generally skeptical of government intervention and put faith in the free market. They tend to draw support from middle class and more affluent voters. But one of the long-standing and distinguishing features of the British party system is the phenomenon of working-class Tories. That is, since the middle of the nineteenth century, a significant proportion (albeit a minority) of working-class voters have supported the Conservatives instead of the leading left-wing party (the Liberals in the nineteenth century and Labour beginning in the twentieth century). This can be traced to the efforts of Conservative leader Benjamin Disraeli who devised an appeal that transcended social class and purported to promote the interests of all Britons.[27] It is also linked to the association in the nineteenth century between industrialists and mill owners and the Liberal Party. As a result of this association, many workers began to support the Conservatives.

The Conservatives have long been, and still are, divided into two ideological tendencies: the Tories (descendents of Disraeli) who emphasize the organic nature of society, the importance of existing institutions, and respect for authority; and the Whigs, whose primary goal is the creation of wealth.[28] Margaret Thatcher, who was prime minister from 1979 to 1990, was closely associated with the latter wing. Indeed, many observers noted the close ideological connections between the Thatcher Conservatives and the Reagan Republicans of the 1980s—especially in their shared antipathy toward government and faith in free market economics.

The Labour Party, Britain's other major party, was formed in 1900, largely by trade unionists and socialists. By 1920, Labour had supplanted the Liberals as the contending party of the left. Like the Conservatives, Labour has also been marked by factional conflict. True to the party's socialist origins, the left wing of the party has remained committed to public ownership of major industries and to greater government control of the market. Labour Revisionists have advocated a greater emphasis on achieving equality within the context of a mixed economy.[29]

The ascendancy of Tony Blair to Labour's leadership in 1994 moved the party away from doctrinaire socialism and toward a more pragmatic form of social democracy. In fact, many observers have noted the similarities between Blair's "New Labour" and Bill Clinton's "New Democrats." Like Clinton's Democrats, Blair's Labour emphasized greater individual responsibility, free market economics, and a reduced role for government. Both Blair and Clinton regarded themselves as "third way" politicians—pragmatic progressives who were not hostage to the traditional left-wing doctrines of their parties.

Only one other political party—the centrist Liberals—achieved any consistent parliamentary representation in the postwar period. From 1945 to 1970, the Liberal Party consistently elected a handful of representatives, the number ranging between six and fourteen Members of Parliament (MPs). As noted above, in the nineteenth century the Liberals were the main party on the left. In

1988, the Liberals merged with the Social Democrats (another centrist party formed in 1981) and became known as the Liberal Democrats. In the 1992 election, the Liberal Democrats won 18 percent of the popular vote, but elected only twenty MPs (out of 659). In subsequent elections, the Liberal Democrats managed to maintain about the same share of the vote and more than double its number of legislators, in spite of Labour's move to the center. With a substantial number of MPs, the Liberal Democrats have secured their place as a centrist alternative to the two major parties.

Other minor parties with regional bases have at times done reasonably well in British elections. Both the Scottish National Party (SNP) and Plaid Cymru (the Welsh nationalists) have maintained a Parliamentary presence since the 1960s and 1970s. Both of these parties have advocated devolution of power and greater home rule. In fact, the creation of elected assemblies in both Scotland and Wales allowed the SNP and Plaid Cymru to emerge as major players within the legislatures of these regions.

British parties have long been considered strong: they are centralized and able to translate party program into government policy.[30] This is largely a product of the parliamentary system, the fusion of legislative and executive power, and the need for party discipline in order for a government to survive. It also encourages voters to cast a ballot on the basis of party, not candidate. As is the case in other parliamentary systems, voters do not vote directly for the prime minister; rather they vote for the candidate of their preferred party, and the party electing the most MPs forms the government. Some have argued that the United States ought to adopt a British-style party system—with members of Congress eligible to serve in the cabinet.[31]

Canada

The Canadian party system is a direct descendent of the British system, with strong, centralized parties. Canada was a British colony until it achieved independence in 1867 and formed a confederation. Unlike the United States, where independence followed a revolutionary war, Canada's independence from Great Britain was granted through an act of the British Parliament. Several scholars have pointed out that although both Canada and the United States are dominated by two political parties, there is greater ideological diversity within the Canadian party system.[32] Because of the lingering influence of French colonial power, as well as the presence of United Empire Loyalists who fled the United States after the American Revolution, collectivism, paternalism, and a strong state have long been important political values in Canada; whereas in the United States, the Lockean philosophy of maximal individual freedom and limited government became the dominant ideological strand.[33] These differences are reflected in the party system.

As is the case elsewhere in the Anglo-American democracies, Canada has two major parties that alternate power. The Liberals are the party of the center-left and the Conservatives are the party of the center-right. As we see in Table 6.1, since the end of World War II, the Liberals have dominated elections, winning almost twice as many elections as the Conservatives.

Until the 1990s, the Canadian party system was remarkably stable. The Conservatives predate Canadian Confederation and formed the first government when Canada achieved independence. Similarly, the Liberals also predate Confederation, and formed their first government in 1873. Initially, the Conservatives were made up of a coalition of businessmen, conservatives from Lower Canada (Quebec), and British-style Tories in Upper Canada (Ontario), while the Liberals were formed by radicals from Quebec and reformers in Ontario. Over the years, there have been important differences between the two major parties on issues ranging from free trade with the United States, to military conscription, to devolution of power to the provinces (in particular Quebec).

But unlike the United States, where the role of government has long been the central dividing line between the two contending parties, this issue has been less salient in Canada. This is due in part to the marked ideological diversity *within* Canadian parties. The Canadian Conservatives, like their British counterparts, have long housed a faction that emphasizes hierarchy, order, stability, and community.[34] This wing of the party is open to a vigorous government role to pursue these goals (not unlike the Federalists, under Washington and Hamilton). In power, Canadian Conservatives have been responsible for the establishment of important government-owned corporations, such as the Canadian Broadcasting Corporation and the Canadian National Railway. In the 1972 campaign, moreover, the Conservatives advocated government-imposed wage and price controls to deal with stagflation and economic downturn. In fact, until 1993 the contending right-wing party in Canada was officially known as the Progressive Conservative Party, a name emblematic of the ideological diversity housed within the Canadian right.

The Liberal Party of Canada has also played a large role in producing an ideologically diverse party system. Canadian Liberalism has been divided into two factions: business liberals and welfare liberals.[35] The former, much like American conservatives, believe in the free market as the engine of economic growth and advocate a reduced role for the federal government. But for much of the twentieth century, welfare liberals dominated the Liberal Party, and were largely responsible for the development of Canada's extensive welfare state. Pensions for senior citizens, family allowances, single-payer universal health care, and a government-owned national oil company were all initiatives of Liberal governments.

But there is an additional factor that helps explain the ideological diversity within Canadian parties. Whereas social class has been an important correlate of voting in the other Anglo-American countries, in Canada, regionalism has proven to be far more important. For much of the twentieth century, the Liberals were the party most closely identified with the interests of Central Canada, especially Quebec, while the Conservatives promoted the interests of Western Canadian provinces that felt that they were getting short shrift from a federal government that favored the center. This kind of regional appeal transcends social class; it is similar to the Southern regional identity that was attached to the Democratic Party in the United States until the late 1960s, and to the Republicans since the Reagan years.

There is another factor that undermines the impact of social class on the Canadian party system. Since 1961, a socialist party, the New Democratic Party (NDP), has been Canada's most prominent third party. When it formed in 1961, it forged a close association with Canada's leading labor union, and it has advocated policies such as progressive taxation and extensive social welfare. The party has been divided between more orthodox socialists and more pragmatic social democrats; the latter have dominated the party since its founding. But the NDP is only a third party, and as such, its class-based appeal is limited by the perception that it cannot form the government. As a result, its success among working-class Canadians has been limited; many working-class Canadians have opted to vote for Liberal or Conservative candidates—both of which have advocated statist policies at various points in time. Cross-national studies suggest that class consciousness is weaker in Canada than in many other Western democracies, and that class consciousness is definitely weaker than regional identity as an influence on party support.[36]

Regionalism manifests itself in another way as well. Unlike the United States where Democrats face off against Republicans in national and state elections, many Canadian provinces have party systems that are different from the national party system. Whereas the Liberals and Conservatives form the contending parties nationally, in the province of British Columbia, for example, the Liberals and the NDP have been the only contending parties since the early 1990s; there has been no Conservative Party to speak of in British Columbia provincial politics. In other provinces, one finds different contending parties that may or may not mirror the national party system.

In 1993, the Canadian party system underwent dramatic changes. The incumbent Progressive Conservatives were wiped out at the polls and reduced to minor party status. They won only two seats in the national parliament (out of 295). For the next ten years, Canada was effectively a one-party system, with the Liberals in power, opposed by four minor parties. In addition to the Conservatives and the NDP, two new parties achieved spectacular results. The Bloc Québécois (BQ), a party committed to defending the interests of Quebec and to the promotion of Quebec sovereignty, won fifty-four seats and formed the Official Opposition.[37] This result was spectacular in part because the BQ contests seats only in the province of Quebec; it captured fifty-four out of the seventy-five seats in that province. In addition, a populist, conservative party, rooted in Western Canadian alienation, the Reform Party, won fifty-two seats, all but one in Western Canada. As a consequence, the Canadian party system was turned on its head. It went from being a stable, two-party system with a consistent but fairly small NDP presence, to a five-party system with only one of them (the Liberals) drawing any significant support across the country.

Liberal dominance from 1993 to 2003 was largely the product of a divided right. In effect, two conservative parties contested elections during these years: the more traditional Tory-style Progressive Conservatives and the populist, neo-conservative Reform Party (which morphed into the Canadian Alliance in 2000). The presence of two conservative parties divided anti-Liberal vote and ensured continued Liberal dominance at the polls.

Since 2003 however, the party system has returned to a more conventional form, with two contending parties, and two significant minor parties. In that year, the two conservative parties united and formed the Conservative Party of Canada. And in 2006, the united Conservatives regained power. So with the exception of the BQ that continues to enjoy concentrated support in Quebec, the Canadian party system has returned to its old form, with the Conservatives enjoying more support in the west, the Liberals enjoying greater support in the east, and the NDP having regained its status as Canada's leading third party (outside of Quebec).

Empirical Analysis of Partisanship in Anglo-America

These thumbnail sketches of the party systems in Australia, Britain and Canada reveal important similarities among these three countries. But our major purpose in presenting these cases is to compare them to the United States, and to highlight ways in which parties in the United States are both similar to, and different from, those in the other Anglo-American countries.

One point that should be emphasized at the outset is that there are crucial institutional differences between the United States and the other Anglo-American states, and these differences shape citizens' orientations toward the parties. As noted above, the fusion of executive and legislative power creates political parties that are highly centralized, disciplined, and programmatically responsible. In Australia, Britain, and Canada, every party has an identifiable leader (the prime minister in the case of the governing party and the "elected party leader" in the case of opposition parties). It is also very rare for an elected member of the legislature to publicly dissent from his/her party's official position. In the United States, party leadership is less clear-cut, especially for the party that does not control the White House. And it is commonplace for legislators from the same political party to publicly disagree with each other, and even to vote differently on roll calls. A prime minister and cabinet in other Anglo-American countries can take their party's election platform and, using their majority in the legislature, can translate that platform into public policy with relatively few obstacles. In the United States, on the other hand, the diffusion of power between the executive and the legislature makes it much harder to translate party programs into government policy. This is especially so in the context of divided government, but much conflict over policy can persist, even when the executive and the legislature are in the hands of the same political party. The upshot is that American parties are less unified, more fractious, and ultimately more irresponsible (in the programmatic sense).

Another institutional difference that affects the nature of the parties in these four countries is the method of voter registration. In the United States, states are in charge of voter registration and there is often a partisan element to it, whereas in the other Anglo-American countries, registration is totally nonpartisan and organized by the central government.

In most American states, when voters register to vote, they must indicate a party affiliation or declare themselves to be independent or nonpartisan.[38] These declarations can affect their access to party primary elections. Indeed in about half of the states, voters must register as Democrat or Republican in order to participate in presidential primaries.[39] This may influence how people choose to register. In California and New York, for example, in recent years only about 25 percent of voters have chosen to register as nonpartisan or with a minor political party.[40] Partisan registration is an integral part of the system of voting in much of the United States; there is no analogous procedure in the other Anglo-American democracies. As we pointed out in Chapter 2, all it takes to become a member of an American party is to say that you are a member, and/or to register as one. In contrast, in the other Anglo-American countries, party membership implies carrying a card and paying annual dues. There are no American-style primaries; candidates are nominated through a variety of methods, involving party members, MPs, and groups such as labor unions that are affiliated with the parties.

Yet another crucial difference rests in the very nature of the electoral system. As we noted earlier, for most of its history, the United States has had a stable, two-party system, with power alternating between the Democrats and the Republicans, and with minor parties breaking through on occasion, only to disappear within one or two election cycles. There are many factors that sustain the continued dominance of the Democrats and Republicans. The Electoral College, for example, makes it very hard for minor parties to achieve any breakthrough in presidential elections. Unless a minor party candidate enjoys concentrated regional support (for example, George Wallace in the South in 1968), it is nearly impossible for minor party candidates to win electoral votes. Many states have adopted laws that ensure continued major party access to ballots while imposing onerous requirements on third-party candidates who seek a spot on the ballot. Campaign finance laws provide automatic subsidies to the major party presidential candidates; minor party candidates are only eligible for public funds after an election in which they win at least 5 percent of the national vote. Nationally televised presidential campaign debates, which have become the high point of contemporary campaigns, almost always exclude minor party candidates. Finally, media coverage of campaigns tends to ignore these candidates. All of these factors contribute to a vicious cycle that is almost impossible to break: voters will not vote for third-party candidates because they have no chance of winning. And they have no chance of winning because voters will not vote for them.

In contrast, as noted in our thumbnail sketches, in each of the other Anglo-American countries, minor parties have secured a lasting presence on the electoral scene and have either held the balance of power in the legislature or have participated in governing coalitions. In all of these countries, minor parties receive public funding, generally based upon the number of votes that they received in the previous election.[41] In addition, in Australia, Britain, and Canada, legislation requires television networks to offer free television airtime to registered political parties, including minor parties, during election campaigns.[42] Recent elections in Britain and Canada (although not Australia) have featured televised campaign debates that included minor party leaders.[43] Money, access to airwaves, and guaranteed television time provide at least some national visibility to minor parties and help them win votes and even achieve occasional victory in legislative districts.

There is one additional factor raised in the thumbnail sketches that fosters minor party success. In both Britain and Canada, a very strong sense of regional identity has led to the creation and success of parties whose mission it is to defend regional interests on the national scene. In Britain, small parties seeking to advance the interests of Scotland and Wales have consistently won victories in constituencies in those regions. Similarly, in Canada, minor parties seeking to promote the interests of Quebec and the western provinces have won a significant share of votes and seats in those provinces. It stands to reason that where citizens feel a primary loyalty to a province or a territory rather than to the nation as a whole, they are more likely to support a minor party that promotes those regional interests.

The difference between the United States and the other Anglo-American countries on the issue of major versus minor party support can be seen in Figure 6.1, where we track electoral support for the major parties in each of the four countries, since the end of the Second World War.[44] In most years, almost 100 percent of American voters cast a ballot for one of the major parties. Significant support for third parties is rare. This stands in sharp contrast to the other countries, where the party alignments are more fleeting, and where new parties have emerged with some continuity. As these new parties break through the electoral system, the partisan lineup is reshuffled, voters are faced with new alignments, and citizens' fundamental orientations toward the parties may shift as a consequence.

Comparing the nature and extent of partisan identification across countries is difficult because the measures used by survey researchers are not always the same.[45] Nevertheless, in the various national election surveys that serve as the source for these party identification trends, respondents are ultimately asked whether or not they identify with a party, whether that identification is strong or not very strong; and they are also offered the opportunity to say that they do not identify with any party. In all of these surveys, analysts can construct four-point scales ranging from strong partisans to pure independents.

Figure 6.1 Major Party Support in National Elections

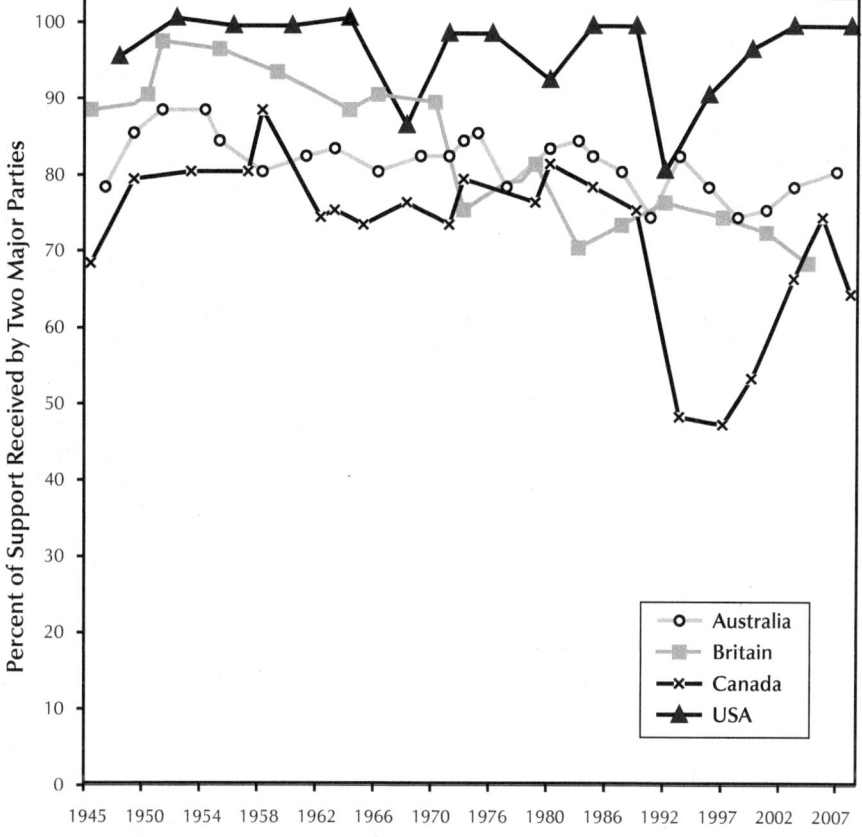

Compiled by authors from following sources: Australia: "Australian Government and Politics," http://elections.uwa.edu.au/; Canada: "Canadian Election Results by Party," http://www.sfu.ca/~aheard/elections/1867-present.html; Great Britain: "Election Information," http://www.politicsresources.net/area/uk.htm; United States: Congressional Quarterly Press Electronic Library, "Vital Statistics on American Politics," http://library.cqpress.com/vsap/toc.php?source=Vital+Statistics+on+American+Politics+2007-2008&mode=vstat-toc&level=2&values=Ch+1+-+Elections+and+Political+Parties.

In Figures 6.2 and 6.3, we compare the levels of strong partisanship (6.2) and independence (6.3) in the four Anglo-American countries.[46] There are several noteworthy patterns.[47] First, since the 1980s, there have been more strong partisans in the United States than elsewhere. During this period, roughly one-third of Americans have claimed that they are strong partisans, a proportion significantly higher than the corresponding figures (in most years) for Australia, Britain, and Canada. Second, in the United States, there has been greater aggregate stability in the level of strong partisanship, especially since the early 1980s.

Figure 6.2 Strong Partisanship in Anglo-America

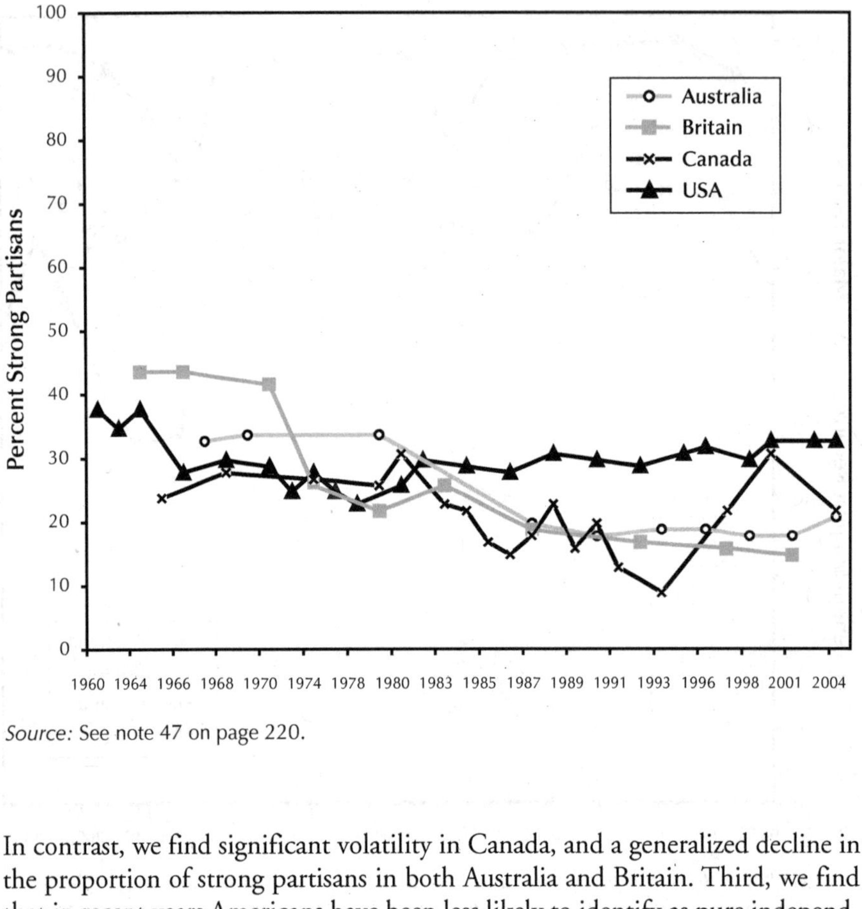

Source: See note 47 on page 220.

In contrast, we find significant volatility in Canada, and a generalized decline in the proportion of strong partisans in both Australia and Britain. Third, we find that in recent years Americans have been less likely to identify as pure independents, and that there has been a fair degree of aggregate stability in these figures.[48] By contrast, there is more volatility in the level of partisan independence in the other countries, especially in Canada; moreover, the proportion of independents or nonpartisans has grown in each of the other countries. These findings are consonant with our description of a more stable and deep-seated partisanship in the United States than in these other countries, especially in recent years.

One way to assess the impact of partisanship is to examine its effect on the vote. To what extent are individuals who identify with a party likely to cast a ballot for that party? Toward that end we examine the connection between partisan identification and vote choice in two recent elections in each of the four countries. The findings, displayed in Figure 6.4, support our contention that party identification is a particularly important factor in Americans' political calculus. Although, it is true that in all four countries a substantial majority of partisan identifiers vote for their own party; in most cases, these majorities are between

Figure 6.3 Nonpartisans in Anglo-America

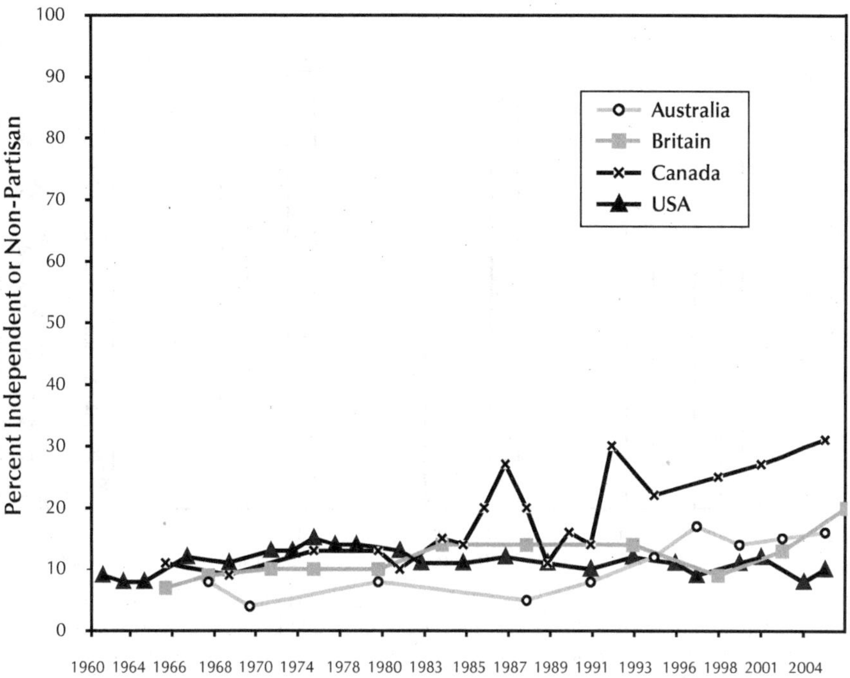

85 and 90 percent. American partisans are at the upper end of this scale—consistently around 90 percent.[49] Here again, third-party alternatives play an important role. In the United States, there has been no consistent third party, while in Australia, Britain, and Canada, third parties are long-standing players on the electoral scene and have maintained a relatively small but constant presence in the respective legislatures. These third parties offer major party partisans who may be temporarily unhappy with their own party the opportunity to express their dissatisfaction without supporting the other contending major party.

The decline of parties in the United States and elsewhere in the latter half of the twentieth century has been well documented.[50] Our main point is that parties have rebounded in the United States, whereas in other countries there is little evidence of resurgence. Our sense is that the offsetting tendencies of the American and the other Anglo-American party systems (initial weakness followed by decline and resurgence in the United States versus initial strength followed by decline without resurgence elsewhere) have made the contemporary parties in the United States and other industrialized democracies more similar than they were in the past. And this new pattern, we believe, is a consequence of stronger parti-

Figure 6.4 Partisan Loyalty in Anglo-America

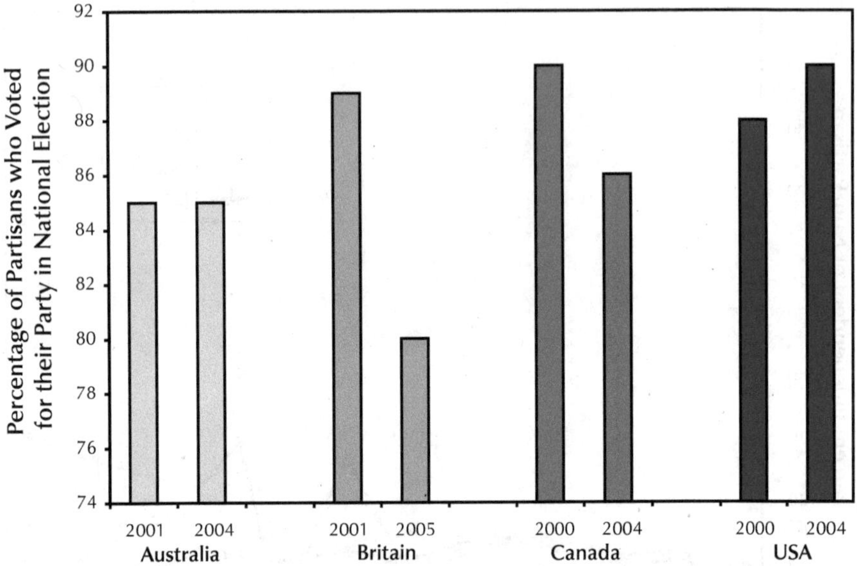

Sources: Australian Election Study, 2001; Australian Election Study, 2004; British General Election Study, 2001; British General Election Study, 2005; 2000 Canadian Election Survey; 2004 Canadian Election Survey; American National Election Study 2000; and American National Election Study, 2004.

san polarization in the United States. The evidence we have assembled supports this contention. In each of the four countries, citizens were asked to place the parties on a left-right scale, although the size of the scale is not always uniform across the surveys and the countries (see Table 6.2). As a result, we standardized the comparison in the last column of Table 6.2, by expressing the mean difference as a percentage of the width of the scale. For example, in Australia in 2001, on average, respondents placed the Liberal Party 1.78 points to the right of the Australian Labor Party on a scale that was eleven points wide. Thus this difference, expressed as a percentage of the width of the scale, is 16.2 percent. Comparing this percentage across countries and across surveys indicates that in recent years, Americans have been more likely to perceive a wider ideological distance between the two major parties than have citizens of the other countries. In both Australia and Britain, perceived party differences grew significantly in the more recent election (2004 and 2005, respectively), but the magnitude of those differences were still smaller than those in the United States. Perceived differences between the major parties have been narrowest in Canada.

There is additional evidence to support the notion that parties are more polarized in the United States than elsewhere. One way to measure polarization is to assess the ideological purity of party identifiers.[51] There is a greater likelihood

TABLE 6.2 Perceptions of Ideological Difference between the Major Parties in Anglo-America

	Mean difference in ideological placements of two major parties	Width of ideological placement scale	Ideological difference as a percentage of width of scale
Australia 2001	1.78	11 points	16.2
Australia 2004	2.73	11 points	24.8
Britain 2001	1.6	11 points	14.5
Britain 2005	2.37	11 points	21.5
Canada 2000	0.32	3 points	10.7
Canada 2004	1.21	11 points	11.0
USA 2000	2.25	7 points	32.1
USA 2004	2.14	7 points	30.5

Sources: Australian Election Study, 2001; Australian Election Study, 2004; British General Election Study, 2001; British General Election Study, 2005; 2000 Canadian Election Survey; 2004 Canadian Election Survey; American National Election Study 2000; and American National Election Study, 2004.

of partisan polarization when party identifiers are ideologically alike and also different from identifiers of the other party. In Table 6.3, we present our findings on the degree of ideological and partisan sorting in recent election years in Anglo-America. There are two noteworthy findings. First, in recent years, American parties, along with their counterparts in Great Britain, are at the top of the ideological purity scale. In 2004, for example, 53 percent of Democratic identifiers considered themselves to be liberal, while 70 percent of Republican identifiers identified as conservative. There is only one case (Britain in 2005) with a higher degree of partisan and ideological sorting. Second, there are large differences in the ideological purity of the contending left and right parties. In all four countries, the contending right party is ideologically purer than the contending left party, and in all cases, these differences are large. As discussed previously, Canadian regionalism contributes to less ideologically defined parties in that country. And, here again, alternative parties would appear to play a large role in these patterns. In both Britain and the United States, where the degree of sorting is the highest, there are no significant minor parties to the left or to the right of the major parties—thus strong ideologues must cast their lot with one of the major parties. However in Canada and Australia, there are minor parties that ideologically outflank their major party rivals (NDP in Canada, One Nation and Green in Australia).

As we saw in the overview of the party systems and in chapters 2 and 3, party differences in Anglo-America have long been associated with social class. In the

TABLE 6.3 Ideological and Partisan Sorting in Anglo-America

	Percentage of left wing party's identifiers that also identify as liberal	Percentage of right wing party's identifiers that also identify as conservative
Australia 2001	42%	56%
Australia 2004	48	62
Britain 2001	40	69
Britain 2005	59	81
Canada 2000	12	48
Canada 2004	36	64
USA 2000	44	68
USA 2004	53	70

Sources: Australian Election Study, 2001; Australian Election Study, 2004; British General Election Study, 2001; British General Election Study, 2005; 2000 Canadian Election Survey; 2004 Canadian Election Survey; American National Election Study 2000; and American National Election Study, 2004.

United States, for example, the Democrats have long been regarded as the party of the common or working man, and the Republicans have long been associated with business and with the more affluent.

In Figure 6.5, we measure the extent to which the major parties have been polarized along lines of class in the four Anglo-American countries. Once again we use income as a measure of social class (see Chapter 3) and we examine the pattern of support across income categories. The vertical axis represents the difference between support for the contending left-wing and right-wing parties—points above the horizontal axis indicate an advantage for the left party, and points below it represent an advantage for the right party. We find that in all cases but two (Australia 2004 and Canada 2004) the association between income and voting is linear and in the expected direction: the left party does best among voters in the bottom third of the income distribution, less well among the middle third, and worst among the top third. When we compare the United States to the other countries, the United States stands out in one important respect. In the cases of the 2000 and 2004 elections, the lines for the United States start well above the horizontal axis and finish well below it. The sharp descent of these lines is indicative of an American electorate that is relatively polarized along class lines and generally evenly divided in its support for the two major parties. Compare this line to the line for Britain in 2005. The slopes are similar, suggesting that moving from one income group to the next produces about the same amount of change in party support. But the British line finishes above the horizontal axis, indicating that among the most affluent, the left party (Labour) still won more votes than did the right party (the Conservatives). Notice also

Figure 6.5 Income and Voting in Anglo-America

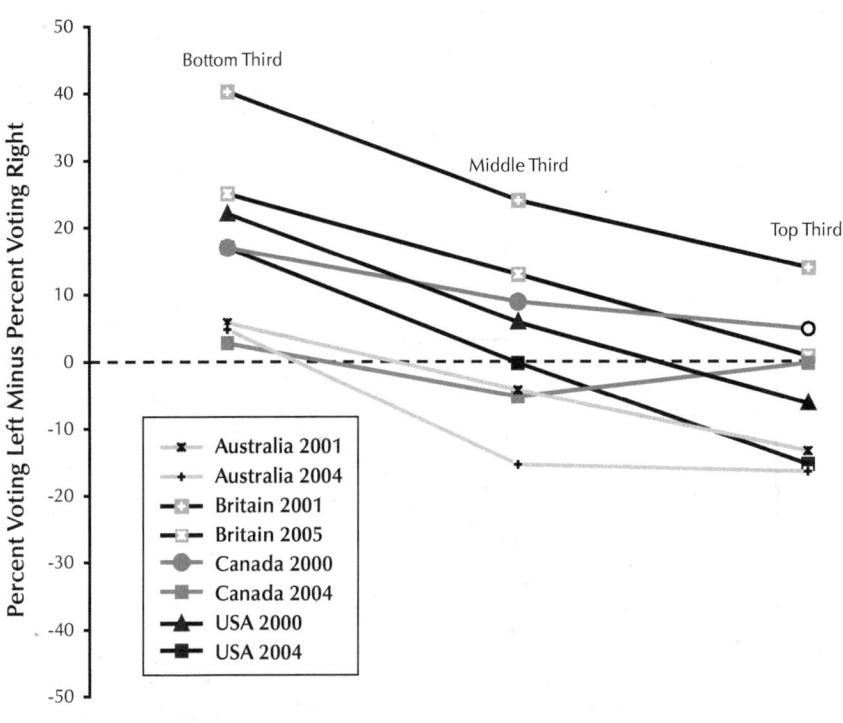

Sources: Australian Election Study, 2001; Australian Election Study, 2004; British General Election Study, 2001; British General Election Study, 2005; 2000 Canadian Election Survey; 2004 Canadian Election Survey; American National Election Study 2000; and American National Election Study, 2004.

that support for the left party in Britain among the bottom third is very high. The pattern in Britain reflects the fact that Labour was the dominant party within the electorate, regardless of social class. The overall patterns suggest that in recent years, social class has functioned as a more important dividing line between the parties in the United States and Great Britain, while we find a weaker class division in Australia and especially Canada.

As we saw in Chapter 3, in recent years cultural issues have joined social class as an important influence on the vote choices that Americans make (see Figure 3.10). We argued that this influence is consistent with sharp differences between the images of the parties on a variety of social/moral issues. We now turn to a comparison between the United States and the other countries on this question of a "morally driven" partisan polarization. Unfortunately our analysis here is limited by the constraints of the survey data: there are relatively few common questions across the countries.[52] The data we have assembled are summarized in Figures 6.6, 6.7, and 6.8.

Figure 6.6 Religious Worship and Voting in Anglo-America

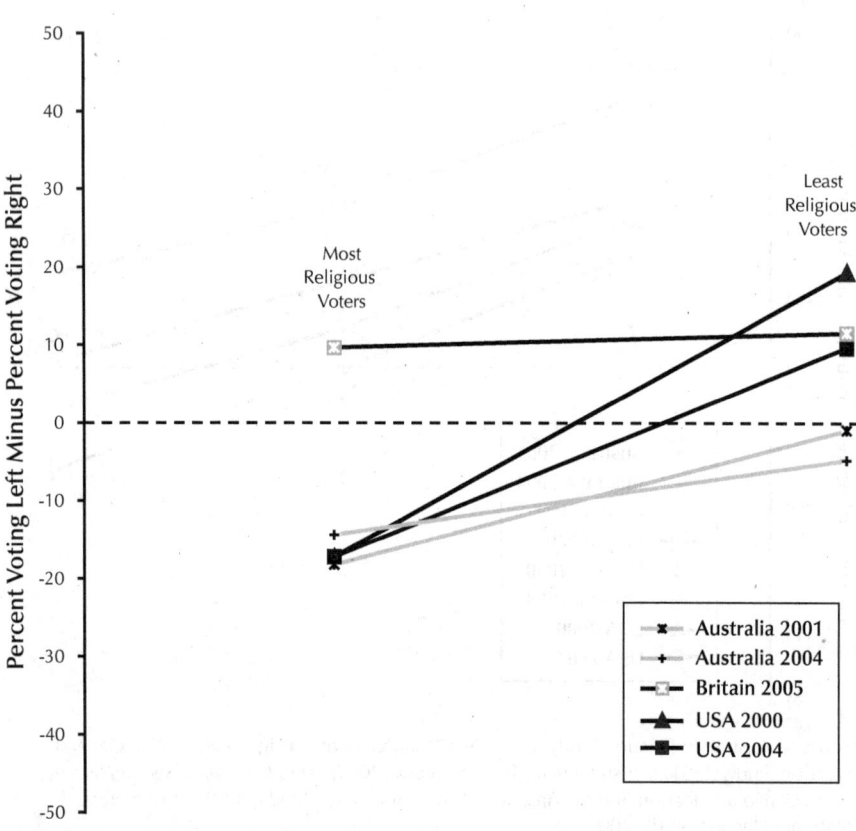

Sources: Australian Election Study, 2001; Australian Election Study, 2004; British General Election Study, 2005; American National Election Study 2000; and American National Election Study, 2004.

These three figures all indicate a similar pattern. The United States stands out from its Anglo-American counterparts in one important way: it displays the largest differences between the voting behavior of religious/pro-life voters and secular/pro-choice voters. In each of these figures, the slope of the line indicates the magnitude of difference in the vote choices of the two groups. In Figure 6.6, we see that in recent elections, the difference in the vote choices of the most religious and least religious Americans is largest.[53] In the 2005 British election, there were almost no differences based on religious worship (the line is almost flat); and in the two Australian elections, weaker slopes, and lines that do not rise above the horizontal axis, indicate a less pronounced partisan division based on religious worship. The patterns in Figure 6.7, where the question asked about the importance of religion to the respondent, are very similar to

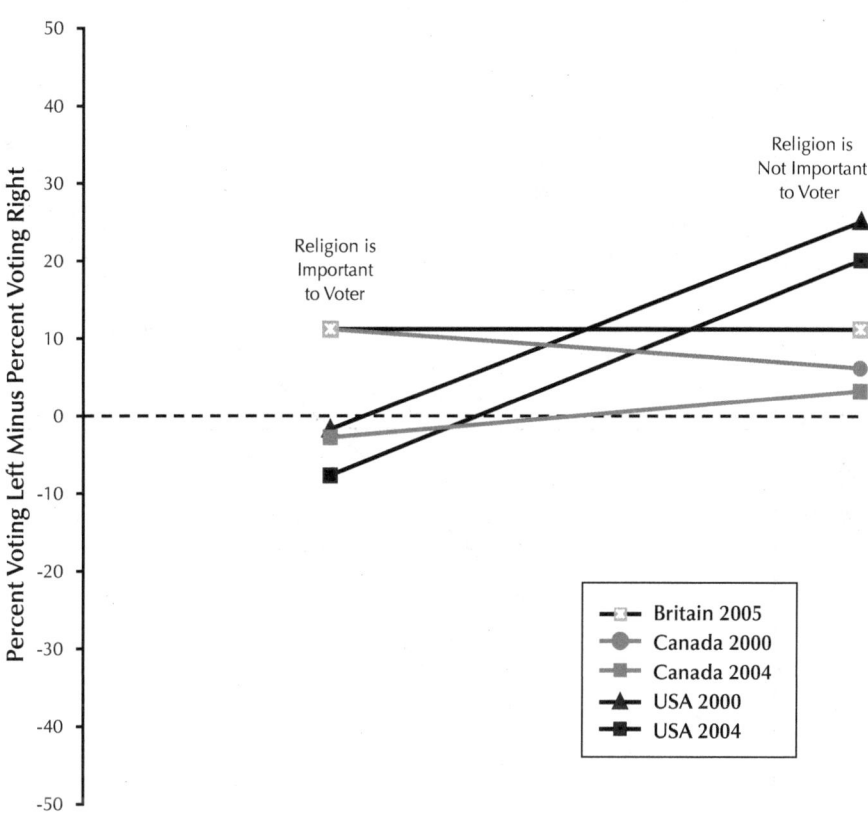

Figure 6.7 Importance of Religion and Voting in Anglo-America

Sources: British General Election Study, 2005; 2000 Canadian Election Survey; 2004 Canadian Election Survey; American National Election Study 2000; and American National Election Study, 2004

those in Figure 6.6, with the two American elections standing out once again. And perhaps most striking are the comparisons on display in Figure 6.8—which examines the relationship between attitudes toward abortion and vote choice. Once again, the American cases stand out. In both elections (2000 and 2004), the two lines that represent the American data suggest a very high degree of partisan polarization based on attitudes toward abortion. It is also noteworthy that in all countries, abortion appears to be a better predictor of vote than attitudes toward religion or religious behavior; we see positive slopes for all of the countries in Figure 6.8—and these relationships are all in the expected direction.

Putting all of this together, we believe that the evidence points to an overall higher degree of partisan polarization in the United States than in Australia,

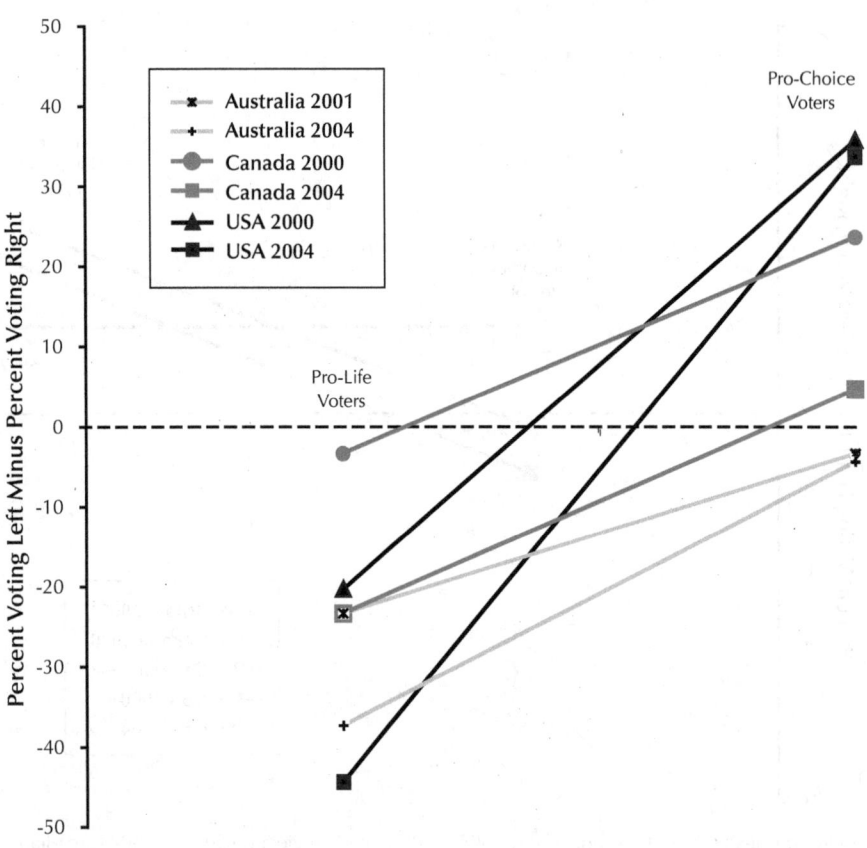

Figure 6.8 Abortion and Voting in Anglo-America

Sources: Australian Election Study, 2001; Australian Election Study, 2004; 2000 Canadian Election Survey; 2004 Canadian Election Survey; American National Election Study 2000; and American National Election Study, 2004.

Britain, or Canada alongside a stronger partisan resurgence. These two phenomena are not unrelated, as we have argued. The parties in Britain and the United States are more cohesive ideologically than in Australia and Canada; in the United States, moreover, citizens see the parties as ideologically further apart, and both income and religiosity/abortion serve as important dividing lines between the parties. As a result, we find more strong partisans and fewer independents in the American electorate, and we also find that partisanship has a very strong impact on vote choice. Certain institutional factors discussed earlier—such as the partisan system of registration, campaign finance, ballot access rules, and the Electoral College—all work to further ensure the dominance of the two major parties. And it is precisely this dominance which inhibits the ability of minor parties to break through and achieve electoral success. As we have argued in our discussion of Anglo-America, the presence of minor parties in the other Anglo-American cases has certain consequences: voters are less wedded to the major parties, they can more easily shift their party identification or their vote without moving over to the rival major party, and the presence of left-wing or right-wing minor parties can undermine major party polarization by blurring class or moral divisions that we associate with the major parties in the United States.

It seems obvious now that the old characterizations of weak American parties versus strong European (and other) parties are no longer accurate. In the United States, we have witnessed a decline and resurgence of the party system, but it is a party system that started out relatively weak. In Europe and elsewhere, there has been more of a steady decline from the 1950s to the present, but the parties started out somewhat stronger. It seems that the contemporary American party system, characterized by two ideologically distinct parties and an electorate that recognizes these differences, is more similar to European party systems than it was in the past.

CHAPTER 7

Looking Backward and Forward: The Election of 2008 and the Future of American Politics

The resurgence of parties that we have documented in the previous chapters was prominently on display during the historic 2008 election campaign. Although Barack Obama emphasized a new spirit of bipartisanship and John McCain played up his reputation as a maverick who was not afraid to buck his own party's line, a substantial majority of the public continued to perceive the parties and candidates as very different from one another; and these perceptions of partisan polarization were rooted in real and significant differences between the parties on a host of issues. In this chapter, we provide a narrative of the 2008 campaign and the first months of the Obama administration, drawing attention to the ways party resurgence and party polarization manifested themselves.

The Nominations

When the 110th Congress began on January 4, 2007, the effects of the momentous 2006 midterm election were on full display. Nancy Pelosi, the first woman to occupy the position of Speaker of the House and the first Democratic Speaker in fifteen years, held the media spotlight. But her command of the political center stage would not last for long. The 2008 presidential race had already begun, as hopefuls were making announcements of their intentions to run. By the end of the month, eight Democrats had thrown their hats into the ring.[1] Republicans were a bit slower in making their formal declarations, but by February the fields on both sides were mostly filled out. The first big event of the campaign—the Iowa Caucuses—would not take place until almost a year later, but the race for the White House was on.

The Democratic contenders included four senators—Hillary Clinton (New York), Barack Obama (Illinois), Christopher Dodd (Connecticut), and Joseph Biden (Delaware); two former senators—John Edwards (North Carolina), who was also the vice presidential candidate in 2004, and Mike Gravel (Alaska); a House member, Dennis Kucinich (Ohio), who ran in 2004; a governor, Bill Richardson (New Mexico); and a former governor, Tom Vilsack (Iowa). On the

Republican side, there was Rudolph Giuliani, the former mayor of New York; Mitt Romney, the former governor of Massachusetts; Mike Huckabee, the former governor of Arkansas; John McCain, senator from Arizona; Sam Brownback, senator from Kansas; Duncan Hunter, House member from California; and Ron Paul, House member from Texas.

This initial cast of characters offered the electorate a good deal to think about. Hillary Clinton, who everyone acknowledged had a good chance to win, offered the possibility of having a woman head a major party presidential ticket for the first time in American history. Obama would be the first nonwhite, Richardson the first Hispanic, and Mitt Romney the first Mormon to do the same. Interestingly enough, polls showed greater public resistance to electing a Mormon than a woman, Black, or Hispanic.[2] Other interesting candidates to emerge during the various speeches and debates during the spring and summer of 2007 were Ron Paul, a Republican libertarian, who opposed the war in Iraq and federal income taxes; Kucinich, who again appealed to the left-wing Democrats with his unequivocal antiwar, anticorporate positions and his support for a single-payer health care system; and Huckabee, who played his guitar and emphasized his fundamentalist religious views.

The early front-runners were Giuliani and Clinton, both of whom enjoyed ten-point leads over their nearest rivals among their respective party voters.[3] But there was a noticeable difference between Democrats and Republicans this time around. Democrats seemed to like their candidates, especially Clinton, Obama, and Edwards, while Republicans seemed unenthusiastic about their slate. Giuliani had trouble with the religious right because of his views on abortion and gay rights; McCain was also viewed negatively by many Republican true believers because of his maverick stands on issues such as campaign finance reform, immigration, and the Bush tax cuts, and because of his past criticism of religious leaders, such as Pat Robertson. Romney was not quite believable as the "true conservative," given his record as governor of Massachusetts and previous statements he had made on abortion and gay rights. This skepticism about the front-runners enabled Huckabee to gradually expand his base of support and led a number of party leaders to encourage Fred Thompson, actor and former senator, to enter the race.

Howard Dean captured a good deal of media and public attention in 2004 by introducing new Internet fund-raising strategies.[4] Obama created a similar stir in 2007, using small donations solicited over the Internet to nearly match Clinton's first-quarter fund-raising total ($25 million to $26 million). Overall, Democrats were raising more than Republicans, with Romney (at $21 million) outdoing Giuliani ($15 million) and McCain ($12.5 million).[5] As expected, all the major candidates opted out of the federal public financing system for the primaries (McCain gave some mixed signals, but later asserted that he was out) so that they would not be subject to state-by-state spending limitations. When it was all over, the prenomination fund-raising totals obtained by the top Democratic candidates were similar to the amounts raised by George W. Bush and

John Kerry in 2004 (Obama did establish a new record), but the top Republicans candidates fell well short of the 2004 levels.[6] The main new development in 2008 was Obama's success in raising large amounts through small donations. Roughly half of his money came from donations of $200 or less.

The debates among the candidates began in the summer of 2007 and extended well into 2008, creating a very long political season. Anyone who was interested had a chance to learn plenty about the candidates. Meanwhile, states were still trying to decide when they would have their primaries and caucuses. Under Democratic rules, Iowa and New Hampshire continued to hold the privilege of going first; other states that sought to go early were encouraged to opt for the "Super Tuesday" date of February 5. California, New York, Illinois, and nineteen other states did this, but Florida and Michigan chose to break the rules and hold their primaries in January. This brought about a promise of punishment (not seating their delegates at the convention) from the Democratic National Committee (DNC), and pledges by the Democratic candidates not to campaign in those states. Nevertheless, not long after the January 29 Florida primary the Clinton campaign began talking about her "victory" there, as well as in Michigan (Obama was not even on the ballot in Michigan).

As a result of all the frontloading, the Iowa Caucus was moved up to January 3, and the New Hampshire primary was set for January 8. Although several of the also-rans had enjoyed some good moments in the various debates, by December of 2007 the serious contenders on both sides had more or less been identified. Clinton, Obama, and Edwards were well ahead of the other Democrats, with Edwards running behind the other two. Thus for Edwards, Iowa was a must, and he spent quite a bit more time there than any other candidate (Democrat or Republican).[7] His message was one of economic populism, emphasizing the need for policies to help the poor and middle class. Obama had established an impressive grassroots organization in Iowa and had staked out an antiwar, big-change-needed-in-Washington position. Clinton, who had once toyed with the idea of passing up Iowa, was hoping her national front-runner status would carry her to victory there.[8] Obama won with 38 percent of the caucus vote, greatly boosting his candidacy. Edwards was second with 30 percent, one point ahead of Clinton.[9]

On the Republican side, Romney and Huckabee had devoted major time and effort to Iowa, while Giuliani and McCain had more or less written it off. Late entry Fred Thompson also was hoping to do well in Iowa. Huckabee scored a surprise victory, beating Romney by nine points (34 percent to 25 percent). Thompson and McCain were far behind at 13 percent each. However, McCain was rising from the ashes of his summer campaign abyss, and was now running even with Romney in preprimary polls in New Hampshire.[10] News that the troop surge in Iraq was working to bring down violence levels there, and his own dogged determination, had catapulted him into the lead in national polls of Republicans.[11] At this point, it was Giuliani's campaign that was sputtering; with no real hope in New Hampshire, he was banking his candidacy on a win in

Florida. Huckabee's support was rising, but few thought he could compete at the national level. Romney had enough money to endure many more primaries, but he needed to win something. He lost New Hampshire to McCain (32 percent to 37 percent), and McCain's path to the nomination became wider and straighter.

The New Hampshire primary produced two "comeback kids": McCain, who relished this description, and Clinton, who seemed more interested in portraying herself as the rightful front-runner. Following his win in Iowa, there was something of a media frenzy to coronate Obama. Preprimary polls showed him with a substantial lead, but Clinton ended this early rush to judgment with a solid win (39 percent to 36 percent; Edwards 17 percent).[12] Her margin of victory came largely from women and low-income voters.[13] But Obama bounced back with a massive win in South Carolina in late January (Obama 53 percent, Clinton 27 percent, Edwards 18 percent), which established a pattern that would be repeated throughout the spring. Obama would do well in states where Democratic voters included large numbers of African Americans, young people, and people with college educations. Clinton would rack up victories in states where most Democrats were women, blue-collar whites, and Hispanics. Obama also did well in states with open primaries; that is, states where Independents or nonpartisans could choose to cast a ballot in one of the party primaries. (Ironically, in some states, Obama's main rival in the battle for Independents was McCain, who proved back in 2000 that he had considerable appeal among Independents.) Clinton's wins occurred mostly in states with closed voting systems.[14]

McCain's success in New Hampshire put him in a very strong position going forward. Romney was able to win in Michigan and Nevada (caucus) in mid-January, but McCain won in Florida at the end of the month, and going into Super Tuesday (February 5), he was poised to put himself out of reach of the other candidates.[15] Giuliani's poor showing in Florida (15 percent) effectively ended his candidacy.[16] Early February polls showed McCain with a twenty-point lead nationally among Republicans, and the results of the February 5 primaries confirmed his dominance. McCain won all the big states (California, New York, Illinois, New Jersey, and Missouri), while Huckabee continued to show strength in the South, winning Georgia, Alabama, Tennessee, and Arkansas. McCain ended the day winning 600 of the 855 delegates that were up for grabs, taking an overwhelming lead over his rivals.[17] On February 8, Romney pulled out of the race, making McCain the presumptive nominee.[18] (Huckabee and Ron Paul stayed in but did not present much of a challenge to McCain in the remaining primaries.)

Most of the Republican primaries were winner-take-all events, which greatly aided McCain in amassing such a large lead after Super Tuesday voting. The Democrats, on the other hand, awarded most of their delegates proportionately, making a longer, more drawn-out selection process somewhat more likely. In California, for example, McCain won by a vote of 42 percent versus 36 percent for Romney, but got 158 of the 170 California delegates. In that same state, Clinton defeated Obama 52 percent to 42 percent, but garnered only 195 delegates compared to Obama's 155.[19] The Democrats also selected nearly twice as many delegates (4,234 to 2,380), and set aside nearly 20 percent of their total for so-called superdelegates (Democratic elected officials, and state and national party leaders). Therefore, it was not altogether surprising that Super Tuesday did not end the Democratic nomination contest. Still few experts were predicting the nomination race would continue until the very last contests on June 3.

Throughout 2007, the Democratic presidential candidates mostly refrained from attacking one another. However, in the days leading up to Iowa, New Hampshire, and South Carolina (January 19), the attacks and counterattacks between Obama and Clinton became more frequent and pointed. He presented himself as the candidate of change; she as the candidate of experience and sound judgment. Edwards withdrew from the race just before Super Tuesday, setting up a head-to-head competition that would last another four months.[20] The Super Tuesday results served up a good deal of satisfaction and disappointment for both Democratic candidates. Clinton won a total of nine primaries, including the big states of California, New York, New Jersey, and Massachusetts, and captured about one hundred more delegates from the primary states (661 to 568) than her opponent. Obama won seven primaries, including Illinois, and swept the six caucus states, which meant that his final Super Tuesday delegate tally was roughly equal to hers.[21] Moreover, the rest of February belonged to Obama, as he won ten consecutive contests (five primaries and five caucuses), including those in several important states such as Virginia, Maryland, Washington, and Wisconsin, to establish a one-hundred-plus delegate advantage that he would never relinquish.

By the time the next big primary date rolled around (March 4), the Clinton-Obama rivalry had increased in intensity and had captured widespread public attention. The Clinton campaign seemed to have been caught off guard by Obama's February surge, and she needed to win in Texas and Ohio to get back on course. Meanwhile, Obama was picking up important endorsements (Ted and Caroline Kennedy, among others), receiving greater support among superdelegates, and speaking to packed houses around the country.[22] National polls, for the first time, showed him ahead of Clinton.[23] Nevertheless, Clinton won the Ohio (54 percent to 44 percent) and Texas (51 percent to 47 percent) primaries, giving her campaign a much needed boost. Still, the boost was far from what the Clinton camp had hoped for—when the March 4 dust had settled, Obama retained his one-hundred-plus delegate lead (1,567 to 1,462).[24] McCain swept the March 4 Republican primaries in Ohio, Texas, Vermont, and Rhode Island, and then claimed the Republican nomination as Huckabee withdrew.[25]

After Ohio and Texas, there were still two months left on the primary calendar. The last really big primary state remaining was Pennsylvania on April 22. But, several additional issues and distractions were swirling around the campaigns. Former President Bill Clinton drew attention for various antics and statements, including his comparison of Obama's candidacy to that of Jesse

Jackson in 1988 after the South Carolina primary, which was widely perceived as a racially laced putdown of Obama. In March, former Democratic vice presidential candidate, and Clinton supporter, Geraldine Ferraro, was quoted as saying: "If Obama was a white man, he would not be in this position. And if he was a woman of any color, he would not be in this position."[26] At the same time, Obama's pastor, Jeremiah Wright, was all over the news as videos of some of his past sermons showed him making remarks that damned America, among other things. Obama confronted the emerging race issue by delivering a major speech on the subject in Philadelphia on March 18.[27] The speech was well received by most commentators, but the image and words of Rev. Wright remained in the news and on television. Clinton unwittingly came to Obama's rescue by fabricating an account of her arrival in Bosnia under "sniper fire" when she was First Lady, which drew considerable media attention.[28] As all of this was going on, the candidates were courting superdelegates (Obama was gaining ground in this arena), and people in and outside the campaigns were wondering what the DNC was going to do about the delegates from Michigan and Florida. The eventual decision to give the delegates from each of these states one half of a vote (made in late May) helped Clinton, but not enough to affect the final outcome.

The whirl of distractions was evident in an April 17 nationally televised debate, moderated by George Stephanopoulos and Charles Gibson, because much of the time was devoted to questions about Rev. Wright, patriotism, and sniper fire, rather than to substantive issues such as health care and foreign policy.[29] When the Pennsylvania voters finally got their chance to speak, they voted 55 percent to 46 percent in favor of Clinton. But she only netted about twelve more delegates than Obama, and his overall delegate lead was now about 150.[30] The hard mathematical reality of the situation post-Pennsylvania was that Clinton had almost no chance of winning more delegates than Obama; her only shot was to deny him the majority he needed to claim the nomination by winning a substantial majority of superdelegates. Still, she vowed to fight on, insisting she could win.

As far as we know, no one predicted that states holding primaries in May of 2008 (North Carolina, Indiana, West Virginia, Kentucky, and Oregon) would play an important role in either party's nomination process. The exit polls from Pennsylvania continued to show the voting pattern discussed earlier: Clinton was winning blue-collar men, older women, Hispanics, and people from nonurban areas; Obama was strong among younger voters, African Americans, the college educated, and those living in urban areas.[31] This meant that North Carolina (large African American contingent) and Oregon (youth and college educated) were likely to go for Obama, while West Virginia and Kentucky (large white, blue-collar contingent) were likely to go for Clinton. Indiana with large numbers of blue-collar whites and African American Democrats was more of a toss-up. Meanwhile, side drama continued as Rev. Wright emerged from seclusion to make some very public and unrepentant statements, which forced Obama to finally renounce him.[32] Wright notwithstanding, Obama won North Carolina and lost narrowly in Indiana on May 6. The rest of the May primaries went as expected, and Obama won the final contests in South Dakota and Montana on June 3. At this point, with the help of superdelegates he had obtained the majority he needed for the nomination.[33]

Clinton ended her campaign with a public endorsement of Obama on June 8. Even though the 2008 Democratic campaign battle was the most extended, and perhaps the most bitter one in history, Clinton's endorsement was made somewhat easier by the fact that the policy positions of candidates Clinton and Obama did not differ substantially. Both were mainstream Democrats who supported greater government involvement in solving social problems, a national health care plan, policies that were environmentally friendly, and a greater emphasis on multilateralism in American foreign policy. As we know now, she would later join his administration as Secretary of State.

The 2008 General Election Campaign and Results

The drawn-out Democratic nomination gave John McCain some time to ready and refine his pitch to voters of all stripes (Republicans, Independents, and Democrats). He went after the Republican base by making anti-abortion, pro–border security and pro–Bush tax cut statements that were at odds with positions he had taken on these issues in the past. He placed greatest emphasis on his advocacy (before it was popular) for the troop surge in Iraq and his readiness to be commander in chief. For Independents and Democrats, he pointed to his support for both climate change legislation and energy independence, and his opposition to torture.[34]

Even though the long nomination campaign revealed several potential weaknesses, Obama and the Democrats probably benefited from being in the spotlight for so long. Many voters had become familiar with the candidate and his positions. And most early polls showed Obama slightly ahead of McCain in the general election.[35] Perhaps more importantly, most of the signs election pundits pay attention to were all pointing against the Republicans. For most of 2008, President Bush's approval ratings hovered around 30 percent, even lower than in 2006.[36] A spring 2008 poll showed 81 percent of Americans thought the country was on the "wrong track," the highest negative judgment of this sort in thirteen years.[37] Moreover, surveys were showing the public to be much more favorable toward Democrats than Republicans, and Republican identification among voters to have fallen a full eleven points below its peak level of 1995.[38] Furthermore, most forecasters had the Democrats adding to their majorities in Congress, an expectation that was bolstered by the fact that Democrats won three special elections for vacated House seats, in districts that were previously Republican, in the spring of 2008.[39] On top of all this, the economy was sputtering badly, and gasoline prices were rising rapidly.

In late June, Obama announced that he was opting out of public financing for the general election—the first major party candidate to do this since the system was established in 1976. This was a naked reversal of a position he had taken earlier, when he stated that he would stay in the public financing system if his general election opponent did (McCain said he would accept the $84 million in public general election funds). Obama justified his move to opt out of public financing by pointing to his large number of small contributors (almost 3 million contributions of $200 or less) and the large advantage the RNC had over the DNC in 2008 fund-raising.[40] Obama proceeded to raise $52 million in June, bringing his total for the year to $237 million and his total for the campaign to $340 million. McCain raised $21.8 million in June, but the RNC had nearly $70 million available to help him (compared to the DNC's $4.5 million), which left the overall money picture fuzzy: the RNC plus McCain had more cash on hand, but Obama had a lot of money and full control over it.[41] By mid-July, Obama's lead over McCain nationally had edged up to about four to six points.[42]

As the two nominees squared off against each other, there was every reason to expect that most of the discussion would be about the issues rather than their respective character flaws. After all, both Obama and McCain had put themselves forward during their nomination campaigns as political leaders who eschewed attack-style politics. But any hopes along these lines were quickly dashed as the attacks began on both sides. To be sure, it was not necessarily the candidates who led the way, as more extreme voices on each side were making all sorts of negative comments about the candidate they opposed.[43] Obama's patriotism was continuously questioned by those on the right, while McCain's ability to govern effectively (often linked to his age) was targeted by the left. As might be expected, gradually the candidates themselves were drawn into the attack mode.

One especially noteworthy juncture occurred in late July when Obama took a well-publicized trip abroad with stops in Afghanistan, Israel, and Germany. In Berlin, Obama spoke to a crowd of more than two hundred thousand, evoking memories of John F. Kennedy and Ronald Reagan, both of whom gave history-making speeches there. The significance of the Obama candidacy to Europeans and others around the world could not be mistaken or ignored by the McCain camp. They responded by criticizing Obama for canceling a visit to an army hospital in Germany, thus questioning his commitment to the troops, and by branding him an international celebrity who was out of touch with average Americans. In one memorable ad they compared Obama to Britney Spears and Paris Hilton; when questioned about this, McCain said he was proud of the spot.[44] Obama's initial reaction was to criticize McCain for resorting to attack politics, but by mid-August, with polls showing the race tightening, he recognized the need for stronger counterattacks.[45]

The preconvention campaign was not only about attacks; the candidates did address the issues as well. Energy and the economy were the principal topics in July, but foreign policy asserted itself in a big way in mid-August, when Russia first threatened, and then invaded, neighboring Georgia as part of an ongoing conflict over disputed territories. Russia's aggressiveness no doubt contributed to Obama's choice of Joe Biden as his running mate because Biden's foreign policy expertise was widely recognized. As the Democratic convention in Denver approached, most polls showed the race to be close. Surveys conducted by the PEW Research Center, for example, showed Obama's lead over McCain declining from a 48 percent to 40 percent advantage in late June, to a 47 percent to 42 percent lead in mid-July, and to a 46 percent to 43 percent edge by mid-August.[46]

The 2008 Democratic National Convention in Denver came off with very few hitches. Unity was the theme, and unity is what the public saw. Memorable speeches by Michelle Obama and the ailing Ted Kennedy got things moving on Monday night, and Hillary Clinton, Bill Clinton, and Joe Biden continued in the upbeat mode on Tuesday and Wednesday. Obama closed things out on Thursday night (August 28) with a speech to more than eighty thousand people at the Denver football stadium on the anniversary of Martin Luther King's "I Have a Dream" speech. Democrats were then poised for the postconvention bounce, but John McCain came forward the next day (August 29) and announced his presidential choice, Governor Sarah Palin of Alaska. Palin would occupy the headlines for the next week or two.

The Republican Convention took place in St. Paul, Minnesota, the next week (September 1–4), and Palin was definitely the star. She gave a rousing speech on Wednesday night, which clearly energized the Republican base. Her most memorable line compared hockey moms (herself) to pit bulls, with the main difference between the two being "lipstick." The enthusiasm for Palin rubbed off on other speakers such as Rudy Guiliani, Mike Huckabee, Mitt Romney, and McCain himself. Neither President Bush nor Vice President Cheney attended the convention, ostensibly because they were overseeing efforts to deal with Atlantic Hurricane Gustav. While both conventions were successful from the standpoint of the party faithful, the general feeling was that the Republicans got the bigger postconvention bounce. By the middle of September, most polls were showing the race to be too close to call.[47]

But rumblings on Wall Street soon overwhelmed any McCain/Palin momentum. The difficulties experienced by the banking sector, stemming from questionable lending practices (subprime mortgages, etc.), had been causing problems for some time. The federal government intervened to help investment house Bear Stearns in the spring, and then went farther to prop up mortgage giants Fannie Mae and Freddie Mac in August and September. But these steps did not quell the crisis, and by mid-September the entire investment banking system was threatening to implode. Lehman Brothers filed for bankruptcy, and mega-insurance company AIG was bailed out by the Federal Reserve. Fed Chairman Ben Bernanke and Treasury Secretary Hank Paulson then proposed a $700 billion bailout scheme, which President Bush endorsed and presented to Congress and the public on September 24.[48] Meanwhile, the first presidential debate was scheduled for September 26, but McCain announced the suspension of his campaign and his intention to go to Washington to deal with the crisis. Obama stated his intention to show up for the debate, commenting that "Presidents are going to have to deal with more than one thing at a time."[49]

McCain left Washington without any agreement on a bailout bill to show for his efforts at statesmanship, and the first presidential debate was held, as scheduled, on September 26 in Oxford, Mississippi.[50] Both sides declared victory after the exchange, which focused on foreign and economic policy. Both candidates acquitted themselves well during the debate; there were no obvious flops, fireworks, or memorable theatrics. Indeed, all three debates went more or less this way, and in the end there was no obvious winner of the debate series.[51] McCain succeeded in presenting himself as competent on the economy and experienced in foreign and military policy; Obama displayed his command of domestic economic issues and presented himself as a plausible, if inexperienced, commander in chief. It soon became clear, however, that by not losing, Obama was winning. By late September he had a four- to five-point lead in most national polls, and that lead gradually stretched in to the seven- to eight-point range in early October.[52]

By early October, the Obama team seemed to have hit its stride. They had their candidate, and he was performing well on the stump and in debates (the second presidential debate took place on October 8, the third on October 15). They had their message—the country needed new leadership in order to bring about a change in course from the policies of the Bush administration; electing McCain would mean more of the same. They had lots of money—Obama raised a record of high of $66 million in August and then more than doubled that by raising a whopping $153 million in September, adding more than $100 million in October.[53] In the end, he would raise nearly $750 million over the course of the campaign.[54] All that money allowed Obama and his team to put on lots of television spots and other ads, massively outspending McCain in this area in October. Furthermore, the Obama team was adept at using new technologies to reach voters, especially young voters. They sent out a constant stream of email messages to their large and growing network of supporters, put up YouTube videos, and did lots of cell phone texting.[55] The steady, "No Drama" Obama gradually convinced the public that he was presidential material.

There was a little drama in early October surrounding the vice presidential debate. Palin had appeared to stumble badly in some predebate interviews, especially one with CBS anchor Katie Couric, and there was a lot of speculation that Palin might embarrass herself (and McCain) in her confrontation with the experienced Joe Biden. But she managed to pull off a credible, if uninspired, performance, and the campaign moved on. No surprises continued to be the theme. There were no big splashes of the "Swift Boat" variety made by outside groups; indeed, the activities of 527 groups were much less noticeable than in 2004. Both the candidates discouraged their more extreme supporters from running potentially unpopular attacks ads, and strived to maintain control over their message, which in both cases had national unity as part of its theme.[56]

As most everyone knows, the key to winning a presidential election in the United States is the Electoral College. Being ahead in the polls nationally is very important, but a candidate still needs to carry enough states to get 270 Electoral College votes. Obama's appealing campaign, and the Bush administration's unpopularity, put a number of states that the Republicans had won in 2000 and 2004 into play in 2008. Some of these were the key swing states from the two previous elections, most prominently Ohio and Florida. Obama won both of these with 51 percent of the vote.[57] Obama also ended up winning several states that many Republicans (and some Democrats) did not think they had to worry about when the general election campaign began. These included Virginia, North Carolina, Indiana, and Colorado, which together represented 48 Electoral College votes and helped to kick Obama's electoral vote total to 364 (McCain 174).

Obama's wins in the states of Florida, North Carolina, Virginia, Ohio, Indiana, Iowa, Colorado, New Mexico, and Nevada, where Bush had won in 2004, did change the electoral map in a significant way, but the basic regional pattern remained intact. McCain won most of the South, all of the Plains states, and most of the Rocky Mountain states. And in many of these states, it wasn't even close. McCain won by a two-to-one margin in Oklahoma, and got more than 55 percent of the vote in fifteen states. In the Democratic strongholds (the two coasts and the upper Midwest), Obama won by wide margins (more than 60 percent of the vote in California, New York, Vermont, Massachusetts, Connecticut, Rhode Island, Delaware, and Maryland). In Washington, DC, Obama received 93 percent of the vote. Thus distinctive regional patterns of partisanship and voting persisted.

The attentive reader should be able to predict the voting patterns. Women (53 percent of the electorate) split 56 to 43 in favor of Obama (five points above their Democratic vote level in 2004). Independents split 52 to 44 in Obama's favor. Obama won by very wide margins among voters under thirty (66 percent to 32 percent), Hispanics (67 percent to 31 percent), single people (65 percent to 33 percent), and of course African Americans (95 percent to 4 percent). (In the case of both Hispanics and youth, Obama's share of the vote was more than ten points higher than John Kerry's in 2004.) McCain won the white vote (55 percent to 43 percent), the elderly vote (53 percent to 45 percent), the married vote (52 percent to 47 percent), and the Southern vote (54 percent to 45 percent). A large percentage of voters (63 percent) thought that the state of the economy was the most important issue in the election, and they favored Obama by a 53 percent to 44 percent margin.[58]

There were several other interesting aspects of the voting in 2008. For example, among those who thought terrorism was the most important issue (only 9 percent), McCain won by a huge margin (86 percent to 13 percent); he did even better with the 29 percent of voters who approved of George W. Bush's performance in office (89 percent to 10 percent). Although 83 percent of Hillary Clinton supporters voted for Obama, this left them well below the level of Obama support among Democrats as a whole.[59] Public perceptions of the parties gave Democrats an unmistakable advantage. Only 23 percent of the NES sample thought that Republicans would do a better job of handling the economy (40 percent thought Democrats would, 38 percent saw little difference); even fewer (14 percent) thought the Republicans would be better at keeping us out of war, while 55 percent thought Republicans were more likely to involve the country in another war. When asked whether they had a favorable reaction to the Democratic Party, 54 percent of the respondents said yes; when asked the same question about Republicans, only 40 percent responded in the affirmative.[60] In this election, public disapproval of the Bush administration's prosecution of the Iraq war appears to have undermined the long-standing Republican advantage in the area of foreign policy and the military. Moreover, as the public's economic anxiety deepened, the Democrats benefited from their long-standing image as defenders of working and middle-class Americans (see Chapter 2).

The Democratic gains in congressional elections in 2008 were especially impressive on the Senate side. They picked up a total of eight seats, with five of them coming from successful challenges to Republican incumbents (Stevens, Alaska; Coleman, Minnesota; Sununu, New Hampshire; Dole, North Carolina; and Smith, Oregon). The vote was very close in several of these, most notably Minnesota, where recounts and court challenges stretched into the summer of 2009 before a winner (former comedian Al Franken) was determined. They won open races in three states that had shifted from Republican to Democrat in the presidential vote: Virginia, Colorado, and New Mexico (the Udall cousins won in the latter two, and Mark Warner (D) replaced John Warner (R) in the former). As discussed previously, these election results, along with the defection of Arlen Specter, gave the Democrats (with Independents Lieberman and Sanders) the magic number of sixty votes in the Senate.

House election results were less spectacular, but a net gain of twenty-one seats represented a solid win for Democrats. They did lose five incumbents (still, their overall incumbent reelection rate was nearly 98 percent), but they retained all of their open seats. Republicans lost twelve open seats and saw fourteen of their incumbents defeated (92 percent reelection rate).[61] The Democratic gains were spread around the map but included several of the same states that figured prominently in the presidential and Senate elections such as Florida, North Carolina, New Mexico, Colorado, and Nevada. The Democratic majority of 257 restored them to the levels they enjoyed throughout the 1980s and early 1990s.[62]

The national congressional party committees were very important players in many of the congressional races around the country. And for the first time in recent history, the Democrats enjoyed a large advantage in fund-raising and spending (much of which was spent independently of the candidates). The Democratic Congressional Campaign Committee (DCCC) spent over $75 million independently in 2008, while the National Republican Campaign Committee (NRCC) spent less than $25 million.[63] Overall spending (direct contributions, coordinated expenditures, and independent spending) was less lopsided; Democrats spent $176 million, Republicans $116 million on House races.[64] Most of the Democratic money was spent for candidates in open races that the national party thought they could win. A competitive challenger could count on the DCCC to spend more than $1 million to support them. The success of Democrats in open races (cited above) speaks to the efficacy of these efforts. The other prime targets for DCCC spending were competitive challengers, who also got more than $1 million each and succeeded in knocking off fourteen Republican incumbents.[65]

A similar pattern played out in Senate elections. Independent spending by the Democratic Senatorial Campaign Committee (DSCC) was $70 million compared to $36 million by the National Republican Senatorial Committee (NRSC).[66] In overall national party campaign committee expenditures for Senate races, the Democrats had an advantage of roughly $70 million ($163 million to $94 million).[67] Most of the money went to eleven Senate races that were considered competitive, and the DSCC spent as much as $3 million in some of these races.[68] The Senate gains by the party suggest that the money was well spent.

One of the most underreported aspects in the aftermath of the election was the extent to which partisan loyalty remained intact. According to the 2008 *American National Election Study*, fully 91 percent of Democratic identifiers voted for Obama, while 90 percent of Republican identifiers supported McCain.[69] This continued a trend established over the past three elections, in which partisans of *both* major parties have demonstrated exceedingly strong loyalty. Prior to 2000, we typically found partisans of one major party being loyal, while a significant share of the other party defected. But as we see in Figure 7.1, the pattern of partisan loyalty that began in 2000 continued unabated through 2008.[70] Recall from Chapter 4 that partisan loyalty in congressional voting was also high from 2000–2008. What changed in 2008 was not the devotion of partisans to their own party; rather, it was the partisan balance (i.e., the proportion of Democratic versus Republican identifiers), and the behavior of Independents.

Although the outcome of the 2008 presidential election was obviously different than the previous two elections, the underlying dynamic has not changed. The electorate is still highly polarized along partisan lines. In Chapter 2, we illustrated the extent of partisan polarization by comparing recent elections (2004 and 2008) to the 1976 election, when the party salience was said to be at a low point. It is instructive to take up this comparison again. In 1976, the nominees of the two major parties, Jimmy Carter and Gerald Ford, were moderates within their own parties, and only 48 percent of NES respondents that year perceived important differences between the parties. Contrast that to 2008. Even though both major party candidates played up their bipartisan credentials, a whopping 78 percent of respondents stated there were important differences between the parties (and 72 percent opined that there were major

Figure 7.1 Partisan Loyalty in Presidential Elections, 1952–2008

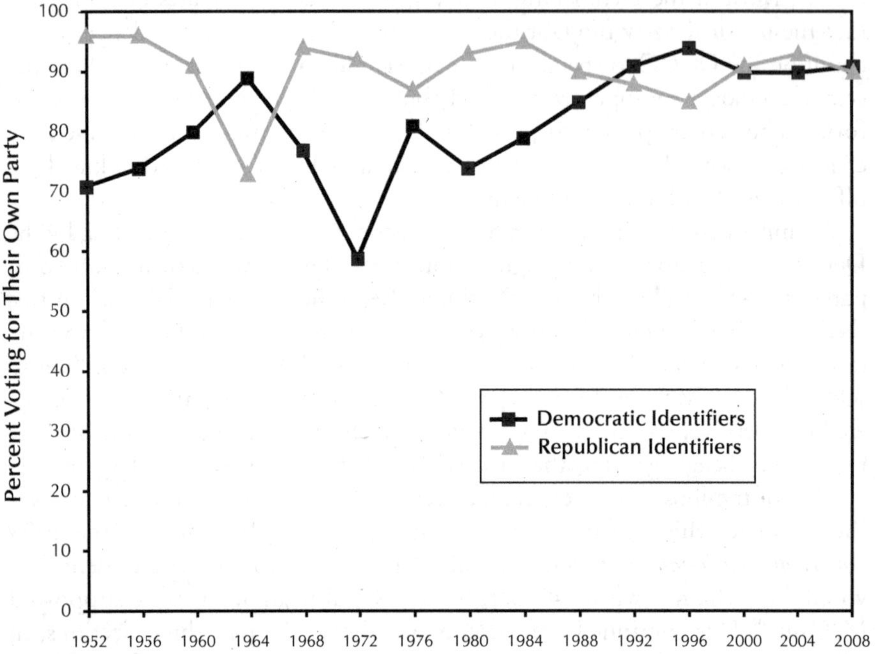

Source: American National Election Studies.

differences between the candidates). In spite of attempts to claim the center, the public perceived genuine and large policy differences between Republican McCain and Democrat Obama.

It is also true that the underlying electoral context has changed a lot since 1976—fewer Americans are now in the middle. Two simple indicators illustrate this point. In 1976, 14 percent of Americans identified as pure Independents; by 2008, that number dropped to only 8 percent. And in 1976, 38 percent of Americans called themselves moderate or middle of the road when asked to situate themselves on an ideological continuum. By 2008, only 29 percent embraced the moderate label.[71]

In Chapter 6, we argued that one of the factors that distinguish American parties from their counterparts elsewhere is their ideological purity. In the United States, we find a stronger correspondence between ideological and partisan identification; that is liberals tend to identify with the Democrats, and conservatives with the Republicans. Once again, it is instructive to compare the pattern in 2008 to that of earlier years. This comparison appears in Figures 7.2a and 7.2b. The story here is straightforward. Republicans are overwhelmingly likely to

Figure 7.2a Ideological Sorting among Republicans

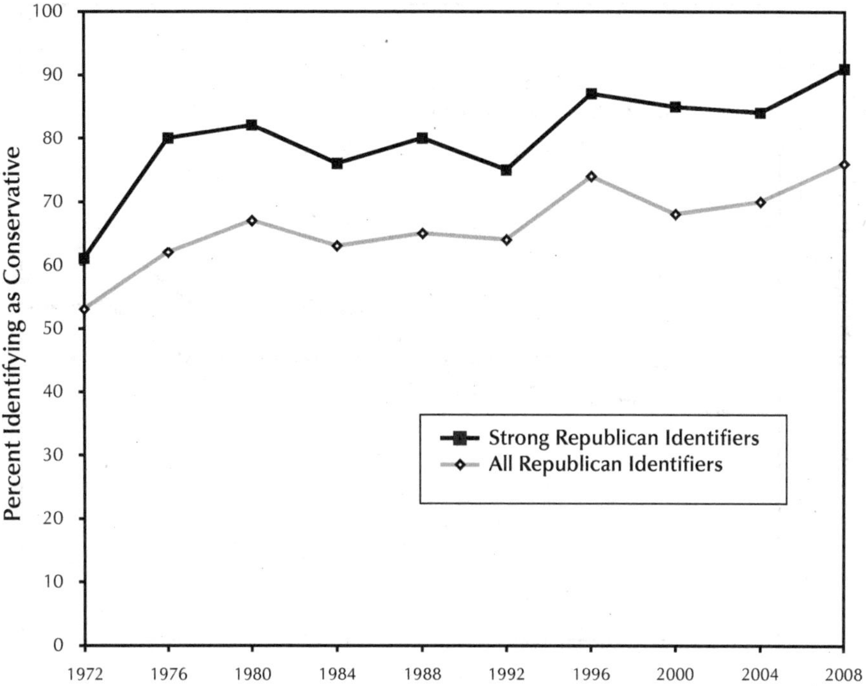

Source: American National Election Studies.

identify as conservatives. In 2008, 76 percent of all Republican identifiers and 91 percent of strong Republicans identified as conservative; both of these represent all-time highs, going back to 1972 (see Figure 7.2a). For the Democrats, the percentages are lower, but the trend is similar (see Figure 7.2b); ideological and partisan sorting was strongest in 2004, with a slight dropoff in 2008. The important point is that recent elections, including 2008, have been fought between partisans and parties that are ideologically purer than they used to be.

This pronounced sorting of partisanship and ideology goes beyond the electorate. Both parties now have elaborate "supporting casts," outside the formal party organization, that support and promote each party's respective point of view and that work to reinforce partisan divisions in the electorate. For example, conservative talk radio host Rush Limbaugh draws between 14 and 30 million listeners to his daily show, which is highly critical of Democrats and liberals. In fact, the line between punditry and partisanship has become so blurred that in the spring of 2009 the political chattering class became embroiled in a debate as to whether or not Rush Limbaugh ought to be considered the leader of the Republican Party![72]

Figure 7.2b Ideological Sorting Among Democrats

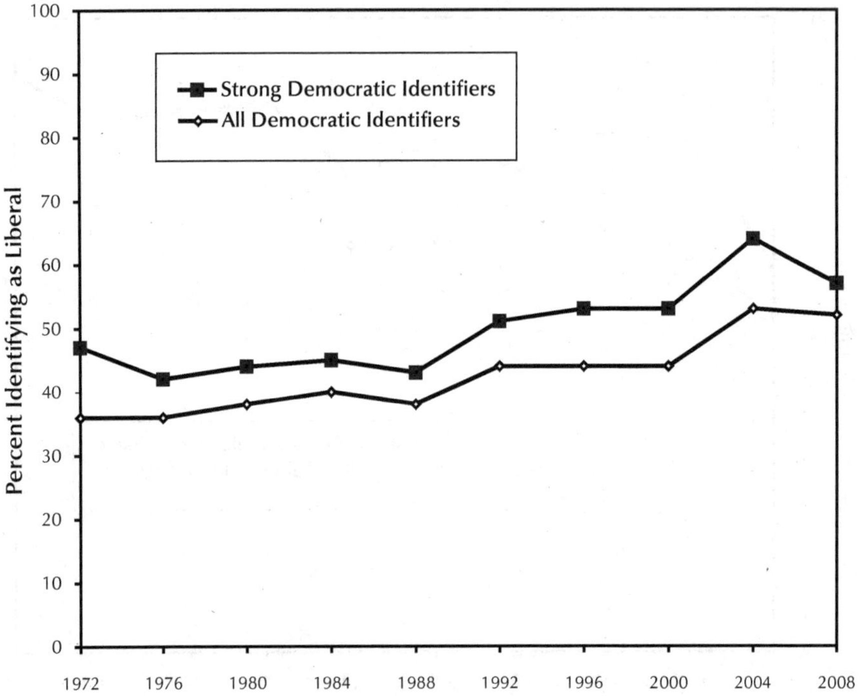

[Chart: Percent Identifying as Liberal, 1972–2008, showing Strong Democratic Identifiers and All Democratic Identifiers]

Source: American National Election Studies.

Along similar lines, the conservative Fox News network draws an audience that is disproportionately Republican and conservative. A 2008 Pew survey found that Fox viewers were disproportionately Republican while CNN and MSNBC viewers were decidedly Democratic. And even within these networks, shows with particular ideological bents such as The O'Reilly Factor (on Fox) and Countdown with Keith Olbermann (on MSNBC) tend to draw audiences that are even more partisan.[73] It should therefore come as no surprise to learn, as Pew did in a study conducted during the 2008 campaign, that Fox News had on balance the most favorable coverage of McCain and the most unfavorable coverage of Obama, while MSNBC displayed the opposite pattern.[74] The general point here is that for many Americans, the information they seek out and receive from the media reinforces preexisting partisan divisions.

A great variety of groups are also part of the supporting cast of each party. Business groups, and issue groups that oppose abortion, gun control, and other conservative causes, usually support the Republican Party and its candidates; unions and liberal cause groups supporting abortion rights, civil rights, and environmental protection tend to support the Democratic Party and its candidates.

Established interest groups and more fleeting advocacy groups have long plumbed campaign finance laws, and the Federal Election Commission's (FEC) enforcement of them, in order to figure out the most effective way they could participate in electoral process. The most straightforward way is for groups to establish affiliated political actions committees (PACs). These groups are then registered with the FEC, collect donations in limited amounts (no more than $5,000 from individuals), and can both contribute funds to candidates ($5,000 limit per election) and parties (limit of $15,000) and act (spend) independently, including making statements of express advocacy (to vote for) a candidate or candidates. As discussed in Chapter 1, most major groups have PACs, and they have been important players, especially in congressional elections, since the 1970s.

In recent years, a number of groups have emerged claiming that they do not want to contribute funds to multiple candidates or parties, but simply want to speak about the issues they care about in elections. Under the Bipartisan Campaign Reform Act (BCRA) these groups, called 527 committees or 501(c) nonprofits (both named after the sections of the IRS code that apply to them) were not subject to most FEC regulations that applied to PACs, were therefore eligible to receive unlimited "soft money" donations, but could not run ads that mentioned the names of candidates with 60 days of an election. However, in the case *FEC v. Wisconsin Right to Life* in 2007, the Supreme Court more or less lifted this ban, allowing advocacy groups to name candidates in their ads as long as they did not urge people to "vote for" or "vote against" a candidate, or the equivalent. Currently both 527 groups and 501(c) nonprofits can raise and spend soft money, most which they use to run ads commenting (usually negatively) on candidates running for office.[75] This allows all sorts of groups, including unions, corporations, and issue groups to form 527 or 501(c) entities and use them as their political mouthpieces. Many groups now have both an affiliated PAC and a 527 or 501(c) in their political arsenals, which enables them to engage in a wide array of election related activities.[76]

In 2004, 527 groups like Swift Boat Veterans for Truth and MoveOn.org made a big splash, spending just more than $425 million in federal elections and drawing attention to the new and complicated world of group participation in American elections. In 2004, liberal 527 groups supporting Democrats outspent conservative 527s by a factor of 4 to 1.[77] As mentioned previously, advocacy groups were somewhat less involved in the presidential campaign in 2008, and thus focused more of their attention on congressional races. The 527 groups again favored Democrats, this time by a margin of 3 to 1, but their overall level of spending was down to $200 million. Picking up the slack were 501(c) organizations that spent about the same amount as the 527s ($200 million), which was much more than the estimated $60 billion they spent in 2004. However, their spending favored Republicans by roughly 3 to 1. Conservative 501(c) groups like Freedom's Watch, whose mission is to defend freedom and Judeo-Christian values and which spent more than $30 million advocating for Republican candidates, helped to level the playing (spending) field among liberal

(Democratic) and conservative (Republican) advocacy groups in 2008. Combined 2008 spending by 527s and 501(c)s of $400 million was slightly lower than the 2004 total for these kinds of groups.[78]

One can also add think tanks into the mix of partisan-infused ideological battles taking place in American political life. Many of these think tanks are unabashedly conservative (such as the American Enterprise Institute or the Heritage Foundation) or liberal (such as the Institute for Policy Studies or the Center for American Progress), and advocate for policies consistent with their ideological positions. According to the Center for Media and Democracy, there are twice as many conservative think tanks as liberal think tanks, and the conservative ones enjoy a significant funding advantage over their liberal counterparts. As a consequence of the growing influence of conservative think tanks, in late 2004 a group of liberal philanthropists established the Democracy Alliance, a group that set out to raise $200 million for a network of liberal think tanks allied with the Democratic Party.[79]

The Obama Administration

Obama's message of change during the 2008 election had a transcendental quality. He invited the public to imagine a postracial and postpartisan society where people of different backgrounds and beliefs worked together to solve the nation's problems.[80] This theme was evident in his Inaugural Address as he promised "to begin again the work of remaking America."[81] The crowd at the Inauguration was huge and enthusiastic, and nearly everyone in the country was touched by the historic significance of a nonwhite man being sworn in as President of the United States. Immediately after Inauguration Day, the Obama administration prepared to get down to business. The economic problems that had helped Obama win the election had only gotten worse as 2008 ended and 2009 began, with most economists now describing the economic slump as the worst one the country had experienced since the Great Depression. The first order of business for the Obama administration was to formulate an economic stimulus bill.

President Obama wanted to work with Congressional leaders on the specifics of the bill, and launched his effort to pass a stimulus package by visiting House Republicans on January 27, 2009—seven days after taking office—to discuss his initial proposal. However, despite some kind words about the president's visit, House Republicans quickly united behind Minority Leader John Boehner, who announced his opposition to the stimulus just before the meeting with the president.[82] The next day, a stimulus bill developed by the White House and Democratic leaders passed the House, with every Republican voting against it.[83]

There was some bipartisanship displayed on the Senate side with regard to stimulus legislation. It consisted mainly of the two Republican Senators from Maine, Susan Collins and Olympia Snowe, working with Nebraska Democrat Ben Nelson, who had announced his opposition to the House stimulus bill, to develop a compromise version that could garner the sixty votes needed to move the legislation forward in the Senate. After a week of negotiation, they reached an agreement on a $780 billion package ($40 billion less than the House version), that addressed the Republican interest in seeing more of the stimulus devoted to tax cuts.[84] Republican Arlen Specter of Pennsylvania joined his colleagues from Maine, all fifty-six Democrats, and the two Independents to first pass a motion for cloture (61 to 36), and to then pass the stimulus bill on February 10 by a vote of 61 to 37. Over the course of the next week, the House and Senate produced a compromise package ($787 billion) that passed both chambers by essentially the same margins as the in the votes the week before (all House Republicans voted against it; three Republicans Senators voted for it).[85] President Obama signed the measure into law on February 17 in an elaborate ceremony in Denver, the site of the Democratic convention. Although the session was only forty days old, an analysis by *Congressional Quarterly* found party polarization in roll call voting in 2009 to be at the highest level ever recorded.[86]

Democrats in Congress successfully pushed two other bills of significance to them as the stimulus debate was unfolding. As in the case of the stimulus bill, this was done by including a small number of Republican Senators in compromise negotiations, and then passing the legislation over nearly unanimous opposition by Republicans in the House. One of these bills effectively overturned a 2007 Supreme Court ruling that made it more difficult for workers to sue their employers for pay discrimination (the Lilly Ledbetter Fair Pay Act); the other was a bill to expand the State Children's Health Insurance Program (SCHIP) by $32 billion, which President Bush had blocked in 2007–2008. The former was the first bill President Obama signed into law (on January 29); he signed the latter on February 4.[87] The next big legislative step was for the president to propose a budget for FY 2010. The proposal he presented to Congress on February 26 called for massive changes in federal tax and spending priorities. It set the stage for major battles between Republicans and Democrats over policy change proposals that Obama had featured during his campaign; debate over these proposals would occupy much of Congress's time and attention in 2009.

The Obama budget outline provided for the elimination of the Bush tax cuts for people in the highest income brackets, along with new limits on the income tax deductions high-income earners could take. These two measures would increase government revenue by nearly $1 trillion over ten years, with some of the savings going to finance Obama's proposed health care overhaul, which was initially estimated to cost more than $600 billion during this same time span. He also proposed a "cap and trade" climate change program that would raise additional revenues for the government by imposing pollution fees on major carbon dioxide producers (electrical utilities and other major industrial facilities). The Obama plan called for much of the pollution fee revenue to be used to continue the "Making Work Pay" tax credit for low-wage workers that was a key feature of his stimulus package. Other significant components of the plan called for changes in corporate income tax regulations that would subject more of the overseas profits of multinational corporations to U.S. taxes, the elimination of tax breaks for hedge fund managers and oil companies, more spending on federal loans for college students, and more tax breaks and spending to encourage renewable energy and green jobs.

The Obama budget plan called for total spending of nearly $3.6 trillion in FY 2010, and projected the federal deficit falling from a record breaking $1.7 trillion in 2009 (much of which was attributable to the TARP program enacted under the Bush administration and Obama's stimulus) to $1.2 trillion in 2010, then descending to $500 billion by 2014. These deficits would result in the national debt rising from $5.8 trillion in 2008 to $12 trillion by 2014.[88] One thing both Democrats and Republicans could agree on after the budget plan was unveiled was that it was dramatically different than the budget priorities advanced by Republican presidents, and that it would set the country on an importantly different course in several areas of policy. Many of the standard policies (and images) of the Democrats were on display—more spending for health care, education, and the environment, fewer tax breaks for the wealthy, and more tax relief for the working class. The health care overhaul was perhaps the most prominent lightning rod for controversy given its importance, its potential price tag, and the Clinton administration's failure to enact a plan of similar proportion in 1993–1994. Obama avoided Clinton's mistake of presenting a full-blown proposal to Congress with little input from congressional leaders. Indeed, Obama made it clear that Congress would have to determine many of the specifics. And he said he wanted the process by which a final bill would be formulated to be bipartisan.

The first step in establishing a budget for an upcoming fiscal year is for Congress to enact a Budget Resolution, which is not binding on Congress and is not subject to either a presidential veto or filibusters in the Senate. It is, however, an important statement of Congress's intention to meet certain spending and revenue goals. The Democratic Budget Committees in both the House and Senate presented their colleagues with Budget Resolutions that conformed closely to President Obama's wishes, and when the votes were taken in early April, the resolutions failed to garner a single Republican vote in either chamber. Twenty Democrats in the House voted against their resolution, as did two Democrats in the Senate.[89] After a House-Senate conference had worked out the differences in the resolutions, a final vote on the 2010 Budget Resolution took place on April 29, exactly one hundred days after Obama took office, and the votes were the same as before—no Republican supporters in either chamber.[90] Democrats congratulated one another; Republicans prepared for the fight over subsequent legislation that would add definition to the aspirations contained in the Budget Resolution.

Although partisan differences figured prominently in the legislative activities of the first session of the 111th Congress, it would be inaccurate to suggest that national policymaking was devoid of bipartisan cooperation in the spring and summer of 2009. Republicans did participate in the development and enactment of several policies that became part of President Obama's multifaceted economic recovery effort, the principal objectives of which were to shore up the banking system, get credit moving to small businesses and individuals, and to create jobs (or prevent jobs from being lost).[91] During the spring, public anger erupted over news reports that many of the same banks the government had bailed out with TARP funds were now gouging their credit card customers with new fees and higher interest rates. Congress went to work and passed legislation that placed new restrictions on credit card fees and bank billing practices, which passed by large margins in both the House (361 to 64) and Senate (90 to 5), and was signed by Obama on May 22.[92] Similarly, a bill aimed at making it easier for homeowners in trouble to get assistance in order to avoid foreclosure passed by wide margins in both chambers, and was signed by the president on May 20.[93] These two pieces of legislation complemented other economic recovery steps being taken by the Obama administration through the Treasury Department, the Federal Reserve, Federal Deposit Insurance Company (FDIC), and other executive agencies.

As suggested above, health care was probably the biggest fish in Obama's sea of reforms. The issues involved were classic bait for partisan warfare. Who should pay for the expansion of coverage to the uninsured? Obama and most Democrats said wealthy taxpayers, private insurance companies, doctors, and hospitals; Republicans said no to most of these possibilities. Should there be a government-run health insurance program to compete with private health care insurance? Many Democrats said yes; Republicans said no. Should the health care benefits paid by employers for their employees be subject to income taxes? McCain and many Republicans said yes; Democrats said no (initially). Should medical malpractice lawsuits be curbed to help doctors reduce the cost of doing business? Republicans said yes; Democrats said no (initially). Obama began the process of formulating actual legislation by meeting with health care industry leaders (insurance providers, drug companies, hospital associations, and physician groups) on May 12 and announced afterward that these groups had pledged voluntarily to cut costs within the industry by $2 trillion over a ten-year period.[94] A few days later, some of those participating said that Obama had misconstrued the commitments made in the meeting and that savings would be more modest.[95]

The Obama goal of making health care available to all citizens was going to be expensive, probably more expensive than his budget proposal suggested (closer to $1 trillion over ten years).[96] Yet the president insisted, in public statements and speeches around the country, that any plan he approved would have to pay for itself through cost savings and new revenues. The search for ways to do this led some Democrats to put McCain's idea of taxing employer health benefits back on the table. Others considered some kind of value-added or consumption tax.[97] Some Democrats, most prominently Senate Finance Committee Chairman Max Baucus (Montana), began to back away from the idea of a public program and introduced an alternative they described as an "insurance cooperative."[98] In addressing the American Medical Association on June 15, Obama indicated his willingness to compromise on medical malpractice lawsuits, but he also set an early August deadline for both the House and Senate to pass some version of health care reform.[99]

Meanwhile, the Republicans were ramping up their attacks on what they began to describe consistently as "a Washington takeover of health care," which was directed primarily at the Democratic insistence on having a government-run insurance program. Legendary Republican political consultant Frank Luntz had put together a memorandum suggesting the language Republicans should use in fighting the Democrats on health care. The gist of it was "No Washington bureaucrat or health care lobbyists should stand between your family and your doctor. The Democrats want to put Washington politicians in charge of your health care."[100] As expected, both parties were leaving their options open. The Senate Finance Committee promised a bipartisan bill, while Democrats on the House Ways and Means, Education and Labor, and Energy and Commerce committees were consulting with other House Democrats (the more conservative "Blue Dog" Democrats), but not Republicans. Thus Democrats would be in a position to either try to ram through a partisan bill, or settle for a compromise. Republicans were poised to either go public with their opposition (using Luntz's words), or try to get some credit for being part of a bipartisan reform program.

As the summer of 2009 unfolded, it became increasingly clear that Congress would not meet the president's deadlines for action, and that the attacks on the health care overhaul would not be confined to Luntz's relatively polite language. The House Bill (H.R. 3200), which was still being tinkered with in the Energy and Comerce Committee, and a draft bill that had passed through the Senate Health, Education, Labor and Pensions Committee, were drawing intense scrutiny from conservative groups. Physician Advisory Boards that elderly patients could, but were not required to, consult for treatment options were dubbed "death panels" by Sarah Palin and others. Anti-abortion groups claimed the House bill would open up the floodgates for government-funded abortions. Most conservatives claimed the overhauls would lead to "socialized medicine." Others claimed that illegal aliens would be eligible for coverage.[101] During their August recess, many Democratic members of Congress were bombarded with questions and accusations at health care town hall meetings around the country. Not surprisingly, surveys showed increasing public concern about the effects of a health care overhaul, as interest groups on both sides spent millions on television ads opposing or supporting the president.[102]

Senate Finance Committee Chairman Max Baucus (Montana), who along with several Democratic colleagues had spent the summer negotiating the particulars of health care reform with three Republicans on the committee (Charles Grassley of Iowa, Olympia Snowe of Maine, and Mike Enzi of Wyoming) was finally ready to make his bill public on September 16, 2009. His plan was less expensive than the House bill, did not include a government-run health insurance option, and placed fewer requirements on employers.[103] The problem was that none of the Republicans, including Snowe, agreed to support it, and several

Democrats, most notably Jay Rockefeller (West Virginia) a Finance Committee member, said they would not vote for the Baucus bill because it did not go far enough. In mid-October, both Snowe and Rockefeller voted in favor of the Finance Committee bill.[104] Once out of committee, the Baucus bill provided a template for further negotiations as the Senate attempted to proceed toward a floor vote on health care.

President Obama worked tirelessly throughout the summer to rally public support for health care reform. The week before the Baucus bill was unveiled, Obama made a prime-time speech to a joint session of Congress, strongly urging them to move forward. But the state of partisan relations was vividly on display when Republican Congressman Joe Wilson (South Carolina) interrupted the speech, yelling, "You lie!" when the president said his health care overhaul would not offer coverage to illegal immigrants.[105] The president persisted in expressing hope for bipartisan compromise, but many in Washington were convinced that his only real hope was Democratic unity.

Of course, Democrats have often had difficulty maintaining unity of purpose and thinking when in power. True to their liberal nature, they often welcome many points of view. This type of liberality is an affliction that rarely strikes Republicans. When in power, Republicans have experienced less difficulty taking a unified stand on policy matters, but their penchant for enacting policies that have strong appeal to fairly narrow segments of the population (the wealthy and the culturally conservative) can sow the seeds of their demise. But as we have seen in 2008–2009, losing power is not altogether bad for Republicans. As the anti-government party, they are comfortable playing the opposition role, especially when it comes to ambitious Democratic plans to use government to solve problems. We hope that Democrats will unify behind their president to pass health care reform and other liberal policies because party unity in the midst of polarization provides voters with a governance record that best facilitates electoral choice and accountability.

Notes

Chapter 1

1. See, for example, Gary Jacobson, *A Divider, Not a Uniter* (New York: Pearson/Longman, 2007).

2. One of those Republican Senate votes came from Arlen Specter of Pennsylvania, who would later (in May 2009) switch parties. On the economic stimulus vote, see Joseph J. Schatz and David Clarke, "Congress Clears Economic Stimulus Package," *CQ Weekly*, February 16, 2009, 352–356.

3. Quoted from James Davison Hunter, "The Enduring Culture War," in James Davison Hunter and Alan Wolfe, *Is There a Culture War? A Dialogue on Values and American Public Life* (Washington, DC: Brookings Institution and Pew Research Center, 2006), 13.

4. Quoted from http://www.buchanan.org/pa-92-0817-rnc.html. Accessed July 19, 2007.

5. Morris Fiorina, with Samuel J. Abrams and Jeremy C. Pope, *Culture War? The Myth of Polarized America*, 2nd ed. (New York: Pearson/Longman, 2006).

6. See John R. Hibbing and Elizabeth Theiss-Morse, *Stealth Democracy: Americans' Beliefs about How Government Should Work* (Cambridge, England: Cambridge University Press, 2002).

7. E. E. Schattschneider, *The Semisovereign People* (Hinsdale, IL: Dryden Press, 1975), 3 and 7.

8. *Webster's New Collegiate Dictionary* (Springfield, MA: G. & C. Merriam Co., 1953).

9. E. E. Schattschneider, *Party Government* (New York: Holt, Rinehart, Winston, 1942), 1.

10. Alexis de Tocqueville, *Democracy in America* (New York: The Modern Library and McGraw-Hill, 1981).

11. Presently, party spending for candidates falls into three categories: direct contributions, coordinated expenditures, and independent spending. Direct contributions refer to money given by party organizations to candidates that becomes part of the candidate's campaign funds and can be spent as the candidate sees fit. Coordinated expenditures are funds the parties spend on behalf of candidates (for polling, ads, etc.) and party officials can consult with the candidate's campaign committee as they are making these expenditures. Independent spending cannot be undertaken in consultation or coordination with a candidate's campaign committee, or in consultation with those making party coordinated expenditures for a candidate. In 2004, party organizations (national and state) could make direct contributions of $20,000 to House

candidates and $40,000 to Senate candidates. These groups could supply up to roughly $75,000 in coordinated expenditures for House candidates, and amounts that vary depending on the population of the state for Senate candidates, with the maximum being almost $2 million for California candidates. Independent party spending for candidates across the country is unlimited. See Paul S. Herrnson, "The Bipartisan Campaign Reform Act and Congressional Elections," in *Congress Reconsidered*, 8th ed., eds. Lawrence C. Dodd and Bruce I. Oppenheimer (Washington, DC: Congressional Quarterly Press, 2005), 107–134. Many of these contribution limits are indexed for inflation and thus increase a bit each election cycle. For example, the total amount national committees could contribute to Senate candidates increased from the 2004 level of $35,000 to $39,900 by 2008. Similar increases occurred for coordinated expenditures. See Harold W. Stanley and Richard Niemi, *Vital Statistics on American Politics 2007–2008* (Washington, DC: Congressional Quarterly Press, 2008), 93.

12. See Alan Rosenthal, *The Decline of Representative Democracy* (Washington DC: Congressional Quarterly Press, 1998), 184–196.

13. See, for example, James L. Sundquist, *The Dynamics of the Party System*, rev. ed. (Washington, DC: Brookings Institution Press, 1983).

14. As cited in Samuel Kernell, Gary C. Jacobson, and Thad Kousser, *The Logic of American Politics*, 4th ed. (Washington, DC: CQ Press, 2008), 573.

15. John M. Blum, Bruce Catton, Edmund S. Morgan, Arthur M. Schlesinger, Jr., Kenneth M. Stampp, and C. Vann Woodward, *The National Experience,* 2nd ed. (New York: Harcourt, Brace & World, Inc., 1968), 243–244; and Kernell et al., *The Logic of American Politics*, 4th ed., 574–575.

16. Blum, et al., *The National Experience*, 2nd ed., 393–397.

17. Ibid., 471.

18. See Richard Hofstadter, *The Age of Reform* (New York: Vintage Books/Random House, 1955).

19. See Kernell et al., *The Logic of American Politics*, 4th ed., 580–582; Hofstadter, *The Age of Reform.*

20. See Richard Hofstadter, *The American Political Tradition* (New York: Vintage Books/Random House, 1974); Blum et al., *The National Expereince*, 535–591.

21. See Schattschneider, *The Semisovereign People*, Chapter 5; Kernell et al., *The Logic of American Politics,* 4th ed., 582–584.

22. Ross M. Robertson, *History of the American Economy,* 2nd ed. (New York: Harcourt, Brace & World, Inc., 1964).

23. Ibid.

24. Committee on Political Parties of the American Political Science Association, "Toward a More Responsible Two-Party System," published as a supplement to the *American Political Science Review*, 44 (September 1950).

25. Stanley and Niemi, *Vital Statistics on American Politics 2007–2008*, 28–29, 40–41.

26. See Robert H. Haveman, ed., *A Decade of Federal Antipoverty Programs* (New York: Academic Press, 1977), especially chapters 2 and 3.

27. See, for example, David S. Broder, *The Party's Over* (New York: Harper & Row, 1971); William J. Keefe, *Parties, Politics, and Public Policy in America*, 3rd ed. (New York: Holt, Rinehart and Winston, 1980); William Crotty, *American Parties in*

Decline, 2nd ed. (Boston: Little, Brown and Company, 1984); or Martin P. Wattenberg, The *Decline of American Political Parties* (Cambridge: Harvard University Press, 1988).

28. Stephen J. Wayne, *The Road to the White House,* 2nd ed. (New York: St. Martin's Press, 1984), 12.

29. Norman J. Ornstein, Thomas E. Mann and Michael J. Malbin, *Vital Statistics on Congress, 1989–1990* (Washington, DC: Congressional Quarterly Press, 1990), Chapter 3.

30. William H. Flanigan and Nancy H. Zingale, *Political Behavior of the American Electorate,* 6th ed. (Boston: Allyn and Bacon, 1987): 30–31; or Flannigan and Zingale, *Political Behavior of the American Electorate,* 11th ed. (Washington, DC: Congressional Quarterly Press, 2006), 73–75.

31. Donald C. Baumer and Howard J. Gold, "Party Images and Party Resurgence," *Social Science Journal,* 44 (2007): 468.

32. For example, in the 1968 *American National Election Study,* less than one-third of respondents expressed the view that political parties keep their promises.

33. Not all PACs are connected to interest groups, but most (around 70 percent) of them are. Some politicians and unaffiliated groups form their own PACs. See, for example, M. Margaret Conway, Joanne Connor Green, and Marion Currinder, "Interest Group Money in Elections," in *Interest Group Politics,* eds. Allan J. Ciglar and Burdett A. Loomis (Washington, DC: Congressional Quarterly Press, 2002), 121.

34. Kernell et al., *The Logic of American Politics,* 4th ed., 640; Ornstein, et al., *Vital Statistics on Congress, 1989–1990,* 85–87.

35. FECA hard money rules, as modified by the McCain-Feingold Act, allow *individuals* to contribute up to $2,000 to a congressional candidate in both the primary and general election, $5,000 to a PAC per year, up to $25,000 to the national party organizations per year, $10,000 per year to state party organizations, with an overall limit of $95,000 every two years; PACs can contribute up to $5,000 per candidate, per election (primary and general), up to $15,000 to national party organizations per year, and up to $5,000 to state party organizations per year. They can also spend as much as they want independently of candidates and parties. For *party* spending rules see note 11 above.

36. In the last two election cycles in which party "soft money" was legal, 1999–2000 and 2001–2002, both national parties raised and spent about $250 million of this type of funds. Stanley and Niemi, *Vital Statistics on American Politics* 2007–2008, 104.

37. As presented by Marjorie Randon Hershey in *Party Politics in America,* 11th ed. (New York: Pearson/Longman, 2005), 76. The actual data were collected by Paul S. Herrnson, and published in three different installments: Herrnson, *Party Campaigning in the 1980s* (Cambridge, MA: Harvard University Press, 1988), 51; Herrnson, "Reemergent National Party Organizations," in *The Parties Respond,* ed. L. Sandy Maisel (Boulder, CO: Westview Press, 1990), 54; and Herrnson, "National Party Organizations at the Century's End," in *The Parties Respond,* 2nd ed., ed. L. Sandy Maisel (Boulder, CO: Westview Press, 1994), 60–61.

38. The DCCC went to great lengths in the late 1980s and 1990s to get their longstanding and safe incumbents to raise and donate money for their younger and more endangered colleagues and promising challengers. See Paul S. Herrnson, *Congressional*

Elections (Washington, DC: Congressional Quarterly Press, 1995), Chapter 4; also Herrnson, *Congressional Elections*, 5th ed. (Washington, DC: Congressional Quarterly Press, 2008), Chapter 4.

39. In the 1989–1990, for example, the Republicans raised roughly $210 million; the Democrats only $90 million. By 1999–2000 the Republicans raised $680 million to the Democrats $510 million. See Kernell et al., *The Logic of American Politics*, 4th ed., 602.

40. See note 11 above.

41. Party independent spending was officially recognized and made legal by the Supreme Court in the case: *Colorado Republican Federal Campaign Committee v. FEC*, 518 U.S. 604, 1996.

42. Hershey, *Party Politics in America*, 11th ed., Chapter 3.

43. See Barbara Sinclair, *Legislators, Leaders and Lawmaking* (Baltimore, MD: John Hopkins University Press, 1995); David Rohde, *Parties and Leaders in the Postreform House* (Chicago: University of Chicago Press, 1991); John M. Barry, *The Ambition and the Power: The Fall of Jim Wright* (New York: Viking, 1989).

44. Baumer and Gold, "Party Images and Party Resurgence," 468.

45. See, for example, Paul Allen Beck, "A Tale of Two Electorates: The Changing Party Coalitions, 1952–2000," in *American Politics: Classic and Contemporary Readings*, 6th ed., eds. Allan J. Ciglar and Burdett A. Loomis (New York: Houghton Mifflin Company, 2005): 218–231.

Chapter 2

1. The *American National Election Study* (NES) series, collected by the Center for Political Studies, Institute for Social Research, the University of Michigan. The data are distributed by the Inter-University Consortium for Political and Social Research. For full information on each biennial election study, see www.icpsr.umich.edu.

2. Nonopinions or nonattitudes are responses people give to survey questions about which they have no genuinely formed opinion or attitude. One of the foremost experts on public opinion polling, Herbert Asher, describes the prevalence of nonopinions as "one of the simplest yet most perplexing problems in public opinion polling." See Herbert Asher, *Polling and the Public*, 7th ed. (Washington, DC: Congressional Quarterly Press, 2007), Chapter 2.

3. Steven H. Chaffee and Stacey Frank, "How Americans Get Political Information: Print Versus Broadcast News," *The Annals of the American Academy of Political and Social Science* 546 (1996): 48–58.

4. The data presented in Table 2.1 for the decade of the 2000s end with responses from the 2004 NES survey because the open-ended party like/dislike questions were not asked in 2006 and the responses to these questions from the 2008 survey were not available when this manuscript went to press.

5. Not all the images just described met the threshold for inclusion in Table 2.1. For a more exhaustive analysis, see Donald C. Baumer and Howard J. Gold, "Party Images and Party Resurgence," *Social Science Journal* 44 (October 2007): 469.

6. The percentage of NES respondents offering at least one party like/dislike response fell from more than 80 percent in the 1950s and 1960s to below 70 percent in many elections in the 1970s, then rose steadily in the 1990s and reached 77 percent

in 2004. The mean number of likes and dislikes followed a similar pattern, decreasing from 3.5 to 4.0 in the 1950s and 1960s to 3 or even fewer in the 1970s, then increasing in the 1980s and 1990s, reaching 4.2 by 2000.

7. See Donald C. Baumer and Howard J. Gold, "Party Images and the American Electorate," *American Politics Quarterly* 23 (January 1995): 33–61; and Baumer and Gold, "Party Images and Partisan Resurgence."

8. See Samuel Kernell, Gary C. Jacobson, and Thad Kousser, *The Logic of American Politics*, 4th ed. (Washington, DC: Congressional Quarterly Press, 2009), 597.

9. This question was not asked in 2004 or 2008.

10. Harris Poll, www.harrisinteractive.com/harris_poll/index.asp?PID=534, accessed June 24, 2005.

11. Baumer and Gold, "Party Images and Partisan Resurgence."

12. See William J. Keefe and Marc J. Hetherington, *Parties, Politics and Public Policy in America*, 9th ed. (Washington, DC: Congressional Quarterly Press, 2003), 11–12.

13. See http://www.fairvote.org/?page=1801, accessed on June 5, 2009; and http://edition.cnn.com/ELECTION/2008/primaries, accessed on June 5, 2009.

14. See Howard J. Gold, "Third Party Voting in Presidential Elections: A Study of Perot, Anderson, and Wallace," *Political Research Quarterly* 48 (1995): 751–773.

15. See Martin Wattenberg, *The Decline of American Political Parties, 1952–1996* (Cambridge, MA: Harvard University Press, 1998).

16. Stephen C. Craig, "The Decline of Partisanship in the United States: A Reexamination of the Neutrality Hypothesis," *Political Behavior* 7 (1985): 57–78.

17. Larry M. Bartels, "Partisanship and Voting Behavior, 1952–1996," *American Journal of Political Science* 44 (January 2000): 35–50; Marc J. Hetherington, "Resurgent Mass Partisanship: The Role of Elite Polarization, *American Political Science Review* 95 (September 2001): 619–631.

18. See, for example, Alan I. Abramowitz and Kyle L. Saunders, "Ideological Realignment in the U.S. Electorate," *Journal of Politics* 60 (August 1998): 634–652; William D. Schreckhise and Todd G. Shields, "Ideological Realignment in the Contemporary U.S. Electorate Revisited," *Social Science Quarterly* 84 (September 2003): 596–612; Marjorie Randon Hershey, *Party Politics in America,* 11th ed. (New York: Pearson Longman, 2005); Donald C. Baumer and Howard J. Gold, "Party Images and Party Resurgence."

19. See Kyle L. Saunders and Alan I. Abramowitz, "Ideological Realignment and Active Partisans in the American Electorate," *American Politics Research* 32 (May 2004): 285–309.

20. See Edward G. Carmines and James A. Stimson, *Issue Evolution: Race and the Transformation of American Politics* (Princeton, NJ: Princeton University Press, 1989); Hetherington, "Resurgent Mass Partisanship."

21. To assess the relative impact of party identification in 1976 and 2008, we selected the five survey items that appeared in the NES survey of both years. All of these items are measured on seven-point scales running from strong liberal (point one) to strong conservative (point seven).

22. See Kernell et al., *The Logic of American Politics*, 4th ed., 476.

23. Ibid., 502; see also Benjamin L. Page and Robert Y. Shapiro, *The Rational Public* (Chicago: University of Chicago Press, 1992).

24. Paul F. Lazarsfeld, Bernard Berelson, and Hazel Gaudet, *The People's Choice; How the Voter Makes Up His Mind in a Presidential Campaign* (New York: Duell, Sloan and Pearce, 1944).

25. See Baumer and Gold, "Party Images and Party Resurgence"; and Michael X. Delli Carpini and Scott Keeter, *What Americans Know about Politics and Why It Matters* (New Haven: Yale University Press, 1996).

26. As explained in note 4, the responses to the open-ended party like/dislike questions from the 2008 survey were not available at the time this manuscript was submitted; therefore, this analysis is based on the 2004 NES survey.

27. See Baumer and Gold, "Party Images and the American Electorate."

28. The dependent variable in Table 2.7 is dichotomous (0 = nonpersuaders, 1 = persuaders). Thus to measure the effect of the independent variables, this model is estimated using logistic regression. Logistic regression coefficients are more difficult to interpret: a one unit increase in X_1 is associated with a b_1 change in the predicted logged odds that the dependent variable takes the value of 1 instead of 0. For ease of interpretation, we have converted these coefficients into probabilities that the dependent variable takes on a 1 rather than a 0. The impact of any given coefficient on the probability that the dependent variable is 1 (as opposed to 0) depends on the values that the other independent variables assume. These probabilities appear in Table 2.8.

29. In the NES, respondents are asked to place each party on a seven-point scale that runs from liberal to conservative for each issue. To measure perceptions of party difference on issues and ideology, we subtracted each respondent's placement of the Democrats from his/her placement of the Republicans on the seven-point scale and then averaged these individual differences. In the 1976 NES, respondents were asked to use the seven-point scale to place the parties on ten different items. In 2004, respondents were asked to use this seven-point scale to place the parties on six different items. All of these party placements appear in Table 2.9. Questions about health insurance, jobs and standard of living, and aid to minorities asked respondents to comment on the government's proper role in these areas.

30. Table 2.10 displays information on the ten items that are measured on a seven-point scale in the 1976 NES and on the eight items that are measured on a seven-point scale in both the 2004 and 2008 NES.

31. Morris Fiorina, with Samuel J. Abrams and Jeremy C. Pope, *Culture War?* 2nd ed. (New York: Pearson/Longman, 2006).

32. Ibid., 99.

33. At one point Fiorina et al. define party activists as "3–5 percent of the citizenry" (that would be about 6 to 10 million people); at another point, they describe the purists in the abortion debate as being "the 10 percent or so of the population that occupy each tail of the distribution of abortion attitudes" (another 20 million people). They also point out that there are purists on a number of issues; they mention that gun control activists represented 2 percent of voters in numerous swing states in 2000 (102). Since issue purists are not necessarily party activists and vice versa, adding up and extrapolating from a few of these examples leads to the conclusion that Fiorina et al. could easily be referring to close to 20 percent of the population, or 40 million people, which is similar to some of our estimates of opinion leaders. See Fiorina et al., *Culture War?*, James Davison Hunter makes a similar point, suggesting that up to

about 60 million Americans are on one side or the other in the culture war. See "Is There a Culture War? Event Transcript" at http://pewforum.org/events/?Event ID=112, accessed January 24, 2008.

34. See James Q. Wilson, *The Amateur Democrat* (Chicago: University of Chicago Press, 1962).

35. See Edward Carmines and James Stimson, *Issue Evolution*; and Saunders and Abramowitz, "Ideological Realignment and Active Partisans in the American Electorate."

36. E. E. Schattschneider, *The Semi-Sovereign People: A Realist's View of Democracy in America* (New York: Holt, Rinehart, and Winston, 1960).

37. The turnout averages are based on self-reported NES data. The loyalty figures come from "Voter News Service General Election Exit Polls, 2000" and "National Election Pool General Election Exit Polls, 2004." These data are distributed by the Inter-University Consortium for Political and Social Research. For a similar calculation, see William H. Flanigan and Nancy Zingale, *Political Behavior of the American Electorate*, 11th ed. (Washington, DC: Congressional Quarterly Press, 2006), 53.

38. For figures on partisan loyalty, see the 2008 exit polls at http://edition.cnn.com/ELECTION/2008/results/polls/#val=USP00p1, accessed on June 5, 2009. The turnout data come from the 2008 *American National Election Study*.

39. Carmines and Stimson, *Issue Evolution*; Bernard R. Berelson, Paul F. Lazersfeld, and William N. McPhee, *Voting: A Study of Opinion Formation in a Presidential Campaign* (Chicago: University of Chicago Press, 1954).

40. See, for example, Doris A. Graber, *Mass Media and American Politics*, 7th ed. (Washington, DC: Congressional Quarterly Press, 2006).

41. Michael P. McDonald, *United States Election Project*, "2004 General Election Turnout Rates" and "2008 General Election Turnout Rates." http://elections.gmu.edu/Turnout.2004G.html, and http://elections.gmu.edu/Turnout.2008G.html, accessed May 28, 2009.

Chapter 3

1. For a different view on the rationality of voters see Bryan Caplan, *The Myth of the Rational Voter: Why Democracies Choose Bad Policies* (Princeton, NJ: Princeton University Press, 2007).

2. For example, in 2004, among respondents in the top third of the income distribution, 48 percent identified as Republican and 46 percent identified as Democrat—thus the Republican advantage in this subgroup was +2. Among all respondents in 2004, 41 percent identified as Republican and 50 percent as Democrat—thus the Republican advantage in the full sample was -9. A score of +2 (for the top third of income distribution) is eleven points higher than a score of -9 (full sample), indicating that the top third of the income distribution was eleven points more Republican than the population at large. If we look at the bottom third of the income distribution in 2004, the Republican partisan advantage was -25 (indicating that the identification of this group was twenty-five points more Democratic than Republican). A score of -25 is sixteen points below the full sample score of -9, indicating that the bottom third of the income distribution was sixteen points more Democratic than the population at

large. The data on which Figures 3.1 to 3.7 are based appear in Appendices B.1 to B.7, at the end of this chapter. The data in this chapter, unless otherwise noted, are from the American National Election Study series.

3. For an in-depth analysis of this point see, Nolan McCarty, Keith T. Poole, and Howard Rosenthal, *Polarized America: The Dance of Ideology and Unequal Riches* (Cambridge, MA: MIT Press, 2006), Chapter 3.

4. See Robert S. Erikson and Kent L. Tedin, *American Public Opinion: Its Origins, Contents, and Impact*, 7th ed. (New York: Pearson/Longman, 2005), 206–210; William H. Flanigan and Nancy H. Zingale, *Political Behavior of the American Electorate*, 11th ed. (Washington, DC: CQ Press, 2006), 133; and Mark D. Brewer and Jeffrey M. Stonecash, *Split: Class and Cultural Divides in American Politics* (Washington, DC: CQ Press, 2007), Chapter 6.

5. See, for example, Edward G. Carmines and James A. Stimson, *Issue Evolution: Race and the Transformation of American Politics* (Princeton, NJ: Princeton University Press, 1989); Erikson and Tedin, *American Public Opinion*, 7th ed., 187–191; Samuel Kernell, Gary C. Jacobson, and Thad Kousser, *The Logic of American Politics*, 4th ed. (Washington, DC: CQ Press, 2008), 497–498.

6. Source: U.S. Census Bureau. 2005 American Community Survey. http://factfinder.census.gov/servlet/DTTable?_bm=y&-ds_name=ACS_2005_EST _G00_&-_geoSkip=0&-mt_name=ACS_2005_EST_G2000_B03001 &-redoLog=false&-_skip=0&-geo_id=01000US&-_showChild=Y&-_lang=en &-_toggle=ACS_2005_EST_G2000_B03001. Accessed on July 19, 2007.

7. Carole Jean Uhlaner and F. Chris Garcia, "Latino Public Opinion," in *Understanding Public Opinion*, 2nd ed., eds. Barbara Norrander and Clyde Wilcox (Washington, DC: CQ Press, 2002).

8. In 1960, only 9 percent of the NES sample had a college degree. This figure increased to 31 percent in 2000.

9. See Erikson and Tedin, *American Public Opinion*, 7th ed., 177–187.

10. See Brewer and Stonecash, *Split*, 118.

11. From 1952 to 1968, the NES asked respondents to indicate how often they worshipped on a scale that included four choices: never, seldom, often, and regularly. Since 1972, respondents place themselves on a scale that contains five choices: never, a few times per year, one to two times per month, almost every week, and every week. In order to achieve a better match with the data from 1952–1968, Figure 3.7 does not include the middle group (one to two times per month) from 1972 to 2004.

12. See also McCarty, Poole and Rosenthal, *Polarized America*, 98–101.

13. For a similar analysis, see Brewer and Stonecash, *Split*, 74–75.

14. See McCarty, Poole, and Rosenthal, *Polarized America*.

15. See, for example, Brewer and Stonecash, *Split*; Morris P. Fiorina, with Samuel J. Abrams and Jeremy C. Pope, *Culture War? The Myth of Polarized America*, 2nd ed. (New York: Pearson/Longman, 2006); and Thomas Frank, *What's the Matter with Kansas? How Conservatives Won the Heart of America* (New York: Metropolitan Books, 2004).

16. For documentation on growing economic inequality in the United States, see Brewer and Stonecash, *Split*, Chapter 2; McCarty, Poole, and Rosenthal, *Polarized*

America, Chapter 4; and Frank Ackerman, et al., eds., *The Political Economy of Inequality* (Washington, DC: Island Press, 2000).

17. See Angus Campbell, Philip Converse, Warren Miller, and Donald Stokes, *The American Voter* (New York: Wiley, 1960), Chapter 12.

18. See, for example, Brewer and Stonecash, *Split,* Chapter 4. They use income as one measure of class, supplemented by answers given by respondents in a poll conducted by the Maxwell School at Syracuse University on "Inequality and Civic Engagement." The kinds of questions asked in this poll included: "Have we become a society of haves and have-nots?" "How serious is inequality as a problem?" and "Should Government do more to reduce inequality?"

19. Because the partisanship of African Americans is so consistently homogeneous, and because income has very little effect on African American partisanship and voting behavior, we have focused our discussion of income effects on whites only, who show more heterogeneity and variation over time. In addition, small numbers of African Americans in NES samples, especially after controlling for income, can produce huge variations in the sample statistics among African American respondents.

20. From 1980 to 2008, high-income married white women, on average, were sixteen percentage points more likely to identify as Republican than were low-income married white women. For single white women, the difference was eight percentage points, and for white men it was nineteen percentage points. With respect to voting, high-income married white women voted Republican at a rate that was 13 percent higher than low-income married white women; for single white women there was essentially no difference between Republican voting at high versus low income (both showed strong support for Democrats); for white men the gap was twenty percentage points (NES data).

21. For whites only, the average difference in Republican affiliation between low- and high-income respondents since 1980 is 23 percent in the South and 15 percent in the non-South; for the full sample (whites and nonwhites) these two averages were 25 percent (South) and 16 percent (non-South). With respect to voting, the average difference in voting for Republican presidential candidates between the high- and low-income groups since 1980 among whites is 24 percent in the South and only 11 percent in the non-South; the comparable figures for the full sample were 34 percent (South) and 14 percent (non-South). The larger disparity in identification and voting between income groups in the South when nonwhites are included shows that low-income white southerners are substantially more supportive of Republicans than all low-income southerners. The same appears to be true, to a lesser extent, for low-income whites in the non-South.

22. In 2006 there were eight more gay marriage ban initiatives on state ballots. Seven of them passed, but for the first time one failed (in Arizona). Monica Davey, "Liberals Find Ray of Hope on Ballot Measures," *New York Times,* November 9, 2006, 16.

23. See James W. Ceaser, Andrew E. Bush, and John J. Pitney, *Epic Journey: The 2008 Elections and American Politics* (Lanham, MD: Rowman and Littlefield, 2009), 182–183.

24. Frank, *What's the Matter with Kansas?,* 17; see also James Davison Hunter, *Culture Wars: The Struggle to Define America* (New York: Basic Books, 1991).

25. In 2008, John McCain only got 55 percent of those attending church services more than once a week (Obama, 43 percent), but white evangelicals backed McCain 74 percent to Obama's 24 percent. For the 2004 exit polls, see National Election Pool, Edison Media Research, and Mitofsky International. "National Election Pool General Election Exit Polls 2004, [computer file]." ICPSR version. Somerville, NJ: Edison Media Research/New York, NY: Mitofsky International (producers), 2004. Ann Arbor, MI: Inter-University Consortium for Political and Social Research (distributor), 2005. For the 2008 exit polls, see http://edition.cnn.com/Election/2008/results/polls/#val+USP00p1, accessed June 2, 2009.

26. Alan Abramowitz, "When Good Forecasts Go Bad: The Time-for-Change Model and the 2004 Presidential Election," in *PS: Political Science & Politics* 37 (October 2004): 745–746.

27. National Election Pool, "National Election Pool General Election Exit Polls 2004, [computer file]."

28. Kevin P. Phillips, *The Emerging Republican Majority* (New Rochelle, NY: Arlington House, 1969).

29. Richard M. Scammon and Ben J. Wattenberg, *The Real Majority* (New York: Coward, McCann, and Geoghegan, 1970), 21.

30. Fiorina et al., *Culture War?*

31. Thomas Frank, "Why They Won"; http://www.commondreams.org/views04/1105-32.htm. Accessed June 26, 2007.

32. Frank, *What's the Matter with Kansas?* For a more recent treatment of this topic that presents a considerable amount of evidence to support the argument that cultural issues have assumed far greater importance in voting behavior in recent elections, and thus transformed the nature of American politics and parties, see Brewer and Stonecash, *Split*.

33. For the wording of the NES question about religious worships, and our grouping of responses for analysis, see note 11 above.

34. The wording of the NES abortion question changed slightly in 1980. See Appendix B.8 for the wording of the question before and since 1980. In the analysis that follows, we contrast pro-choice respondents (option 1) and pro-life respondents (option 4).

35. Donald C. Baumer and Howard J. Gold, "Party Images and the American Electorate." *American Politics Quarterly* 23 (January 1995): 33–61.

36. The NES gives respondents a 100-point feeling thermometer to gauge attitudes toward gays and lesbians. In the analysis that follows, we contrast the responses of those least positive about gays (0 to 24 on the thermometer) and those most positive (75 to 100 on the thermometer).

37. Our analysis of the cultural divide is limited to whites only. Although many African Americans are religious in terms of church attendance and embrace some culturally conservative issue positions, their partisan choices and assessments are overwhelmingly Democratic. Therefore, we exclude them from the analysis here because we want to examine the effects that cultural differences have on partisan assessments, and we know there are very few such effects among African Americans.

38. See Kristin Luker, *Abortion and The Politics of Motherhood*. (Berkeley: University of California Press, 1984); also Melody Rose, *Safe, Legal, and Unavailable?: Abortion Politics in the United States* (Washington, DC: CQ Press 2007).

39. See Brewer and Stonecash, *Split*, Chapter 6.

40. In Table 3.6, for questions that were asked in both 2004 and 2008, we included only the 2008 response; for questions asked in 2004, but not in 2008, we included the 2004 response.

41. The strengthening of the relationship between attitudes on abortion and attitudes on noncultural issues may well have been helped along by organized efforts of conservative leaders. Melody Rose points out that Ralph Reed, one of the leaders of the Christian Coalition, decided in 1991 to emphasize the connection between conservative economic positions, such as low taxes, and conservative social/cultural issues, such as abortion, to his followers. These efforts increased after the Republicans won the House in 1994. See Rose, *Safe, Legal, and Unavailable?*, 9–10. Presently, Tony Perkins and the Family Research Council are engaged in a similar effort. See, http://www.frcaction.org.

42. See Fiorina et al., *Culture War?*, Chapter 2.

43. For example, in 2004, 57 percent of pro-choice respondents in blue states supported gay marriage compared to 5 percent of pro-life respondents in blue states. Similarly, 63 percent of pro-choice respondents in red states supported gay marriage compared to 3 percent of pro-life respondents in red states. Similar patterns appear across all of these issues.

44. Readers should note that our previous multivariate model (Table 3.1) had party identification as the dependent variable. It showed that many of the demographic variables included in this model were independently related to partisanship. What this model implicitly asks is how much effect do all the factors, demographic and otherwise, that we have examined in this chapter have on presidential voting choices independently of party identification? The full model is presented in the Appendix B.8, at the end of this chapter.

45. In Figure 3.10, we have converted the nonstandardized logistic regression coefficients reported in Appendix 3.8 into standardized coefficients. To standardize, we multiplied each coefficient by the variable's sample standard deviation. See Scott Menard, "Six Approaches to Calculating Standardized Logistic Regression Coefficients," *The American Statistician* 58 (August 2004): 218–223.

46. See Larry Bartels. "Partisanship and Voting Behavior, 1952–1996." *American Journal of Political Science* 44 (January 2000): 35–50.

Chapter 4

1. The items in the Contract for America included the following: applying antidiscrimination laws to Congress, giving the president line-item veto power, new crime control legislation, a welfare reform bill, a new law to govern federal unfunded mandates imposed on states, tax reform, social security reform, expanded spending for national security, tort reform, changes in adoption laws, a balanced budget amendment, and term limits for members of the House. See James G. Gimpel, *Fulfilling the Contract* (Boston: Allyn and Bacon, 1996), 5.

2. Ibid., 8; Ceci Connolly, "Legislation Goes Overboard As Members Eye the Exits," *Congressional Quarterly Weekly Report*, October 1, 1994, 2753–2755.

3. Jon Healy, "Jubilant GOP Strives To Keep Legislative Feet on Ground," *Congressional Quarterly Weekly Report*, November 12, 1994, 3210.

4. As cited in Rhodes Cook, "Using Clinton as a Punching Bag May Have Limits as GOP Tactic," *Congressional Quarterly Weekly Reports*, October 22, 1994, 2992–2993; Gary C. Jacobson, *The Politics of Congressional Elections*, 4th ed. (New York: Longman, 1997), 160–62; Gimpel, *Fulfilling the Contract*, 2.

5. As cited in Bob Beneson, "Playing Defense," *CQ Weekly*, April 24, 2006, 1078.

6. See Janet Hook, "Judgment Calls on a Career: The Rostenkowski Vigil," *Congressional Quarterly Weekly Reports*, May 28, 1994, 1359–1361; and Jacobson, *The Politics of Congressional Elections*, 156.

7. Dave Kaplan and Juliana Gruenwald, "Longtime 'Second' Party Scores a Long List if Firsts," and Phil Duncan, "Republicans' Gains Matched Their Rosy Predictions," *Congressional Quarterly Weekly Reports*, November 12, 1994, 3232–3246; Jacobson, *The Politics of Congressional Elections*, 173.

8. Rep. Robert Livingston (R-LA), as quoted by Jon Healy in "Jubilant GOP Strives to Keep Legislative Feet on Ground," *Congressional Quarterly Weekly Report*, November 12, 1994, 3211.

9. George Hager, "Though He Shares Comrades' Elation, Dole Knows the Hazards of Majority Rule," *Congressional Quarterly Weekly Report*, October 22, 1994, 3226–3227.

10. Beth Donovan, "Freshman Focus on the Product, Not on Legislative Process," *Congressional Quarterly Weekly Reports*, November 14, 1992, 3226–3228; Jacobson, *The Politics of Congressional Elections*, 21, 152.

11. See, for example, Samuel Kernell, Gary C. Jacobson, and Thad Kousser, *The Logic of American Politics*, 4th ed. (Washington, DC: CQ Press, 2008), 259.

12. Jacobson, *The Politics of Congressional Elections*, 125.

13. Robert W. Merry, "Voters' Demand for Change Puts Clinton on the Defensive," *Congressional Quarterly Weekly Reports*, November 12, 1994, 3207; also Clyde Wilcox, *The Latest American Revolution?* (New York: St. Martin's Press, 1995), 22–26.

14. Jacobson, *The Politics of Congressional Elections*, 162; Wilcox, *The Latest American Revolution?*, 21.

15. See Gimpel, *Fulfilling the Contract*, Chapter 2.

16. As quoted in Gimpel, *Fulfilling the Contract*, 22.

17. Jacobson, *The Politics of Congressional Elections*, 163.

18. Wilcox, *The Latest American Revolution?*, 14–17.

19. One of the Senate gains was the result of Richard Shelby of Alabama switching party affiliation. See Rhodes Cook, "Dixie Voters Look Away: South Shifts to GOP," *Congressional Quarterly Weekly Reports*, November 12, 1994, 3230–3231; also Wilcox, *The Latest American Revolution?*, 27.

20. Sources for these data are: Voter Research and Surveys/*CBS News*/*New York Times* General Election Exit Poll: National File, 1990; Voter Research and Surveys General Election Exit Polls, 1992; Voter News Service General Election Exit Polls, 1994. Data are distributed by the Inter-University Consortium for Political and Social Research.

21. See John Cochran, "The Influence Implosion," *Congressional Quarterly Weekly*, January 16, 2006, 174–179; Cochran, "The End of the Republican Revolution,"

Congressional Quarterly Weekly, April 10, 2006, 965–972; Bob Benenson, "Playing Defense," *Congressional Quarterly Weekly*, April 24, 2006, 1078–1083.

22. See, for example, Bruce I. Oppenheimer, "Deep Red and Blue Congressional Districts: The Causes and Consequences of Declining Party Competitiveness," in *Congress Reconsidered*, 8th ed., eds. Lawrence C. Dodd and Bruce I. Oppenheimer (Washington, DC: Congressional Quarterly Press, 2005), 135–157.

23. Benenson, "Playing Defense," and "Race by Race," 1078–1095.

24. Larry Sabato, "Culture of Corruption," *Sabato's Crystal Ball*, Vol. IV, Issue. 12, May 10, 2006, goodpolitics@virginia.edu, www.centerforpolitics.org/crystalball.

25. Benenson, "Playing Defense," 1078; Polling Report.com, "President Bush— Overall Job Rating," www.pollingreport.com/BushJob,htm, accessed, January, 20, 2007; Andrew Taylor, "New Revelations on Whitewater Revive GOP Call for Hearings," *Congressional Quarterly Weekly Reports*, March 12, 1994, 586.

26. Jim Rutenberg and Megan C. Thee, "Poll Shows Growing Skepticism in U.S. Over Peace in the Middle East," *New York Times*, July 27, 2006, A20.

27. Bob Benenson, "Blue State Special," *Congressional Quarterly Weekly*, August 14, 2006, 2224–2231.

28. Bob Benenson, "The Battering Ram and the Bulwark," *Congressional Quarterly Weekly*, October 30, 2006, 2868.

29. Adam Nagourney and Janet Elder, "Poll Shows Foley Case Is Alienating Public From Congress," *New York Times*, October 10, 2006, A22; John Cochran, "A Cultural Discontent," *Congressional Quarterly Weekly*, October 9, 2006, 2690–2700.

30. Adam Nagourney and Janet Elder, "Only 25% in Poll Voice Approval of the Congress," *New York Times*, September 21, 2006, A1, A20.

31. The *Congressional Quarterly* political staff, like most other election forecasters, does not make specific predictions, but rather gives a range of outcomes based on a categorization scheme that deems congressional seats to be "safe" (Republican or Democratic), ones where a Democratic or Republican candidate is "favored," ones that "lean" Democrat or Republican, or true "tossups," where there is no clear favorite. Their October House lineup had 210 seats that were either safe, favored, or leaning Democrat and eighteen tossups. Assuming an even split on tossups you get a prediction of 218 seats for the Democrats. Their Senate lineup had forty-nine safe, favored, or leaning seats for the Republicans and three tossups, which leads to a prediction of either fifty or fifty-one Republican Senate seats. See Benenson, "The Battering Ram and the Bulwark," 2866–2879. For a similar October breakdown see Adam Nagourney and Robin Toner, "With Guarded Cheer, Democrats Dare to Believe This Is Their Time," *New York Times*, October 22, 2006, A1, A24.

32. Larry Sabato, "The Big Picture," Sabato's Crystal Ball, Vol. IV, Issue 28, October 28, 2006, goodpolitics@virginia.edu, www.centerforpolitics.org/crystalball.

33. Charles Cook, *The Cook Political Report*, "Charlie Cook's National Overview," www.cookpolitical.com/overview/default/php, accessed Feb. 15, 2007.

34. Adam Nagourney and Megan C. Thee, "With Iraq Driving Election, Voters Want New Approach," *New York Times*, November 2, 2006, A1, A22.

35. Ian Urbina, "Democrats See Black Turnout as a Challenge," *New York Times*, October 27, 2006, A1, A15.

36. See Sheryl Gay Stolberg, "GOP Moves Fast to Reignite Issue of Gay Marriage," *New York Times*, October 27, 2006, A1, A14; David Kirkpatrick, "In Ohio, Democrats Show a Religious Side to Voters," *New York Times*, October 31, 2006, A19.

37. Christopher Drew, "Automated Telemarketing Tactic Steers Voters Toward Republicans," *New York Times*, November 6, 2006, A1, A16.

38. See Michael P. McDonald, United States Election Project, "2006 Election Data," http://elections.gmu.edu/voter_turnout.htm, accessed Jan. 30, 2007; Laurie Goodstein, "Religious Voting Data Show Some Shift, Observers Say," *New York Times*, November 9, 2006, P7.

39. David Nather, "On a Mission to the Middle," *Congressional Quarterly Weekly*, December 4, 2006, 3225–3231.

40. Anthony Corrado and Katie Varney, "Party Money in the 2006 Election: The Role of National Party Committees in Financing National Campaigns," www.cfinst.org/parties, accessed December 21, 2007; also, Federal Election Commission, *Campaign Finance Summary Releases*, "National Party Financial Activity Summarized," www.fec.gov/press/press2004/summaries2004.shtml, accessed January 30, 2007. If state and local party organizations are included, the Republican total goes to $602 million and the Democratic total to $483 million. See Paul Herrnson, *Congressional Elections*, 5th ed. (Washington, DC: Congressional Quarterly Press, 2008), 92.

41. Campaign Finance Institute, *Money and the Battle for Congress 2006*, Table: "National Party Receipts and Cash on Hand, 2002–06," http://www.cfinst.org, accessed January 30, 2007; also Herrnson, *Congressional Elections*, 118.

42. Colorado Republican Federal Campaign Committee v. FEC, 518 U.S. 604, 1996; FEC v. Colorado Republican Federal Campaign Committee, 513 U.S. 431, 2001.

43. See Anne E. Kornblut and Jim Rutenberg, "Federal Rules Help Shield Creators of Political Advertisements," *New York Times*, October 27, 2006, A1.

44. Federal Election Commission, "Electronically Filed Independent Expenditures," http://www.fec.gov/finance/disclosure/ie_reports.shtml, accessed January 22, 2007.

45. See Marie Horrigan, "Midterm Meanness," in *Congressional Quarterly Weekly*, October 16, 2006, 2755–2760.

46. Adam Nagourney, *New York Times*, September 17, 2006, A1, A24.

47. See Michael Malbin, "Candidate Spending Was Up, But Party Spending Was Way Up, and Crucial," Campaign Finance Institute, *Money and the Battle for Congress 2006*, www.cfinst.org, accessed January 30, 2007.

48. Jeff Zaleny and Megan C. Thee, "Exit Polling Shows Independents, Citing War, Favored Democrats," *New York Times*, November 8, 2006, A1, P9.

49. Table: "Survey of Voters, Who They Were," *New York Times*, November 9, 2006, P7; see also Gary C. Jacobson and Samuel Kernell, *The Logic of Politics Under Divided Government; The Legacy of the 2006 Elections* (Washington, DC: Congressional Quarterly Press, 2008), 4.

50. The sixteen noncompetitive or "safe" Senate elections were won by Democratic incumbents Dianne Feinstein (CA), Thomas Carper (DE), Daniel Akaka (HI), Ted Kennedy (MA), Jeff Bingaman (NM), Hillary Clinton (NY), Kent Conrad (ND), Robert Byrd (WV), and Herb Kohl (WI); and Republican incumbents Richard Lugar (IN), Olympia Snow (ME), Trent Lott (MS), John Ensign (NV), Kay Bailey Hutchinson (TX), Orrin Hatch (UT), and Craig Thomas (WY).

51. See "Election 2006," *Congressional Quarterly Weekly*, November 13, 2006, 2962–3077.

52. David Nather and John Cochran, "Gender Gap at the Ballot Box," *Congressional Quarterly Weekly*, January 29, 2007, 310–317.

53. Figures are from NES. Low-income voters include those in the bottom third of the income distribution.

54. Gary C. Jacobson and Samuel Kernell, *Strategy and Choice in Congressional Elections*, 2nd ed. (New Haven, CT: Yale University Press, 1983).

55. See Gary Jacobson, *The Politics of Congressional Elections*, 6th ed. (New York: Longman, 2004).

56. The Harrison administration was widely perceived as catering to the rich and the privileged, especially by the Populists, whose movement was in full swing at this time. The economy was also headed for trouble. See John M. Blum et al., *The National Experience*, 2nd ed. (New York: Harcourt, Brace & World, Inc., 1968), 500–502.

57. See, for example, Wilcox, *The Latest American Revolution?*, 10–11.

58. See Jacobson, *The Politics of Congressional Elections*, Ch. 6; also Alan Ehrenhalt, *The United States of Ambition* (New York: Times Books, 1992).

59. See Wilcox, *The Latest American Revolution?*, 10–11; also Oppenheimer, "Deep Red and Deep Blue Congressional Districts: The Causes and Consequences of Declining Party Competitiveness," 135–157.

60. This was also the period when the "party decline" school of thought prevailed among political scientists (see Chapters 1 and 2).

61. As shown in Appendix C.1 and C.2, much of the falloff in 2008 was attributable to the voting of weak and leaning Democrats in Senate races.

62. Oppenheimer presents persuasive evidence for a decline in "personal incumbency advantage" by 2000 and after. He concludes that this is largely a reflection of redistricting in 1992 and 2002 that created many more heavily Republican and heavily Democratic congressional districts. He did find evidence of personal incumbency advantage in competitive districts. See Oppenheimer, "Deep Red and Deep Blue Congressional Districts: The Causes and Consequences of Declining Party Competitiveness," 136–157. Oppenheimer attributes the distinction between "personal incumbency advantage" and "partisan incumbency advantage" to John R. Alford and David W. Brady, "Personal and Partisan Advantage in U.S. Congressional Elections, 1946–1986" in *Congress Reconsidered*, 4th ed., eds. Lawrence C. Dodd and Bruce I. Oppenheimer (Washington, DC: Congressional Quarterly Press, 1993), 153–169.

63. We obtained these data on presidential and House election results from 1994 through 2002, broken down by congressional district, at http://www.polidata.us/books/default.htm. For 2006, we obtained the data from http://www.nytimes.com/ref/elections/2006/House.html. Both Web sites were accessed in December 2007. For a similar analysis using presidential elections returns as a measure of partisan strength, see Robert S. Erikson and Gerald C. Wright, "Voters, Candidates, and Issues in Congressional Elections" in *Congress Reconsidered*, 8th ed., eds. Lawrence C. Dodd and Bruce I. Oppenheimer (Washington, DC: Congressional Quarterly Press, 2004), 77–106. See also Oppenheimer, "Deep Red and Deep Blue Congressional Districts: The Causes and Consequences of Declining Party Competitiveness," 135–157.

Chapter 5

1. See note 1 in Chapter 4 for a listing of the items in the contract.
2. See, for example, John B. Bader, *Taking the Initiative* (Washington, DC: Georgetown University Press, 1996), 199–205; or Carl E. Van Horn, Donald C. Baumer, and William T. Gormley, Jr., *Politics and Public Policy*, 3rd ed. (Washington, DC: Congressional Quarterly Press, 2001), Chapter 3.
3. Bader, *Taking the Initiative*, 145.
4. Ibid., 128; Jon Healy, "Clinton Success Rate Declined To a Record Low in 1995," *Congressional Quarterly Weekly Report*, January 27, 1996, 193–198.
5. Van Horn et al., *Politics and Public Policy*, 169; also Andrew Taylor, "Few In Congress Grieve as Justices Give Line-Item Veto the Ax," *Congressional Quarterly Weekly*, June 27, 1998, 1747–1749.
6. See Roger H. Davidson, Walter J. Oleszek, and Frances E. Lee, *Congress and Its Members*, 11th ed. (Washington, DC: Congressional Quarterly Press, 2008), 164.
7. Earmarking is a practice whereby individual members of Congress are allowed to designate certain projects, usually highway or other construction projects, that will receive funding in appropriations bills. A transportation appropriation bill will contain literally thousands of such earmarks, also called "pork." Critics contend that many of these projects are wasteful and that Congress should take steps to curb this practice. Pay-as-you-go (PAYGO) budget rules require Congress to pay for any increases in spending in entitlement programs, such as Social Security, Medicare, Medicaid, and others, that are the result of newly passed legislation by either raising taxes, or cutting spending in another program. Similarly, new tax cuts, which deprive the government of revenue, had to be offset in the same way. These rules were in place throughout the 1990s, and many believe they were importantly responsible for the success Congress and President Clinton had in balancing the federal budget in the late 1990s.
8. Martin Kady II, "New Majority, New Rules," *Congressional Quarterly Weekly*, January 8, 2007, 122–124.
9. See Edward Epstein and Bart Jansen, "Role Reversal Yields Stalemate," *Congressional Quarterly Weekly*, January 7, 2008, 18–21.
10. See David Nather, "A Waning Season for Making Law," *Congressional Quarterly Weekly*, July 9, 2007, 2008–2016.
11. Josh Rogin, "War Supplemental Frozen in Senate," *Congressional Quarterly Weekly*, November 19, 2007, 3482–3483.
12. See Steven Lee Myers, "Despite 'High Note,' Bush Scolds Congress as Wasteful," *New York Times*, December 21, 2007, A22; Carl Hulse and Robert Pear, "Republican Unity Trumps Democratic Momentum," *New York Times*, December 21, 2007, A22.
13. See Drew Armstrong, "Democrats Try to Retry SCHIP Expansion," *Congressional Quarterly Weekly*, October 22, 2007, 3091–3092.
14. See Nather, "A Waning Season for Making Laws."
15. See Bart Jensen, "Details of the Lobbying Rules Law," *Congressional Quarterly Weekly*, September 17, 2007, 2692–2694; Libby George, "Broad Student Aid Overhaul Clears" *Congressional Quarterly Weekly*, September 10, 2007, 2620–2621.
16. See Dina Capiello, "Slimmer Energy Bill Reaches Finish Line," *Congressional Quarterly Weekly*, December 17, 2007, 3722–3723; Myers, "Despite 'High Note,' Bush Scolds Congress as Wasteful."

17. David Nather, "A Crisis of Confidence," *Congressional Quarterly Weekly*, October 22, 2007, 3061–3067.

18. See Davidson et al., *Congress and Its Members*, 13; and Bob Dole, *Historical Almanac of the United States Senate* (Washington, DC: U.S. Government Printing Office, 1989), 20.

19. Eric Schickler, "Institutional Development of Congress," in *The Legislative Branch*, eds. Paul J. Quirk and Sarah A. Binder (New York: Oxford University Press, Institutions of American Democracy Series, 2005), 35–62.

20. Ibid., 39; also Thomas E. Mann and Norman J. Ornstein, *The Broken Branch* (New York: Oxford University Press, 2006), 27.

21. Randall B. Ripley, *Congress: Process and Policy*, 3rd ed. (New York: W. W. Norton, 1983), 61.

22. Ibid., 63.

23. John M. Blum, Bruce Catton, Edmund S. Morgan, Arthur M. Schlesinger, Jr., Kenneth M. Stampp, and C. Vann Woodward, *The National Experience*, 2nd ed. (New York: Harcourt, Brace & World, 1964), 325.

24. Sarah A. Binder, *Stalemate* (Washington, DC: The Brookings Institution Press, 2003), 13.

25. See Blum et al., *The National Experience*, 373–383; and Samuel Kernell, Gary C. Jacobson, and Thad Kousser, *The Logic of American Politics*, 4th ed. (Washington, DC: Congressional Quarterly Press, 2008), 149–151.

26. Ripley, *Congress: Process and Policy*, 61; Schickler, "Institutional Development of Congress," 41.

27. For more on these changes and their significance see Schickler, "Institutional Development of Congress," 41–45; Steven S. Smith and Gerald Gamm, "The Dynamics of Party Government in Congress," in *Congress Reconsidered*, 8th ed., eds. Lawrence C. Dodd and Bruce I. Oppenheimer (Washington, DC: Congressional Quarterly Press, 2005), 181–205; and Joseph Cooper, "From Congressional to Presidential Preeminence: Power and Politics in Late Nineteenth-Century America and Today," in *Congress Reconsidered*, 363–393; also Mann and Ornstein, *The Broken Branch*, Chapter 2.

28. Schickler, "Institutional Development of Congress," 44–45; Smith and Gamm, "The Dynamics of Party Government in Congress," 189–195.

29. Schickler, "Institutional Development of Congress," 42.

30. Ibid., 46–47; Cooper, "From Congressional to Presidential Preeminence," 370–371.

31. Ibid., 371.

32. Blum, et al, *The National Experience*, 515–518.

33. Woodrow Wilson, *Congressional Government* (Boston: Houghton Mifflin, 1913).

34. See Kenneth Shepsle, "The Changing Textbook Congress," in *Can Congress Govern?*, eds. John Chubb and Paul Peterson (Washington, DC: The Brookings Institution Press, 1989), 238–262.

35. See William S. White, *The Citadel: The Story of the United States Senate* (New York: Harper & Row, 1956); and Donald R. Matthews, *U.S. Senators and Their World* (Chapel Hill: University of North Carolina Press, 1960).

36. Schickler, "Institutional Development of Congress," 48–51.

37. The Committee was named after its cochairs, legendary Progressive Robert LaFollette of Wisconsin and Democrat Mike Monroney of Oklahoma.

38. See Donald C. Baumer, "Senate Democratic Leadership in the 101st Congress" in *The Atomistic Congress*, eds. Allen D. Hertzke and Ronald M. Peters, Jr. (Armonk, New York: M. E. Sharpe, 1992), 293–332.

39. House Republicans, Senate Democrats, and Senate Republicans call the meetings of their party members conferences; House Democrats use the name caucus to describe these meetings.

40. There are many accounts of this episode and related events. See for example, Leroy N. Rieselbach, *Congressional Reform: The Changing Modern Congress* (Washington, DC: Congressional Quarterly Press, 1994); David W. Rhode, *Parties and Leaders in the Post-Reform House* (Chicago: University of Chicago Press, 1991); Barbara Sinclair, *Majority Leadership in the U.S. House* (Baltimore: Johns Hopkins University Press, 1983); Schickler, "Institutional Development of Congress," 51–55.

41. See Barbara Sinclair, "Parties and Party Leadership in the House," in *The Legislative Branch*, eds., Quirk and Binder, 224–254; and Baumer, "Senate Democratic Leadership in the 101st Congress."

42. *Congressional Quarterly Weekly*, April 16, 2007, 1084.

43. As we discuss later in this chapter, the Republican House leadership in 2000–2006 facilitated widespread earmarking by members, thus using pork as an instrument of centralized leadership. See, for example, Mann and Ornstein, *The Broken Branch*, 175–179.

44. It should be noted, however, that the committee/subcommittee system of the modern Congress rests on a foundation of party unity when it comes to matters of organization. If Democrats have a majority, they always vote as a bloc in the House and Senate to sustain their standing committee plans and Republicans vote as a bloc against them. When Republicans are in the majority, the reverse is true. This enables the majority party to have majority membership on all the legislative committees, and to control all the committee and subcommittee chairmanships (the minority party has what are called "ranking members" on these groups). Without this unity, the system would crumble. Thus, even at the height of decentralized committee/subcommittee power in the 1970s, the potential advantages of cohesive party voting were apparent to observant members of Congress.

45. See David E. Price, "Congressional Committees in the Policy Process," in *Congress Reconsidered*, 3rd ed., eds. Lawrence C. Dodd and Bruce I. Oppenheimer (Washington, DC: Congressional Quarterly Press, 1981), 161–188; and Christopher J. Deering and and Steven S. Smith, "Subcommittees in Congress," in *Congress Reconsidered*, 3rd ed., eds. Dodd and Oppenheimer, 189–210; Rieselbach, *Congressional Reform*, or Davidson et al., *Congress and Its Members*, 11th ed., Chapter 7.

46. See Barbara Sinclair, *The Transformation of the U.S. Senate* (Baltimore: Johns Hopkins University Press, 1989); Barbara Sinclair, "The New World of U.S. Senators," in *Congress Reconsidered*, 8th ed., eds. Dodd and Oppenheimer; and Steven S. Smith, "Parties and Leadership in the Senate," in *The Legislative Branch*, eds. Quirk and Binder, 255–278.

47. David R. Mayhew, *Congress: The Electoral Connection* (New Haven: Yale University Press, 1974).

48. Ibid., Part 2.

49. Norman J. Ornstein, Thomas E. Mann, and Michael J. Malbin, *Vital Statistics on Congress, 1989–1990* (Washington, DC: Congressional Quarterly Press, 1990), 56–57.

50. Ripley, *Congress: Policy and Process*, 219.

51. Sinclair, *Majority Leadership in the U.S. House*.

52. The Democratic leadership teams during this period were: Thomas "Tip" O'Neil, Speaker; Jim Wright, majority leader (1977–1987); and John Brademas (1977–1980) and Tom Foley (1980–1987), whips. Then Wright, Speaker; Foley, majority leader; and Richard Gephardt, whip (1987–1989). They were followed by Foley, Speaker; Gephardt, majority leader; and David Bonior, whip (1989–1995).

53. An example of a specialized rule of this sort would be one that explicitly prohibited floor consideration of an amendment to a bill that would force party members to vote in a way that might hurt or embarrass them politically. Thus in considering an energy package, the leadership might try to exclude amendments to their preferred bill that would cut gasoline taxes, which would be popular with constituents, but would be damaging to the overall package.

54. See Sinclair, "The Evolution of Party Leadership in the Modern House," in *The Atomistic Congress*, eds. Hertzke and Peters, 259–292; Barbara Sinclair, "House Majority Party Leadership in the Late 1980s," in *Congress Reconsidered*, 4th ed., eds. Lawrence C. Dodd and Bruce I. Oppenheimer (Washington, DC: Congressional Quarterly Press, 1989), 307–330; and John Barry, *The Ambition and the Power* (New York: Penguin Books, 1990).

55. Theda Skocpol, *Boomerang* (New York: W. W. Norton & Company, 1996).

56. The Budget Enforcement Act of 1990 changed the previous budget control legislation, commonly known as Gramm-Rudman-Hollings, by moving away from deficit reduction targets and across-the-board spending cuts to what is known as PAYGO (pay-as-you-go) discipline covering entitlement programs (see note 7 above), and annual caps on discretionary spending (the funding contained in appropriations bills). See, for example, Allen Schick, *The Federal Budget: Politics, Policy, Process*, revised ed. (Washington, DC: The Brookings Institution, 2000).

57. See Carl E. Van Horn et al., *Politics and Public Policy*, Chapter 9.

58. See Paul J. Quirk, "The Legislative Branch: Assessing the Partisan Congress," in *A Republic Divided*, ed. Kathleen Hall Jamieson (New York: Oxford University Press, 2007), 121–156.

59. See James G. Gimpel, *Fulfilling the Contract* (Boston: Allyn and Bacon, 1996); Bader, *Taking the Initiative*; and Sinclair, "Parties and Party leadership in the House"; also Smith and Gamm, "The Dynamics of Party Government in Congress"; and Eric Schickler and Kathryn Pearson, "The House Leadership in an Era of Partisan Warfare," in *Congress Reconsidered*, 8th ed., eds. Dodd and Oppenheimer.

60. Davidson et al., *Congress and Its Members*, 213.

61. See Baumer, "Senate Democratic Leadership In the 101st Congress."

62. Schickler, "Institutional Development of Congress," 57.

63. Davidson et al., *Congress and Its Members*, 214.

64. The Senate can and does achieve floor consideration and debate arrangements that are similar to those in the House through what are called "Unanimous Consent

Agreements." As the name implies, these require the consent of all senators, and are negotiated by the majority and minority leaders. The use and/or threat of filibusters in the contemporary Senate has also developed into something of an art form. Party leaders commonly threaten to deploy them, and they can be used at several steps along the way to a final floor vote, and even after that with regard to appointing a conference committee. Often leaders will call for cloture votes (sixty votes are needed to stop filibusters) at the beginning of Senate consideration of a bill to see whether they have the votes to break filibusters. With all the options and maneuvers available to leaders and ordinary senators, sometimes members are not sure whether or not a filibuster is taking place. Smith "Parties and Leadership in the Senate"; and C. Lawrence Evans and Daniel Lipinski, "Obstruction and Leadership in the U.S. Senate," in *Congress Reconsidered*, 8th ed., eds. Dodd and Oppenheimer; and Sarah A. Binder and Steven S. Smith, *Politics or Principle? Filibustering in the United States Senate* (Washington, DC: The Brookings Institution Press, 1997).

65. See Baumer, "Senate Democratic Leadership in the 101st Congress."

66. See Binder, *Stalemate*; and Daniel J. Palazzolo, *Done Deal?* (New York: Chatham House Publishers, 1999).

67. For an extended, and much more critical, assessment of this era, see Mann and Ornstein, *The Broken Branch*.

68. See Gary C. Jacobson, *A Divider, Not A Uniter* (New York: Perason/Longman, 2007), 1.

69. See Lori Nitschke, "Tax Cut Deal Reached Quickly As Appetite for Battle Fades," *Congressional Quarterly Weekly*, May 26, 2001, 1251–1255.

70. See Tom Daschle, *Like No Other Time* (New York: Crown Publishers, 2003), 130–131.

71. See, Gebe Martinez, "Concerns Linger for Lawmakers Following Difficult Vote for War," *Congressional Quarterly Weekly*, October 12, 2002, 2671–2678; David Nather, "Compliments for the 107th: Lessons for a New Congress," *Congressional Quarterly Weekly*, December 14, 2002, 2332–2335.

72. Mann and Ornstein, *The Broken Branch*, 178. The overall number of earmarks in 2005 was 13,491, see Robert Pear, "Earmarks Seen Likely to Continue, but With Details," *New York Times*, January 22, 2008, A13.

73. See John Cranford "Key Votes Highly Partisan," *Congressional Quarterly Weekly*, January 3, 2004, 24; for a more extended treatment see, Mann and Ornstein, *The Broken Branch*, 1–6.

74. Cranford, "Key Votes Highly Partisan," 24–39.

75. See *2005 CQ Almanac Plus*, ed. Jan Austin (Washington, DC: Congressional Quarterly Press, 2006), 1–3.

76. Ibid., 14–8–9.

77. See *2006 CQ Almanac Plus*, ed. Jan Austin (Washington, DC: Congressional Quarterly Press, 2007), 1–6.

78. See 2005 *CQ Almanac Plus*, 1–3; and 2006 *CQ Almanac Plus*, 1–6.

79. The groups are: Americans for Democratic Action, the American Civil Liberties Union, the American Federation of State County and Municipal Employees, the League of Conservation Voters, the Information Technology Council, National Tax-

payers Union, Chamber of Commerce, the American Conservative Union, the Club for Growth, and the Family research Council. The scores from each group run from 1 to 100, with liberal members of Congress getting low scores from conservative groups and high scores from liberal groups, while the opposite is true for conservative members. See Michael Barone and Richard E. Cohen, *The Almanac of American Politics 2008* (Washington, DC: National Journal Group, 2008).

80. Aage R. Clausen, *How Congressmen Decide* (New York: St. Martin's Press, 1973). While Clausen's approach yielded several distinct policy dimensions, Poole and Rosenthal were eventually able to capture most of the variation in floor voting in a single dimension (see below).

81. Keith T. Poole and Howard Rosenthal, *Congress: A Political Economic History of Roll Call Voting* (New York: Oxford University Press 1997); also Poole's Web site, www.voteview.com.

82. For a fuller description of the Congressional Quarterly scores and scoring system, see *2006 CQ Almanac Plus*, Appendix B.

83. For the 1961–2006 scores, see *2006 CQ Almanac Plus*, B-15; for the 2007 scores, see Catharine Richert, "United We Stand Opposed," *Congressional Quarterly Weekly*, January 14, 2008, 144; for the 2008 scores, see Shawn Zeller, "Parties Dig In On Fractured Hill," *Congressional Quarterly Weekly*, December 15, 2008, 3332–3335.

84. See, for example, Jonathan Rauch, *Demosclerosis: The Silent Killer of American Government* (New York: Times Books, 1994); Lester Thurow, *Zero Sum Society* (New York: Penguin Books, 1981); David A. Stockman, *The Triumph of Politics* (New York: Harper & Row, 1986). For other perspectives, see *Interest Group Politics*, 6th ed., eds. Allan J. Cigler and Burdett A. Loomis (Washington, DC: Congressional Quarterly Press, 2002).

85. Some of the actions taken against powerful interests in the 1970s and 1980s include the deregulation of several industries such as the airline and telephone (breakup of AT&T) industries, the passage and subsequent strengthening of various environmental policies (Clean Air, Clean Water, and Superfund), a tax reform law (1986) that seemed to help average citizens and hurt special interests, and later the prolonged and largely successful attack on the cigarette industry that was once thought to epitomize the power of interest groups in American politics. See Kernell et al., *The Logic of American Politics*, 643–647; also Allan J. Cigler and Burdett A. Loomis, "From Big Bird to Bill Gates: Organized Interests and the Emergence of Hyperpolitics," in *American Politics: Classic and Contemporary Readings*, 6th ed., eds. Allan J. Ciglar and Burdett A. Loomis (Boston: Houghton Mifflin Co., 2005); John R. Wright, *Interest Groups and Congress* (Boston: Allyn and Bacon, 1996); and Martha Derthick, *Up in Smoke*, 2nd ed. (Washington, DC: Congressional Quarterly Press, 2005).

86. David Mayhew, *Divided We Govern: Party Control, Lawmaking and Investigations, 1946–1990* (New Haven: Yale University Press, 1991); Mayhew, *Divided We Govern: Party Control, Lawmaking and Investigations, 1946–2002* (New Haven: Yale University Press, 2005).

87. As cited in Morris Fiorina, *Divided Government* (New York: Macmillan Publishing Company, 1992), 88; see also Mayhew, *Divided We Govern: 1946–1990*; Binder, *Stalemate*, 44.

88. Ibid., Chapter 3; also George C. Edwards III, Andrew Barrett, and Jeffrey Peake, "The Legislative Impact of Divided Government," in *American Journal of Political Science* 41 (April 1997): 545–563.

89. Binder created her legislative agendas for each congressional session by counting the number of issues that appeared in editorials in the *New York Times*, which called for some kind of congressional action, from 1947 to 2000. She ended up with an agenda of some 3,152 items. See Binder, *Stalemate*, 38 and Appendix A. Her analysis of the causes of gridlock is the most complete and quantitatively sophisticated one we have encountered. Other examples of similar efforts include Gary Cox and Matthew McCubbins *Legislative Leviathan* (Berkeley: University of California Press, 1993); and Nolan McCarty, Keith T. Poole, and Howard Rosenthal, *Polarized America* (Cambridge, MA: The MIT Press, 2006), Chapter 6.

90. The policy differences between the House and Senate in each session were calculated by comparing the percentage of the vote in favor of legislation that was considered in exactly the same form in each chamber (conference reports). Using this information Binder was able to determine the median policy position in each chamber and average them over the number of conference reports that were voted upon. She found that the overall average difference was roughly 7 percent, with the range being 2 to 11 percent over the Congresses covered. See Binder, *Stalemate*, 62–63 and Appendix B.

91. Ibid., 80; Fiorina et al., *Divided Government*, Chapter 6; also McCarty, Poole, and Rosenthal, *Polarized America*, Chapter 6.

92. See Mayhew, *Divided We Govern: 1946–2002*; Van Horn et al., *Politics and Public Policy*, Chapter.5.

93. See Eric Lipton and David Johnston, "Gonzales's Critics See Lasting, Improper Ties to White House," *New York Times*, March 15, 2007, A18.

94. See David Nather, "GOP Quick to Tread Shaky New Ground," *Congressional Quarterly Weekly*, March 21, 2005, 704–706; and David Nather and Seth Stern, "A Classic Creed Supplanted," *Congressional Quarterly Weekly*, March 28, 2005, 778–785.

95. David R. Mayhew, "Actions in the Public Sphere," in *The Legislative Branch*, eds. Quirk and Binder, 63–105; and David R. Mayhew, *America's Congress: Actions in the Public Sphere, James Madison through Newt Gingrich* (New Haven: Yale University Press, 2000).

Chapter 6

1. See Steven J. Rosenstone, Roy L. Behr, and Edward H. Lazarus, *Third Parties in America*, 2nd ed. (Princeton, NJ: Princeton University Press, 1985), 111.

2. See Russell J. Dalton, *Citizen Politics*, 4th ed. (Washington, DC: Congressional Quarterly Press, 2006): 180.

3. See Eric Schickler and Donald Philip Green, "The Stability of Party Identification in Western Democracies: Results from Eight Panel Surveys," *Comparative Political Studies* 30 (August 1997): 450–483.

4. Dalton, *Citizen Politics*, 184.

5. Russell J. Dalton, "The Decline of Party Identifications" in *Parties without Partisans*, eds. Russell J. Dalton and Martin P. Wattenberg (Oxford: Oxford University Press, 2000), 25. For additional evidence on decline of parties, see Ian McAllister,

"Political Parties in Australia: Party Stability in a Utilitarian Society" in *Political Parties in Advanced Industrial Democracies*, eds. Paul Webb., David M. Farrell, and Ian Holliday (Oxford: Oxford University Press, 2002), 388–389; R. Kenneth Carty, "Canada's Nineteenth-Century Parties at the Millennium," in *Political Parties in Advanced Industrial Democracies*, eds. Paul Webb, David M. Farrell, and Ian Holliday, 354–355; and Philip Norton, *The British Polity*, 4th ed. (New York: Longman, 2001), 159–162.

6. Dalton, "The Decline of Party Identifications" in *Parties without Partisans*, 29–30.

7. H. Clarke, D. Sanders, M. Stewart, and P. F. Whiteley (Principal Investigators), "British General Election Study, 2001 (computer file)." Distributed by the UK Data Archive.

8. Russell J. Dalton, "Political Cleavages, Issues, and Electoral Change," in *Comparing Democracies 2: New Challenges in the Study of Elections and Voting*, eds. Lawrence LeDuc, Richard G. Niemi, and Pippa Norris (London: Sage Publications, 2002), 189–209. See also, Ronald Inglehart, "The Changing Structure of Political Cleavages in Western Society," in eds. Russell Dalton, Scott Flanagan, and Paul Beck, *Electoral Change in Advanced Industrial Societies* (Princeton, NJ: Princeton University Press, 1984).

9. Quoted in Dalton, "Political Cleavages, Issues, and Electoral Change," 192.

10. Robert R. Alford, *Party and Society: The Anglo-American Democracies* (Chicago: Rand McNally, 1963), 79–86. Alford uses occupational status to define social class.

11. Dalton, *Citizen Politics*, 153.

12. See Dalton, *Citizen Politics*, 155–156 for a summary of some of these findings.

13. Ibid., 159.

14. Ibid., 161.

15. Alford, *Party and Society*, 2.

16. The data in Table 6.1 were assembled from the following sources: "Australian Government and Politics Database," The University of Western Australia, http://elections.uwa.edu.au/listelections.lasso?skiprecords=0; "British Governments and Elections since 1945," http://www.psr.keele.ac.uk/area/uk/uktable.htm; "Canadian Elections," http://www.sfu.ca/~aheard/elections; and Office of the Clerk of the House of Representatives, "Party Divisions of the House of Representatives (1789 to Present)," http://clerk.house.gov/art_history/house_history/partyDiv.html. All were accessed June 8, 2009.

17. Patrick Weller and Jenny Fleming, "The Commonwealth" in *Australian Politics and Government*, eds. Jeremy Moon and Campbell Sharman (Cambridge: Cambridge University Press, 2003), 23.

18. Ibid.

19. McAllister, "Political Parties in Australia: Party Stability in a Utilitarian Society," 381.

20. Ibid., 386.

21. See, Center for Responsive Politics, OpenSecrets.org, "Political Parties Overview," http://www.opensecrets.org/parties/index.php?cmte=&cycle=2008, accessed June 14, 2009.

22. In a first-past-the-post electoral system, the candidate with a plurality of the total vote wins the election. With more than two candidates in a race, the victorious candidate may win with less than 50 percent of the vote.

23. McAllister, "Political Parties in Australia: Party Stability in a Utilitarian Society," 385–387.

24. Weller and Fleming, "The Commonwealth," 20. Unlike Australia, Britain and Canada have appointed upper chambers.

25. Norton, *The British Polity*, 125.

26. Ibid., 127.

27. Ibid.

28. Ibid., 128.

29. Ibid., 140.

30. Ibid., 123–124.

31. *A Bicentennial Analysis of the American Political Structure* (Committee on the Constitutional System, 1987).

32. See Louis Hartz, *The Liberal Tradition in America* (New York: Harcourt, Brace, and World, 1955); Gad Horowitz, "Conservatism, Liberalism and Socialism in Canada: An Interpretation," *The Canadian Journal of Economics and Political Science* 32 (May 1966): 143–171; and Seymour Martin Lipset, *American Exceptionalism* (New York: W. W. Norton, 1996).

33. Rand Dyck, *Canadian Politics: Critical Approaches*, 5th edition (Toronto: Thomson Nelson, 2008), 243.

34. Ibid., 347.

35. Ibid., 346.

36. Ibid., 368.

37. In the British parliamentary system, the party that wins the second highest number of seats in the legislature becomes the Official Opposition. The Official Opposition forms a shadow government, with its leader and leading members becoming the "shadow cabinet." The party that forms the Official Opposition typically enjoys financial benefits, such as enhanced research support, as well as a more prominent role in proceedings of the legislature.

38. Rhodes Cook, "A New Electorate in the Making." In *Larry J. Sabato's Crystal Ball*, July 17, 2008. http://www.centerforpolitics.org/crystalball/print.php?article=FRC2008071701. Accessed May 15, 2009.

39. See Voting and Democracy Research Center, "Primaries: Open and Closed," http://www.fairvote.org/?page=1801, accessed on June 5, 2009; and CNN Election Center 2008, "Primaries and Caucuses," http://edition.cnn.com/ELECTION/2008/primaries/, accessed June 5, 2009.

40. See California Secretary of State, "Historical Close-of-Registration Statistics for Statewide Special Elections," http://www.sos.ca.gov/elections/ror/ror-pages/15day-stwdsp-09/hist-reg-stats.pdf, accessed on June 17, 2009; and New York Secretary of State, "New York State Voter Enrollment by Congressional District, Party Affiliation, and Status, Voters Registered as of March 1, 2008," http://www.elections.state.ny.us/NYSBOE/enrollment/congress/congress_mar08.pdf. Accessed May 8, 2008.

41. Kenneth R. Mayer, "Sunlight as the Best Disinfectant: Campaign Finance in Australia." Discussion paper for Democratic Audit of Australia. See http://www.democraticaudit.anu.edu.au/papers/20061026mayerfin.pdf, accessed June 5, 2009; Elections Canada, "Annual Allowance for Political Parties," http://www.elections.ca/content.asp?section=loi&document=fs08&dir=gui&lang=e&textonly=false, accessed

on June 8, 2009; and The U.K. Electoral Commission, "Public Funding of Parties," http://www.electoralcommission.org.uk/party-finance/results_and_analysis, accessed June 8, 2009.

42. See Fritz Plasser and Gunda Plasser, *Global Political Campaigning: A Worldwide Analysis of Campaign Professionals and Their Practices*. (Westport, CT: Praeger Publishers, 2002), 181–204; Alan Grant, "Party and Election Finance in Britain and America: A Comparative Analysis," *Parliamentary Affairs* 58, 2005: 71–88; and Elections Canada, "Broadcasting and Other Media Issues," http://www.elections.ca/content.asp?section=pas&document=br&dir=39ge/mer/guide&lang=e&textonly=false, accessed June 8, 2009.

43. Harold Clarke, David Sanders, Marianne Stewart and Paul Whiteley, "Britain: Modeling Campaign Effects in the 2005 British Election Study." Presented at the Conference on Cyberinfrastructure and National Election Studies, Essex, United Kingdom, June 8, 2007; http://www.essex.ac.uk/bes/2007%20nes%20conference/papers.htm, accessed June 8, 2009; Nick Squires, "Rudd beats Howard in Australia election debate," *Daily Telegraph*, October 21, 2007, http://www.telegraph.co.uk/news/worldnews/1566885/Rudd-beats-Howard-in-Australia-election-debate.html, accessed June 8, 2009; and Greg Quinn, "Green Party Candidate Can Participate in Canada's TV Election debates," *Bloomberg Press*, September 10, 2008, http://www.bloomberg.com/apps/news?pid=20601082&sid=aD7Z0bQfDigA&refer=canada, accessed June 8, 2009.

44. To measure major party support in Britain and Canada, we use legislative elections (House of Commons). For Australia, we use the primary (first preference) vote in lower house (House of Representatives) legislative elections. And for the United States, we use presidential elections.

45. See "Andre Blais, Elisabeth Gidengil, Richard Nadeau, and Neil Nevitte, "Measuring Party Identification: Britain, Canada, and the United States." *Political Behavior* 23 (2001): 5–22; and Dalton, *Citizen Politics*, 180 and 199.

46. In the 2000–2005 period, each of the four Anglo-American countries held two elections. We chose this relatively narrow time frame to conduct the empirical analysis in this chapter. We used the following data sources. **Australia:** Clive Bean, David Gow, and Ian McAllister (principal investigators), "Australian Election Study, 2001 (computer file)"; and Clive Bean, Ian McAllister, Rachel Gibson, and David Gow (principal investigators), "Australian Election Study, 2004 (computer file)"; both distributed by the Australian Social Science Data Archive, The Australian National University. **Britain:** Harold Clarke, David Sanders, Marianne Stewart, and Paul Whiteley (principal investigators), "British General Election Study, 2001 (computer file)"; and David Sanders, Paul Whiteley, Harold Clarke, Marianne Stewart, and Kristi Winters (principal investigators), "British General Election Study, 2005 (computer file)"; both distributed by the UK Data Archive, University of Essex. **Canada:** Andre Blais, Elisabeth Gidengil, Richard Nadeau, and Neil Nevitte (principal investigators), "2000 Canadian Election Survey (computer file)"; and Andre Blais, Elisabeth Gidengil, Neil Nevitte, Patrick Fournier, and Joanna Everitt (principal investigators), "2004 Canadian Election Survey (computer file)"; data available at http://ces-eec.mcgill.ca/surveys.html#2004. **United States:** University of Michigan, Center for Political Studies, "American National Election Study, 2000: Pre-and Post-Election Survey [computer

file]." Ann Arbor, MI: Inter-university Consortium for Political and Social Research [distributor], 2008-04-11; and University of Michigan, Center for Political Studies, "American National Election Study, 2004: Pre-and Post-Election Survey [computer file]." Ann Arbor, MI: Inter-university Consortium for Political and Social Research [distributor], 2006-02-17.

47. The historical party identification data come from the following sources. Australia 1967–2001: Ian McAllister, "Political Parties in Australia: Party Stability in a Utilitarian Society;" 388; Britain 1964–2001: Paul Webb, "Political Parties in Britain: Secular Decline or Adaptive Resilience," in *Political Parties in Advanced Industrial Democracies*, eds. Webb, Farrell, and Holliday, 20; Canada 1965–1997: R. Kenneth Carty, "Canada's Nineteenth-Century Parties at the Millennium," 355; USA 1960–2004: University of Michigan, Center for Political Studies. American National Election Studies Cumulative Data File, 1948–2004 [computer file]. Ann Arbor, MI: Inter-university Consortium for Political and Social Research [distributor], 2007-09-25; Party identification figures for the more recent years come from each country's respective general election study, cited in the previous note; and from University of Michigan, Center for Political Studies, "American National Election Study, 2008, [computer file]," data available at http://www.electionstudies.org.

48. In the American case, independents are pure independents (that is, respondents who initially identify as independent and subsequently state that they do not lean toward either party). For the other three countries, independents are those who do not identify as strong, fairly strong, or not very strong partisans.

49. In Australia, Britain (2001), and Canada, these figures are based on those respondents who identify as partisan in the initial question about party identification. Because of the structure of the questions, this includes strong, fairly strong, and not very strong partisans. (There was no strength of partisanship question in the 2005 British Election Study.) For the sake of comparison, we included in the American case strong and weak partisans as well as respondents who initially identify as independent but who say they lean toward one of the parties. If we include respondents who identify as only strong and weak, then the proportion of American partisans who vote for their own party jumps from 88 percent to 94 percent in 2000 and from 90 percent to 93 percent in 2004.

50. See note 5 above, as well as Chapter 2.

51. See Morris P. Fiorina and Matthew S. Levundusky, "Disconnected: The Political Class versus the People." In *Red and Blue Nation? Volume I*, eds. Pietro S. Nivola and David W. Bradt (Washington, DC: Brookings Institution Press, 2006), 55–58.

52. We selected questions where we could find comparable survey questions for the United States and any two other Anglo-American countries.

53. Figure 6.6 contrasts the vote choice of those who worship most frequently and those who never worship.

Chapter 7

1. John M. Broder and Patrick Healy, "Rush of Entries Gives 2008 Race Early Intensity," *New York Times*, January 22, 2007, A1, A14.

2. In an August 2007 PEW poll, 25 percent of the respondents said that they were less likely to support Mormon candidates than others, while only 15 percent expressed this sentiment about Hispanic candidates, 12 percent about women candidates, and 6 percent about Black candidates. See Scott Keeter and Gregory Smith, "Public Opinion About Mormons," *PEW Forum on Religion and Public Life*, December 4, 2007, http://pew research.org/pubs/648/romney-mormon, accessed August 8, 2008.

3. In the spring of 2007, Giuliani was favored by 35 percent of Republicans, McCain had 25 percent, and Romney 10 percent. At this same time, Clinton was the first choice of 40 percent of Democrats, Obama was favored by just less than 30 percent, and Edwards had 20 percent. See the PEW Research Center for the People and the Press, "McCain and Huckabee Catch Up to Giuliani Nationwide," January 2, 2008, http://people-press.org/report/381/mccain-and-huckabee-catch-up-to-giuliani-nation wide, accessed August 8, 2008.

4. See, for example, Stephen J. Wayne, *The Road to the White House 2008*, 8th ed. (Boston: Thomson Wadsworth, 2008), 53.

5. Adam Nagourney, "The Early '08 Fund-Raising Has Clear Blue Tint," *New York Times*, April 5, 2007, A1, A12.

6. In 2004, Kerry raised $234.5 million in the prenomination phase of his campaign, while George Bush raised $268. In 2008, Obama's prenomination total was $326.3 million, Clinton came in at $212.7, McCain's total was $137.7 million, and Romney's was $108.7 million. See Wayne, *The Road to the White House*, 52, and Campaign Finance Institute, "Obama's Small Contributions Surge in June, but McCain's Party-Based Strategy Gave the GOP a Combined Advantage on June 30," Table 2: Presidential Candidates' Fundraising Activity Jan. 1, 2007, through June 30, 2008, http://www.cfinst.org/pr/prRelease.aspx?ReleaseID=195, accessed August 9, 2008.

7. Edwards spent 179 days campaigning in Iowa, compared to 113 for Obama. Romney and Huckabee also spent over 100 days in Iowa. See Marc Santora, "McCain Senses Momentum is Starting to Help Him," *New York Times*, December 8, 2007, A22.

8. Adam Nagourney, "Clinton Resists Aide's Advice to Skip Iowa," *New York Times*, May 24, 2007, A20.

9. All the primary and caucus results reported in this chapter come from the "CQ Politics 2008 Primary Guide," http://innovation.cq.com/primaries, accessed August 9, 2008. See also "Primaries and Caucuses," http://www.washingtonpost.com/wp-srv/politics/interactives/campaign08/primaries.

10. "The 2008 Campaign: Looking to New Hampshire" *New York Times*, January 4, 2008, A15.

11. PEW Research Center, "McCain and Huckabee Catch Up to Giuliani Nationwide," January 2, 2008, http://people-press.org/report/381/, accessed June 16, 2009.

12. Seven polls had Obama ahead going into the New Hampshire primary by margins running from 5 percent to 13 percent. See Adreil Bettelheim, "A Greater Margin for Error," *Congressional Quarterly Weekly*, August 4, 2008, 2112.

13. See, "Low-Income Voters, Women Without Full-Time Jobs, Boosted Clinton," January 10, 2008, http://blogs.cqpolitics.com/polltracker/2008/01, accessed August 10, 2008.

14. According to exit polls conducted among voters in the Super Tuesday Democratic primaries on February 5, 2008, 56 percent of Independents voted for Obama and 36 percent voted for Clinton. Source: National Election Pool, "Super Tuesday Exit Poll," http://www.abcnews.go.com/images/PollingUnit/SuperTuesdayDemCrossSurvey.pdf, accessed June 15, 2009. See also Craig Gilbert, "Advantage for Obama: Independent voters now likely to choose Democratic primary," *Milwaukee Journal-Sentinel*, February 8, 2008, http://www.jsonline.com/news/president/29445104.html, accessed June 15, 2009.

15. Both the Democratic and Republican National Committees threatened to punish Florida and Michigan for holding their primaries early (the delegates from each state were to be reduced by half), but unlike the Democrats, the Republican candidates campaigned actively in both states.

16. See Michael Powell and Michael Cooper, "Dizzying Fall for Ex-Mayor," *New York Times*, January 30, 2008, A1, A17.

17. Delegate figures from Patrick Healy, "In Close Race, Democrats Brace for Long Haul," *New York Times*, February 7, 2008, A1, A21.

18. Elisabeth Bumiller and David D. Kirkpatrick, "Romney Is Out; McCain Emerges as GOP Choice," *New York Times*, February 8, 2008, A1, A16.

19. "With the Results In, How the Delegates Are Shaking Out," *New York Times*, February 7, 2008, A22; James W. Ceaser, Andrew E. Busch, and John J. Pitney, Jr., *Epic Journey: The 2008 Elections and American Politics* (Lanham, MD: Rowman and Littlefield, 2009), 77.

20. See, Elizabeth Bumiller, "Edwards Is Out; Giuliani Quits and Backs McCain," *New York Times*, January 31, 2008, A1, A20.

21. Patrick Healy, "In Close Race, Democrats Brace for the Long Haul," *New York Times*, February 7, 2008, A1, A22.

22. Adam Nagourney and Farhana Hossain, "Old Clinton Ties and Voters' Sway Tug at Delegates," *New York Times*, February 17, 2008, A1, A20.

23. See, Robin Toner and Dalia Sussman, "Obama's Support Grows Broader, New Survey Says," *New York Times*, February 26, 2008, A1, A15.

24. Adam Nagourney and Carl Huse, "Clinton Success Changes Dynamic in Delegate Hunt," *New York Times*, March 6, 2008, A1, A23.

25. Adam Nagourney, "McCain Claims Nomination as Democrats Duel," *New York Times*, March 5, 2008, A1, A17.

26. Katharine Q. Seelye and Julie Bosman, "Ferraro's Obama Remarks Become Issue in Race," *New York Times*, March 12, 2008, A23.

27. Jeff Zeleny, "Obama Urges U.S. to Grapple with Racial Issues," *New York Times*, March 19, 2008, A1, A14.

28. Patrick Healy, "Clinton Seeks to Soften Impact of Misstatement," *New York Times*, March 26, 2008, A17.

29. Jacques Steinberg, "Who Lost the Debate? Many Say the Moderators," *New York Times*, April 18, 2008, A14.

30. Adam Nagourney, "Obama Struggling to Add Support to Key Blocs," *New York Times*, April 24, 2008, A1, A20.

31. Poll Tracker, "Tracking Exit Polls in Pennsylvania," April 22, 2008, http://blogs.cqpolitics.com//polltracker/2008/04/tracking-the-early-exit-polls.html, accessed August 11, 2008.

32. Jeff Zeleny and Adam Nagourney, "An Angry Obama Renounces Ties to Ex-Pastor," *New York Times,* April 30, 2008, A1, A17.

33. Adam Nagourney and Jeff Zeleny, "After Epic Battle, Obama Claims the Nomination," *New York Times,* June 4, 2008, A1, A19.

34. Elisabeth Bumiller, "Is McCain Like Bush? It Depends On the Issue," *New York Times,* June 17, 2008, A1, A14.

35. See, for example, Poll Tracker, "This Week: Obama Always Ahead, but By Varying Margins," June 21, 2008, http://blogs.cqpolitics.com/polltracker/2008/06, accessed August 12, 2008.

36. Polling Report.Com, "President Bush—Overall Job Rating in National Polls," http://www.pollingreport.com/Bush/Job/htm, accessed August 13, 2008.

37. David Leonhardt and Marjorie Connelly, "81% in Poll Say Nation is Headed on the Wrong Track," *New York Times,* April 4, 2008, A1, A18.

38. See The PEW Research Center for The People and The Press, Convention Backgrounder, "A Closer Look at the Parties in 2008," http://pewresearch.org/pubs/933/a-closer-look-at-the-parties-in-2008, accessed August 14, 2008. According to this report, the Republican identification level (strong, weak and leaners) was 38 percent in 2008; Democrats, 51 percent. As shown in Chapter 2, the NES had the partisan identification (all three categories) split at 51 percent (D) and 37 percent (R), which is essentially the same as the 2008 PEW Report.

39. See, Bob Berenson, "With Enemies Like These . . . " in *Congressional Quarterly Weekly,* April 28, 2008, 1086–1106; Adam Nagourney and Carl Hulse, "Election Losses For Republicans Stir Fall Fears, *New York Times,* May 15, 2008, A1, A26.

40. Michael Luo and Jeff Zeleny, "Obama in Shift, Says He'll Reject Public Financing," *New York Times,* June 20, 2008, A1, A18.

41. Campaign Finance Institute, "Obama's Small Contributions Surged in June, but McCain's Party-Based Strategy Gave the GOP a Combined Advantage on June 30," July 22, 2008, http://www.cfinst.org/pr/prRelease.aspx?ReleaseID=201, accessed August 15, 2008. For the entire 2007–2008 election cycle, the Republican National Committee raised and spent about $170 million more than the Democratic National Committee ($428 million to $260 million). See, Center for Responsive Politics, OpenSecrets.org, "Political Parties Overview," http://www.opensecrets.org/parties/index.php?cmte=&cycle=2008, accessed June 14, 2009.

42. See PEW Research Center for the People and the Press, Election 08 Headquarters, "General Election: McCain vs. Obama," http://people-press.org, July 31, 2008, accessed August 15, 2008; or Alan Abramowitz, Thomas E. Mann and Larry J. Sabato, "The Myth of A Toss-Up Election," Sabato's Crystal Ball, Vol. VI, Iss. 28, July 24, 2008, goodpolitics@virginia.edu, http://centerforpolitics.org/crystalball/.

43. See Jim Rutenberg, "Political Freelancers Use Web to Join the Attack," *New York Times,* June 29, 2008, A1, A17.

44. See Jim Rutenberg, "With Commercial McCain Gets Much More Than His Money's Worth," *New York Times*, July 30, 2008, A15; Jim Rutenberg, "McCain Is Trying to Define Obama as Out of Touch," *New York Times*, July 31, 2008, A1, A15.

45. Also in mid-August, Jerome Corsi, who had authored a book attacking John Kerry's military record in Vietnam that was published in the summer of 2004, came out with a book called *Obama Nation*, which portrayed Obama as a leftist radical with "extensive connection to Islam." The book quickly became a best-seller. See Jim Rutenberg and Julie Bosman, "Book Attacking Obama Hopes To Repeat '04 Anti-Kerry Feat," *New York Times*, August 13, 2008, A1, A14.

46. PEW Research Center for the People and the Press, "Presidential Race Draws Even, GOP Base Getting Behind McCain," August 13, 2008, http://people-press.org/report/443/presidential-race-draws-even, accessed September 10, 2008; also, Michael Cooper and Dalia Sussman, "Poll Shows Tight Race With Focus On Economy," *New York Times*, August 21, 2008, A13, A16.

47. See Robin Toner and Adam Nagourney, "McCain Seen as Less Likely To Bring Change, Poll Finds," *New York Times*, September 18, 2008, A1, A22; Ceaser et al., *Epic Journey*, 144; and PEW Center for the People and the Press, "McCain Gains on the Issues, but Stalls as Candidate of Change," September 18, 2008, http://people-press.org/report/450/presidential-race-remains-even, accessed June 9, 2009.

48. "Bush to Hold Meeting on Bailout; First Debate Up in Air," *New York Times*, September 25, 2008, A1.

49. See Patrick Healy, "In a Time Of Crisis, Is Obama Too Cool?," *New York Times*, September 26, 2008.

50. The Bush administration's first bailout bill failed in the House of Representatives in a dramatic vote on September 29. Rank and file members, mostly Republicans, refused to go along with the wishes of their leaders and President Bush. A revised bailout bill, creating the Troubled Asset Relief Program (TARP), did eventually pass on October 3. See Benton Ives and Alan K. Ota, "Financial Rescue Becomes Law," *Congressional Quarterly Weekly*, October 6, 2008, 2692–2699.

51. See Jim Rutenberg, "A Day After McCain and Obama Face Off, a Debate Over Who Won," *New York Times*, September 28, 2008, A21.

52. See, for example, Pew Center for the People and the Press, "Obama Boosts Leadership Image and Regains Lead Over McCain," October 1, 2008, http://people-press.org/report/456/obama-regains-lead, accessed June 9, 2009; Alan I. Abramowitz, "Thirty Days and Counting," Sabato's Crystal Ball, Vol VI, Iss 39, October 9, 2008, goodpolitics@virginia.edu, http://centerforpolitics.org/crystalball/.

53. See Jeff Zeleny and Michael Luo, "Obama Raised a Record $66 million in August," *New York Times*, September 15, 2008, A1, A16; Marion Currinder, "Campaign Finance: Fundraising and Spending in the 2008 Election," in *The Elections of 2008*, ed. Michael Nelson (Washington, DC: CQ Press, 2010), 175; Ceaser et al., *Epic Journey*, 150.

54. Michael Luo, "Obama Hauls in Record $750 million For Campaign, With Plenty Left To Spend," *New York Times*, December 5, 2008, A28.

55. See David Carr, "A Campaign Not Filtered By the Press," *New York Times*, August 25, 2008, C1, C6.

56. In 2004, 527 groups spent $426 million in federal elections, this fell to around $200 million in 2008. Part of the reason 527 groups were less vigorous in 2008 is that the Federal Election Commission placed new restrictions on their fundraising ability. The restrictions had the effect of limiting the amount individuals could contribute to these groups to $5,000 (same as PACs) if the groups were going to be involved in political activities directed at candidates. See Currinder, "Campaign Finance: Fundraising and Spending in the 2008 Election," 164–176.

57. See Jonathan Allen, "The Nation as Community: Organizing Obama's Win," *Congressional Quarterly Weekly*, November 10, 2008, 2970–2975; Ceaser et al., *Epic Journey*, 153–156.

58. All of the figures presented in this paragraph come from the 2008 exit polls. See http://edition.cnn.com/ELECTION/2008/results/polls/#val=USP00p1, accessed June 15, 2009.

59. These figures also come from the 2008 exit polls.

60. These figures on perceptions of the parties are from the 2008 *American National Election Study*.

61. See Gary C. Jacobson, "Congress: The Second Democratic Wave," *The Elections of 2008*, ed. Nelson, 101.

62. Gregg Giroux, *Congressional Quarterly Weekly*, Nov. 10, 2008, 314–318.

63. Figures from the Campaign Finance Institute, "A First Look at Money in the House and Senate Elections," http://wwwcfinst.org/pr/prRelease.aspx?ReleaseID=215; cited in Gary C. Jacobson, "Congress: The Second Democratic Wave," *The Elections of 2008*, ed. Nelson, 107.

64. Figures from OpenSecrets.org, Center for Responsive Politics, "Political Parties Overview," http://opensecrets.org/parties/index.php?cmte=&cycle=2008, accessed June 14, 2009.

65. Jacobson, "Congress: The Second Democratic Wave," 101–109.

66. Ibid., 107.

67. Opensecrets.org, "Political Parties Overview."

68. Currinder, Campaign Finance: Fundraising and Spending in the 2008 Election," 181–182.

69. Party identifiers include independents who lean to one of the parties. The 2008 exit poll figures for partisan loyalty are almost identical to the 2008 NES figures. According to the exit polls, 89 percent of Democrats and 90 percent of Republicans supported their party's candidate. See http://edition.cnn.com/ELECTION/2008/results/polls/#val=USP00p1, accessed June 15, 2009.

70. The data in Figure 7.1 are based on percentage of the two-party vote.

71. See James E. Campbell, "Polarization Runs Deep, Even by Yesterday's Standards," in *Red and Blue Nation? Volume One*, eds. Pietro S. Nivola and David W. Brady (Washington, DC: The Brookings Institution Press, 2006), 153.

72. See, for example, Thomas Schaller, "Rush Limbaugh is the leader of the Republican party," *Salon*, March 1, 2009, http://www.salon.com/news/feature/2009/03/01/limbaugh, accessed June 16, 2009. See also Paul Farhi, "No rush to measure Limbaugh's ratings," *Los Angeles Times*, March 9, 2009, http://articles.latimes.com/2009/mar/09/entertainment/et-limbaugh9, accessed June 16, 2009.

73. "Key News Audiences Now Blend Online and Traditional Sources," The Pew Research Center for the People and the Press, August 17, 2008, http://people-press.org/report/?pageid=1353, accessed June 16, 2009.

74. "The Color of News: How Different Media Have Covered the General Election," Pew Research Center's Project for Excellence in Journalism, http://www.journalism.org/node/13436, accessed June 16, 2009.

75. The FEC did get tougher on 527s in the 2007–2008 election cycle; see note 56 above.

76. See Campaign Finance Institute, "Soft Money Political Spending by 501(c) Nonprofits Tripled in 2008 Election," http://wwwcfinst.org/pr/prRelease.aspx?Release ID=221, accessed June 14, 2009.

77. Samuel Kernell, Gary C. Jacobson, and Thad Kousser, *The Logic of American Politics*, 4th ed. (Washington, DC: CQ Press, 2008), 538.

78. Campaign Finance Institute, "Table 1: 501(c) Groups' Spending at least $200,000 on the Federal Elections in the 2008 Cycle," http://www.cfinst.org/interest_groups/pdf/np527/527_08_24M_Table1.pdf, accessed June 16, 2009; Campaign Finance Institute, "Soft Money Political Spending by 501(c) Nonprofits Tripled in 2008 Election."

79. See Center for Media and Democracy, "Think tanks," http://www.sourcewatch.org/index.php?title=Think_tanks accessed on June 16, 2009; see also David Teather, "Liberals Pledge Millions to Revive U.S. Left," *The Guardian*, August 8, 2005, http://www.guardian.co.uk/world/2005/aug/08/usa.davidteather accessed June 16, 2009.

80. See Ceaser et al., *Epic Journey*, 15–18.

81. Peter Baker, "A Milestone in History," *New York Times,* January 21, 2009, A1, P2.

82. Jackie Calmes and Carl Hulse, "Obama, Visiting G.O.P. Lawmakers, Is Open to Some Compromise on Stimulus," *New York Times,* January 28, 2009, A17.

83. See Joseph J. Schatz and Richard Ruben, "House Democrats Pass Stimulus," *Congressional Quarterly Weekly*, February 2, 2009, 254–256.

84. The Senate compromise not only included more tax cuts, but also less spending on education and health care than the bill the House passed. See, Joseph J. Schatz, "Senate Scales Back Its Stimulus," *Congressional Quarterly Weekly*, February 9, 2009, 306–308.

85. The final version split the stimulus between $212 billion in tax cuts and $575 billion in new spending. See Joseph J. Schatz and David Clarke, "Congress Clear Stimulus Package," *Congressional Quarterly Weekly*, February 16, 2009, 352–356.86. John Cranford, "This Change Isn't Very Hepful," *Congressional Quarterly Weekly*, February 16, 2009, 335.

87. See Karoun Demirjian and Lydia Gensheimer, "House Clears Time-to-File Extension for Pay Discrimination Lawsuits," *Congressional Quarterly Weekly*, February 2, 2009, 259; Drew Armstrong, "House Set to Clear SCHIP Measure," *Congressional Quarterly Weekly*, February 2, 2009, 257. The other major Democratic holdover from the 110th Congress (see first section of Chapter 5) was ending the Bush ban on government-sponsored stem cell research. Obama did this by executive order in early March, 2009.

88. See David Clarke and Joseph J. Schatz, "Big Plans, Big Costs, Big Deficits," *Congressional Quarterly Weekly*, March 2, 2009, 472–475.

89. David Clarke and Paul M. Krawzak, "Chambers Adopt Budget Resolutions," *Congressional Quarterly Weekly,* April 6, 2009, 781.

90. David Clarke, "Budget Moves on Hard Party Lines," *Congressional Quarterly Weekly*, May 4, 2009, 1036–1037.

91. See Adriel Bettelheim, "Cautious Cheerleading," *Congressional Quarterly Weekly*, May 25, 2009, 1204–1211.

92. Phil Mattingly, "Credit Card Restriction Enacted," *Congressional Quarterly Weekly*, May 25, 2009, 1214–1215.

93. David Clarke, "Obama Signs Measure that Eases Eligibility for Mortgage Aid," *Congressional Quarterly Weekly*, May 25, 2009, 1220.

94. Robert Pear, "Health Care's Early Pledges," *New York Times*, May 12, 2009, A1, A16.

95. Robert Pear, "Health Care Leaders Say Obama Overstated Their Promise to Control Costs," *New York Times*, May 15, 2009, A18.

96. Ariel Bettelheim, Underwriting the Overhaul," *Congressional Quarterly Weekly*, June 15, 2009, 1356–1358.

97. Robert Pear and Jackie Calmes, "Obama Advances His Case: Health's Bill's Cost Challenged," *New York Times*, June 16, 2009, A1, A13.

98. Sheryl Gay Stolberg and Robert Pear, "Obama Makes Care Case With the People," *New York Times*, June 12, 2009, A15.

99. Sheryl Gay Stolberg and Robert Pear, "Obama Open to Reigning in Medical Suits," *New York Times,* June 15, 2009, A1, A14; Sheryl Gay Stolberg, "Much Riding on Health Care Fight," *New York Times*, July 22, 2009, A13

100. Robert Pear, "Democrats to Develop Plan to Sell Health Care," *New York Times,* May 14, 2009, A14.

101. Robert Pear and David M. Herszenhorn, "As Bombast Escalates, a Primer on the Details of the Health Care Overhaul," *New York Times*, August 10, 2009, A8, A10; Jim Rutenberg and Jackie Calmes, "A New Playbook in Health Care Debate," *New York Times*, August 11, 2009, A1, A11.

102. Adam Nagourney and Megan Thee-Brenan, "New Poll Finds Growing Unease on Health Plan," *New York Times*, July 30, 2009, A1, A17; Katharine Q. Seelye, "Competing Ads on Health Care Plan Swamp Airwaves," *New York Times*, August 16, 2009, A1, A22.

103. Robert Pear and David M. Herszenhorn, "Senator Unveils Bill to Overhaul U.S. Health Care," *New York Times*, September 17, 2009, A1, A21.

104. Robert Pear and David Herszenhorn, "A Senate Health Bill Gains with One Republican Vote," *New York Times*, October 14, 2009, A1, A18.

105. Sheryl Gay Stolberg and Jeff Zeleny, "Obama, Armed with Details, Challenges Congress," *New York Times*, September 10, 2009, A1, A18.

Index

Abortion, 55, 148
  and Clinton, 94
  in comparative context of other countries, 166–168
  and cultural divisions and war, 72–78, 79, 96–97, 98
  and health care, 192
  and images of parties, 21, 22, 23, 71, 72
  and multivariate analysis of voting behavior, 80, 81–82, 90
  and "supporting casts" of parties, 186
  and 2008 election, 172, 177
Abramoff, Jack, 101
Abramowitz, Alan, 70
Adams, John, 122
Affirmative action, 137
Afghanistan, 121, 178
Age, 49, 53–55, 57, 58, 61, 79, 87
AIG, 179
Aldrich, Nelson, 124
Alford Index, 147
Alito, Samuel, 135
Allen, George, 105
The Almanac of American Politics, 136
American Enterprise Institute, 188
American Medical Association, 191
American Political Science Association (APSA), 9–10

The American Voter, 82
Anderson, John, 30
Apathy, 34, 82
Armey, Richard, 93–94
Australia, 148, 149–151, 156, 158, 159, 160, 161, 162, 163, 164, 165, 166, 167, 168
Australian ballot, 7
Australian Labor Party (ALP), 149, 150, 151
Austria, 146, 148, 149

Baby boom generation, 24, 55
Bailouts, 179, 180, 191
Baucus, Max, 191, 192, 193
Bear Stearns, 179
Belgium, 148
Bernanke, Ben, 179
Biden, Joseph, 171, 179, 180
Binder, Sarah, 141–142
Bipartisan Campaign Reform Act (BCRA), 187
Blair, Tony, 152
Bloc Québécois (BQ) Party (Canadian), 150, 155, 156
Boehner, John, 188
Bork, Robert, 15
British General Election Study (2001), 147
Brownback, Sam, 172
Bryan, William Jennings, 7
Buchanan, Patrick, 1–2

229

Budget
    and Clinton, 94, 134
    and "Contract with America," 96, 119–120
    and George H. W. Bush, 132, 133
    and Obama, 189–190, 191
    and "pay as you go," 120
    and Reagan, 15, 131
    and Republicans, 21, 190
    Resolution, 190
Budget and Enforcement Act (1990), 131
Bull Moose Party, 8
Burns, Conrad, 105
Bush, George H. W., 2
    and budget, 132, 133
    and 1988 election, 27, 110
    and 1992 election, 94
Bush, George W., 1
    and approval ratings, 101, 177, 181
    and bailouts, 179
    and Congress, 120, 134, 135–136, 142, 189
    and gay marriage, 103
    and Iraq, 101–102, 120–121, 142, 182
    and September 11, 134
    and TARP program, 190
    and 2008 election, 46, 172, 177, 179, 180, 181
    and 2004 election, 52, 67, 70, 81, 103, 172–173, 181
    and 2007 successes, 121
    and 2006 election, 100–101, 104
    and 2002 election, 114
    and white men, 65

Calhoun, John C., 123
Canada, 146, 148, 149, 150, 153–156, 158, 159, 160, 161, 162, 163, 164, 165, 167, 168
Cannon, Joseph "Uncle Joe," 123, 124, 125, 131
Carter, Jimmy, 133, 183
Cass, Lewis, 5
Center for American Progress, 188
Center for Media and Democracy, 188
Cheney, Richard, 179
Christian Coalition, 96
Christian-Democratic Party (German and Italian), 148
Civil rights, 24, 70, 71, 136, 137, 148, 186
Civil War, U.S., 5, 6, 9, 122, 123
Class-action litigation bills, 135
Clausen, Aage, 136
Clay, Henry, 5, 122
Cleveland, Grover, 6
Climate change, 177, 189
Clinton, Bill
    and approval ratings, 101
    and budget, 134
    and Congress, 133
    and "Contract with America," 119–120
    and culture war, 1–2
    and fund-raising, 14
    and Gingrich, 132, 134
    and health care, 130, 190
    and impeachment, 33
    and "New Democrats," 152
    and 1994 election, 94, 96, 114
    and 1996 election, 120
    and 1992 election, 30, 94, 110
    and 2008 election, 175–176, 179
Clinton, Hillary
    and culture war, 1–2
    and 2008 election, 171, 172, 173, 174–175, 176, 177, 179, 181
CNN, 186
Coelho, Tony, 14
Coleman, Norm, 182

Collins, Susan, 188
Conflict
    and extremism, 46
    and parties, 2–3, 17, 47
    and Schattschneider, 2–3
Congress
    and approval ratings, 101, 121
    big swings in elections for, 109–110
    and centralized versus decentralized organization, 128, 131–132
    and committees, 122, 124–125, 126, 127–128, 129, 130, 131, 132, 133
    and debate and filibusters, 123, 124, 128, 133, 135
    in early and mid-twentieth century, 8, 10–11, 123–125
    in eighteenth and nineteenth centuries, 6, 121–124
    evolving role of partisanship in, 121–125
    explaining elections for, 107–109
    and first-past-the-post method of voting for, 151
    and health care, 190, 191–193
    and investigations and oversight, 142, 143
    and Iraq, 120–121
    and legislative supremacy, 125
    modern, 125–126, 131
    and 1994 election, 93–100
    and parties and party leaders, 4, 15, 122, 123, 124–125, 126–133, 136–143
    and partisan loyalty in elections for, 110–117, 183
    and polarization's effect on legislative process, 138, 141–143
    and presidents, 133–136, 143
    and redistricting, 110
    and reelection, 129, 182
    and scandals, 94–95, 101, 102, 104
    and symbolism, 142, 143
    "textbook," 125–126, 129
    and 2008 election, 182–183
    and 2006 election, 93, 100–107, 171
    voting trends in, 136–138, 139, 140, 143, 189
    See also Democratic Party: and Congress; Republican Party: and Congress
Congress: The Electoral Connection (Mayhew), 129
Congressional Quarterly, 101, 102, 138, 189
Conservative coalition, 9
Conservative Party (British), 147, 148, 150, 151–152, 164
Conservative Party (Canadian), 150, 154, 155, 156
"The Contract with America," 93–94, 96, 110, 119–120, 132
Cook, Charles, 102
Coolidge, Calvin, 8
Corker, Bob, 104, 105
Countdown with Keith Olbermann, 186
Couric, Katie, 180
Credit card legislation, 191
Cultural divisions and war
    abortion as best measure of divide, 74–78, 79
    defining and measuring the divide, 72, 74
    and Democratic Party, 71
    and Fiorina, 2, 71, 78
    and gay marriage, 70
    and Hunter, 1–2
    and 1994 election and revolution, 96–97
    and 1960s, 70–71
    and noncultural issues, 75, 76–78, 79

and partisanship, 1–2, 71, 72–74, 75, 78, 79
and the press, 70, 71
and 2000 and 2004 elections, 70
and voting, 72–74, 75, 79
Cultural issues
and Clinton, 1–2, 94
in comparative context of other countries, 165–168
and support for Republicans, 69, 71–74
and voting, 72–74, 75, 82, 165–168
and working class, 63, 71–72
See also particular cultural issues
Culture War? The Myth of a Polarized America (Fiorina et al.), 2, 45
Cunningham, Randy "Duke," 101

Dalton, Russell, 146–147, 148
Dangerfield, Rodney, 26
Daschle, Tom, 132, 134
Dean, Howard, 172
Death penalty, 78, 79
Debates, campaign, 46, 157, 158, 173, 176, 179–180
DeLay, Tom, 101, 134, 135
Democracy Alliance, 188
Democratic Congressional Campaign Committee (DCCC), 14, 103, 127, 182–183
Democratic National Committee (DNC), 14, 103, 173, 176, 178
Democratic Party
composition of, 49–62, 64–69, 79
and Congress, 4, 8, 10–11, 15–16, 24, 94, 95, 97, 98, 101, 102, 103, 104–106, 109, 110–115, 120, 121, 123, 124, 125, 126–127, 128–131, 132, 133, 134, 135, 137–138, 139, 140, 142, 177, 182–183, 189, 190, 191–193

and conservative defections, 28
and "Contract with America," 119
and cultural divisions, 71
and dominance of two-party system, 157
and fund-raising, 14, 103, 104, 172, 173, 178, 180, 182–183
and Great Society, 10–11
and health care, 191–193
images of, 16, 19–23, 71, 75, 79, 82, 164
as integrative agent, 3–4
and issues and ideology, 34–35, 38–39, 49, 148, 163, 184–185, 186
and Jefferson, 5
and mobilizing voters, 150
and negative campaign ads, 19, 104
and New Deal, 8–9, 10, 24
and New Directions for America, 120
number of legislative elections won since 1945, 150
and opinion leaders, 38–44
and party identification, 24–30
and Populist Movement, 7
and post–Chicago 1968 reforms, 12
and speeches, 19
and "supporting cast," 186
and think tanks, 188
and 2008 election, 171, 172, 173, 174–175, 176, 177, 179, 182–183
Democratic Senate Campaign Committee (DSCC), 14, 103, 183
Disraeli, Benjamin, 152
Dodd, Christopher, 171
Dole, Robert, 95, 119, 133

Economic stimulus legislation, 188–189, 190, 191

Education
  and multivariate analysis of voting behavior, 80, 90
  and party salience, 145, 146–147
  and political beliefs and orientation, 49, 55, 56, 57, 58, 61, 88, 174, 176
Edwards, John, 171, 172, 173, 174, 175
Eisenhower, Dwight, 9, 21, 109
Elections (by time period and year)
  1800s, 5–8, 109, 124
  early 1900s, 8, 125
  mid-1900s, 9, 10, 11, 12, 13, 27, 28, 36, 47, 109
  1968, 11, 12, 28, 30, 47, 48, 145, 157
  1972, 11, 12, 28, 47, 110
  1974, 109
  1976, 13, 47, 183, 184
  1980, 30, 47, 48, 110
  1984, 30, 47, 82
  1988, 27, 47, 133
  1990, 100, 110
  1992, 30, 47, 48, 94, 95, 98, 100, 110
  1994, 93–100, 101, 109, 110, 113, 114, 115
  1996, 47, 48, 120
  1998, 113, 114, 115
  2000, 16, 28, 30, 46, 47, 48, 65, 70, 81, 101, 103, 162, 163, 164, 165, 166, 167, 168, 174, 181
  2002, 101, 103, 105, 106, 107, 113, 114, 115
  2004, 16, 28, 31, 33, 36–37, 46, 47, 52, 55, 65, 67, 70, 72, 81, 101, 103, 105, 107, 135, 162, 163, 164, 165, 166, 167, 168, 172, 173, 180, 181, 185, 187
  2006, 93, 100–107, 109, 111–112, 113, 114, 115, 134, 142, 171
  2008, 28, 31, 46, 47, 52, 65, 70, 81, 82, 106, 109, 111, 112, 114, 171–188
Elections (general)
  big swings in congressional, 109–110
  "candidate-centered" versus "party-centered," 13
  explaining congressional, 107–109
  and financing, 12–15, 101, 103, 104, 108, 127, 157, 158, 168, 172–173, 177–178, 180, 182–183, 187
  and incumbents, 93, 95, 105, 107–108, 109, 110, 111–112, 114, 129
  and Jacksonian democracy, 5
  and name recognition, 108
  in other countries, 146, 149, 150–151, 152, 153, 154, 158, 159, 160–161, 162, 163, 164, 165, 166, 167, 168
  perceptions of rigging, 103
  and post–Chicago 1968 reforms, 12
  and Progressive Movement reforms, 7
  and proportional representation, 151
  and surge and decline theory, 109–110
  and two-party system, 157–158
  and voter registration, 157
  winner-take-all, 17
  See also Parties: and elections; Voting
Electoral College, 6, 10, 70, 157, 168, 181
Elementary and Secondary Education Act (ESEA), 11
Emanuel, Rahm, 103, 127
Energy bills, 120, 121, 130, 135
Enzi, Mike, 192

Fannie Mae, 179
Fazio, Vic, 14
Federal Deposit Insurance Company (FDIC), 191
Federal Election Campaign Act (FECA), 12–13, 14
Federal Election Commission (FEC), 187
Federal Reserve Act (1913), 125
Federal Trade Commission, 125
Federalist Party, 5, 154
Feingold, Russ, 101, 103
Ferraro, Geraldine, 176
Fifteenth amendment, 6
Finland, 148
Fiorina, Morris, 2, 45, 46, 71, 78
501(c) groups, 187–188
527 groups, 180, 187–188
Foley, Mark, 102
Food Stamps, 11
Ford, Gerald, 109, 183
Ford, Harold E., Jr., 104
Fourteenth amendment, 6
Fox News, 186
France, 146, 147, 148, 149
Frank, Thomas, 71–72
Franken, Al, 138, 182
Freddie Mac, 179
Free Soil Party, 6
Freedom's Watch, 187
Frist, Bill, 97, 133, 135
Fund-raising
    See Democratic Party: and fund-raising; Elections (general): and financing: Parties: and financing; Hard money; Political Action Committees (PACs); Republican Party: and fund-raising; Soft money

Garfield, James, 6
Gays
    attitudes toward, 72–74
    and Foley, 102
    marriage and rights, 22, 70, 71, 78, 79, 103, 104, 172
    in military, 79, 94
Gender
    as issue, 34, 35, 40, 41, 42, 43, 44, 147
    and multivariate analysis of voting behavior, 80, 90
    and political beliefs and orientation, 49, 50, 52, 57, 58, 60, 64–66, 67, 69, 78–79, 85, 98, 100, 105, 106
    and 2008 election, 172, 174, 176, 181
Germany, 146, 147, 148, 178
Gibson, Charles, 176
Gingrich, Newt
    and House organization, 132, 134
    and 1995 legislative session, 119
    and 1994 election and revolution, 33, 93–94, 95, 96, 110, 120, 134
    and Wright, 16
Giuliani, Rudolph, 172, 173, 174, 179
Goldwater, Barry, 10, 28
Gore, Al, 81
Grassley, Charles, 192
Gravel, Mike, 171
Great Britain, 10, 145, 146, 147, 148, 149, 150, 151–153, 156, 158, 159, 160, 161, 162, 163, 164–165, 166, 167, 168
Great Depression, 8, 24, 109, 188
Great Society, 10–11, 70, 131, 133, 136
Green parties, 150, 163
Gridlock, 94, 119, 141–142
Gulf War, 94
Gun control, 3, 79, 94, 186

Hamilton, Alexander, 5, 6, 154
Hard money, 13–14, 103

Harding, Warren, 8
Harrison, Benjamin, 6, 109
Harrison, William Henry, 5
Hastert, Dennis, 102, 132, 134, 135
Hayes, Rutherford B., 6
Head Start, 11
Health care, 34, 35, 40, 41, 42, 52, 76, 77, 78, 94, 130, 154, 172, 176, 177, 189, 190, 191–193
Heritage Foundation, 188
Hilton, Paris, 178
Home foreclosure bill, 191
Homeland Security, Department of, 134
Hoover, Herbert, 8
House Democratic Caucus, 125, 126–127, 128–129, 130
House of Representatives
  evolution of, 119, 121–125
  and party machinery, 126–128
  and party resurgence, 128–133
  and polarization's effect on legislative process, 141, 142
  and presidency, 134, 135, 136
  and reelection, 129
  and textbook Congress, 125–126, 129
  voting trends in, 137–138, 139
House Rules Committee, 127–128, 129, 130, 132
House Ways and Means Committee, 129, 192
Huckabee, Mike, 172, 173, 174, 175, 179
Hunter, Duncan, 172
Hunter, James Davison, 1–2
Hurricane Katrina, 100–101

Ideology
  and images of parties, 22, 23
  and moderates, 184
  and opinion leaders, 38–44
  and parties in other countries, 145, 148, 153, 154, 162–163, 164, 168, 184
  partisan divide over, 33–36, 49, 184–185, 186
  and party choices, 79
  and social, economic, and demographic factors, 49
  and think tanks, 188
  and voting, 79–80, 80–81, 82, 90
  and voting trends in Congress, 136–138, 139, 140
Ignorance, 34, 36, 82
Income and social class
  defining class, 63–64
  and multivariate analysis of voting behavior, 80, 81, 82, 90
  in other countries, 62, 63, 147, 154, 155, 164–165
  and parties in other countries compared to U.S. parties, 62, 147, 155, 163–165
  and party systems, 147
  and political beliefs and orientation, 49, 50, 51, 57, 58, 59, 62–69, 72, 79, 83, 106, 107, 147, 164–165, 168, 174, 176
Independents, 189
  appeal and disadvantages of being one, 26–27
  increase in, 13, 17, 27
  leaners and pure, 26, 27, 28, 31
  and 1990–1994 congressional elections, 100
  in other countries compared to United States, 158, 159, 160, 161, 168
  and party identification, 24–30
  and Republican incumbents in Congress, 110, 111, 112
  and significant third party candidates, 30

and social, economic, and demographic variables, 55, 57
and surge and decline theory of midterm elections, 109
and 2008 election, 174, 177, 181, 182, 183, 184
and 2006 election, 104, 105, 106, 109
Institute for Policy Studies, 188
Interest groups, 12, 13, 141, 186–188, 192
Internet, 172
Iraq, 100, 101–102, 104, 120–121, 134, 135, 142, 172, 173, 177, 182
Israel, 101, 178
Issues
 and 527 groups, 187
 new, 145, 147
 and 1994 and 2006 elections, 93, 104
 and opinion leaders, 38–44
 partisan divide over, 33–36, 49
 See also particular issues
Italy, 146, 148, 149

Jackson, Andrew, 5, 12
Jackson, Jesse, 175–176
Jacobson, Gary, 96, 107, 108
Jefferson, Thomas, 5, 9, 12
Jeffords, James, 134
Johnson, Lyndon, 10–11, 28, 131, 133

Kennedy, Caroline, 175
Kennedy, Edward, 134, 138, 175, 179, 182
Kennedy, John F., 10, 27, 178
Kernell, Samuel, 107
Kerry, John, 67, 70, 81, 135, 173, 181
King, Martin Luther, Jr., 179
Kucinich, Dennis, 171, 172
Kyl, John, 105

Labor Party (Australian), 150, 162
Labor unions, 3, 9, 24, 62, 147, 149, 152, 155, 157, 186, 187
Labour Party (British), 147, 148, 150, 151, 152, 153, 164, 165
LaFollette-Monroney Committee, 126
Landmark laws, 141
Lazarsfeld, Paul, 36
Lebanon, 101
Legislative Reorganization Act (1946), 126
Lehman Brothers, 179
Liberal Democrats Party (British), 146, 150, 153
Liberal Party (Australian), 149–150, 162
Liberal Party (British), 151, 152–153
Liberal Party (Canadian), 150, 153–154, 155, 156
Lieberman, Joe, 105, 182
Lilly Ledbetter Fair Pay Act, 189
Limbaugh, Rush, 96, 185
Lincoln, Abraham, 6, 136
Lipset, Seymour Martin, 147
Lobbying rules, 120, 121
Lott, Trent, 133
Luntz, Frank, 192

Madison, James, 5
Marital status, 105, 106–107, 181
Mayhew, David, 129, 141
McCain, John, 46, 52, 65, 81, 101, 103, 171, 172, 173, 174, 175, 177–181, 183, 184, 186, 191
McGovern, George, 12, 28
McKinley, William, 8
Media, 145, 147, 157
Medicare and Medicaid, 11, 120, 135
Mehlman, Ken, 104
Middle East, 101
Minimum wage, 120, 121

Mitchell, George, 132, 133
Monroe, James, 5
MoveOn.org, 187
MSNBC, 186
Muhlenburg, Frederick, 122

Nader, Ralph, 30
National Election Study (NES), 20–23, 24, 27, 30, 31, 36, 39, 41, 44, 52, 53, 63, 74, 75, 125, 182, 183
National Front Party (French), 146
National Party (Australian), 149–150
National Republican Congressional Committee (NRCC), 14, 182
National Republican Senatorial Committee (NRSC), 14, 183
National Rifle Association (NRA), 96
Nelson, Ben, 188
Netherlands, 148
New Deal, 8–9, 10, 24, 55, 82, 125, 133, 136
New Deal coalition, 9, 16, 17
New Democratic Party (NDP) (Canadian), 150, 155, 156, 163
New Freedom program, 125
New York Times, 101, 102, 104, 141
New Zealand, 146
Nineteenth amendment, 7
Nixon, Richard, 11, 12, 21, 30, 110
No Child Left Behind, 134
North American Free Trade Agreement (NAFTA), 94
Norway, 148

Obama, Barack, 1, 127
   administration of, 188–193
   and bills in Congress, 188–189, 190–191
   and budget, 189–190, 191
   and health care, 189, 190, 191–193

and 2008 election, 28, 46, 70, 81, 171, 172, 173, 174–181, 183, 184, 186, 188
and 2010 election, 114
Obama, Michelle, 179
One Nation Party (Australian), 150, 163
Opinion leaders
   and the apathetic and ignorant, 34, 36
   identifying, 36–39, 44–45
   number of, 44–45
   and polarization, 39–44, 45–46
   See also Voting: and opinion leaders
The O'Reilly Factor, 186

Palin, Sarah, 179, 180, 192
Pannetta, Leon, 14
Parties
   and APSA report, 9–10
   composition of, 49–62, 64–69, 78–79
   and conflict, 2–3
   and Congress, 4, 15, 122, 123, 124–125, 126–133, 136–143
   and "dealignment," 17, 147
   decline of, 11–13, 16, 30–31, 34, 44, 145, 146–147, 161, 169
   distrust of, 26
   and elections, 4, 8, 12, 14–15, 16, 103–104, 108–109, 127
   in Europe and other countries, 62, 145, 146–147, 148–156
   in Europe and other countries: compared to United States, 156–169
   and financing, 12–15, 103–104, 108, 127, 150, 172, 177–178, 182–183, 187
   functions of, 3–4
   history of, 4–17
   and images, 16, 19–23, 36, 37, 38, 39, 40, 41, 44, 45, 48, 49, 71, 72, 75, 76, 78, 79, 82, 165

and machines, 6, 7, 8, 15
and membership, 26, 157
and mobilizing voters, 150
and negative campaign ads, 19, 104
and neutrality, 31, 32
new, 146, 158
and 1994 and 2006 elections, 93
overview of systems in Anglo-American democracies, 148–156
as political compasses, 33, 80
and preferential voting, 151
resurgence of, 14–17, 31–33, 34, 93, 128–133, 145, 161, 168, 169, 171
rising dissatisfaction with, 147
and strategic choice model, 108–109
and "supporting casts," 185–187
systems of, 4–17
"weak" versus "strong," 10, 11–12, 13, 169
See also Democratic Party; Partisanship; Party differences; Party identification; Republican Party; Voting: and parties
Partisanship
and age, 53–55, 57, 61
and cultural divisions, 72–74, 75, 78, 79
defining, 24, 26
degrees of, 26
and education, 55, 57, 61
in Europe and other countries, 145, 146, 147, 148, 149
in Europe and other countries: compared to United States, 156–169
evolving role in Congress of, 121–125
and gender, 50, 57, 60, 64–66, 67, 69
and grinding of institutional gears and gridlock, 119–120, 141, 142
and ideology, 33–36, 184–185
and income and social class, 50, 57, 59, 62–69
and issues, 33–36
and legislative outcomes, 119
and loyalty, 82, 110–117, 145–146, 162, 183, 184
measuring, 24–26, 31, 32
and opinion leaders, 38, 39, 43, 44, 45
and party composition, 50, 78–79
and polarization, 1–2, 33, 35, 45, 74, 136–138, 139, 140, 141, 161–163, 165, 167, 169, 171, 183
and punditry, 185–186
and race, 52, 53, 57, 60, 69
and region, 50, 57, 59, 66–68
and religion, 55, 57, 62
renewal of, 31–33, 93, 113
and strategic choice model, 108–109
trends in, 27
and utility, 24
and voter registration, 157
and voting behavior, 27–30, 32, 33, 34, 46, 47, 49, 65–69, 80, 82, 104, 110–117, 146, 160–161, 162, 168, 169, 181
and voting trends in Congress, 136–138, 139, 140
See also Party identification
Party differences
and images, 20, 22, 23, 163–164
in 1972–1984, 80
and opinion leaders, 38, 39, 40, 41, 46
and perceptions in other countries, 162–163
public's recognition of, 2, 3, 16, 31, 47, 49, 80–81, 168, 169, 171, 183–184
and 2008 election, 171, 183–184

and voting, 4, 16, 17, 31, 47, 49, 80–81, 82
Wallace quote on, 145
Party identification
and age, 54, 57, 58, 87
and cultural divisions, 72–74, 75
defining, 24, 26
and education, 56, 57, 58, 88
in Europe and other countries, 145–146, 158, 160, 162–163, 169
and gender, 52, 57, 58, 66, 85
and ideology, 184–185, 186
and income and social class, 51, 57, 58, 66, 68, 69, 83
and loyalty, 145–146, 183, 184
measuring, 24–26
and opinion leaders, 39
and party composition, 50
and party images, 79
and race, 52–53, 57, 58, 86
and region, 51, 57, 58, 68, 84
and religion, 56, 57, 58, 89, 147–148
stability of, 146
trends in, 27
and voting behavior, 27–30, 65–69, 79, 80–81, 82, 90, 110–117, 146, 160–161, 169
See also Partisanship
Patriot Act, 134, 135
Paul, Ron, 172, 174
Paulson, Henry, 179
Pelosi, Nancy, 120, 132, 134, 171
Perot, Ross, 28, 30, 94
Phillips, Kevin, 70
Plaid Cymru Party (British), 150, 153
Playboy Company, 104
Polarization
in comparative context of other countries, 145, 148, 162–163, 164, 165, 167, 169
and conflict, 3

and cultural divisions, 1–2, 70, 72, 74, 78, 79
and opinion leaders, 39–44, 45–46
partisan, 1–2, 33, 35, 45, 74, 82, 136–138, 139, 140, 141, 162–163, 165, 167, 169, 171, 183, 189, 193
and public policy, 138, 141–143
Political Action Committees (PACs), 12–13, 187
Poole, Keith, 136–137
Populist Movement and Party, 6–7, 8
Poverty, 10–11
Prayer, 22, 55, 79
Prescription drug bill, 135
Presidency
and Congress, 125, 133–136, 143
evolution of, 119
and line-item veto power, 120
Progressive Conservative Party (Canadian), 148, 154, 155, 156
Progressive Movement, 6, 7–8

Race
as divisive force in working class, 63
as issue, 35, 40, 41, 42, 43, 44, 52, 71, 76, 77
and multivariate analysis of voting behavior, 80, 81, 82, 90
and political beliefs and orientation, 49, 50, 52–53, 57–58, 60, 64–66, 69, 78–79, 81, 86, 98, 100
and 2008 election, 172, 174, 176, 181
and voting trends in Congress, 137
Reagan, Ronald, 15, 30, 33, 65, 82, 110, 131, 133, 152, 155, 178
The Real Majority (Scammon and Wattenberg), 71
Red Tories Party (Canadian), 148
Reed, Thomas B., 123, 124, 131
Reform Party (Canadian), 155, 156

Region
   and Canada, 154–155, 156, 158, 163
   and Great Britain, 158
   and multivariate analysis of voting behavior, 80, 90
   and political beliefs and orientation, 49, 50, 51, 57, 58, 59, 66–68, 70, 79, 84, 99, 181

Reid, Harry, 133

Religion
   in comparative context of other countries, 166–167, 168
   and cultural divide, 63, 72, 73, 74, 75, 103
   as issue, 19, 55, 63
   and party systems, 147–148
   and political beliefs and orientation, 49, 55, 56, 57, 58, 62, 70, 89, 147–148, 166–167
   and 2008 election, 172

Republican Conference, 127, 132, 133

Republican National Committee (RNC), 14, 103, 104, 178

Republican Party
   and British Conservatives, 152
   Civil War legacy of, 9
   composition of, 49–62, 64–69, 79
   and Congress, 4, 8, 93–100, 100–107, 109, 110–117, 123, 126, 127, 129, 131, 132, 133, 134, 135–136, 137–138, 139, 140, 142, 182–183, 188–189, 190, 191–193
   and "Contract with America" and 1994 revolution, 93–94, 96–100, 119–120
   and control of national politics in late nineteenth and early twentieth centuries, 8
   and dominance of two-party system, 157
   and economic stimulus bill, 188–189
   emergence of, 6
   and Franklin Roosevelt era, 24
   and fund-raising, 14, 101, 103, 104, 172, 173, 178, 182–183
   and health care, 191–193
   images of, 16, 19–23, 71, 75, 76, 79, 82, 164
   as integrative agent, 3
   and issues and ideology, 34–35, 38–39, 49, 163, 184–185
   and Jefferson, 5
   and mobilizing voters, 150
   and negative campaign ads, 19, 104
   number of legislative elections won since 1945, 150
   and opinion leaders, 38–44
   and party identification, 24–30
   and speeches, 19
   and "supporting cast," 185–186
   2008 decline in identification with, 177
   and 2008 election, 171, 172, 173–174, 175, 177, 179, 181, 182–183
   and 2006 election, 100–107
   and white Southerners, 16, 17, 28, 50, 67, 68, 79, 97–98, 99
   See also Cultural issues: and support for Republicans

Richardson, Bill, 171, 172
Roberts, John, 135
Robertson, Pat, 172
Rockefeller, Jay, 193
Roe v. Wade (1973), 72
Romney, Mitt, 172, 173, 174, 179
Roosevelt, Franklin D., 8–9, 10, 24, 62, 109, 125, 133

Roosevelt, Theodore, 8, 94
Rosenthal, Howard, 136–137
Rostenkowski, Dan, 95
Rove, Karl, 101
Russia, 178–179

Sabato, Larry, 101, 102
Sanders, Bernie, 182
Scammon, Richard, 70–71
Schattschneider, E. E., 2–3
Schiavo, Terri, 142
Schumer, Charles, 103, 127
Scottish National Party (SNP) (British), 150, 153
Senate
    evolution of, 119, 121–125
    and individualism, 129
    and party machinery, 126–128
    and party resurgence, 129, 132–133
    and polarization's effect on legislative process, 138, 141, 142
    and presidency, 134, 135, 136
    and reelection, 129
    and textbook Congress, 125–126, 129
    voting trends in, 137–138, 140
Senate Finance Committee, 191, 192, 193
September 11, 2001, attacks, 134
September 11 Commission, 120
Seventeenth amendment, 7
Sinclair, Barbara, 130
Sixteenth amendment, 7
Snowe, Olympia, 188, 192
Social class. *See* Income and social class
Social Security, 9, 11, 20, 136
Socialist and Communist parties, 147, 149
Soft money, 13–14, 15, 103, 108, 187

Spears, Britney, 178
Specter, Arlen, 138, 182, 189
State Children's Health Insurance Program (SCHIP), 121, 189
Stem cell research, 120, 121
Stephanopoulos, George, 176
Stevens, Ted, 182
Strategic choice model, 107–109, 110, 111
Student loans, 120, 121, 190
Subprime mortgages, 121, 179
Sumner, Charles, 123
Sununu, John, 182
Swift Boat Veterans for Truth, 187
Switzerland, 148

Taft, William Howard, 8
TARP program, 190, 191
Tax cuts, 16, 19, 21, 50, 119, 131, 134, 135, 172, 177, 189, 190
Taylor, Zachary, 5
Term limits, 119
Terrorism, 75, 76, 134, 181
Tester, Jon, 105
Thatcher, Margaret, 152
Think tanks, 188
Thompson, Fred, 97, 172, 173
Tilden, Samuel, 6
Tocqueville, Alexis de, 3
Tories (British), 151–152
Transportation bills, 135
Truman, Harry, 9, 109

Udall, Mark, 182
Udall, Tom, 182
Union for a Popular Movement Party (French), 147

Van Buren, Martin, 5–6
Vietnam War, 24, 147
Vilsack, Tom, 171

Voting
  and Australian ballot, 7
  multivariate analysis of, 80–82, 90–91
  and opinion leaders, 36–38, 39, 40, 41, 43, 44, 45, 47
  and parties, 4, 16, 26, 27–30, 31, 32, 33, 49, 145, 146, 151, 153
  percent voting for third party in presidential elections, 48
  percent voting Republican in presidential elections, 47
  preferential, 151
  and registration, 15, 157, 168
  and social class in the United States, Great Britain, Germany, and France, 147
  turnout: in congressional elections, 108
  turnout: in other countries, 150
  turnout: late 1800s and early 1900s, 8
  turnout: mid-to-late 1900s, 13
  turnout: Republicans versus Democrats, 46
  turnout: 2000s, 46, 47, 103
  See also Congress: voting trends in; Cultural divisions and war: and voting; Cultural issues: and voting; Partisanship: and voting behavior; Party differences: and voting; Party identification: and voting behavior
Voting Rights Act (1965), 11

Waldholtz, Enid, 96
Wallace, George, 28, 30, 145, 157
War on Poverty, 10, 11
Warner, John, 182
Warner, Mark, 182
Washington, George, 4–5, 154
Washington Post, 141
Watergate, 109, 147
Wattenberg, Ben, 70–71
Weaver, James, 7
Webb, Jim, 105
Webster, Daniel, 5, 123
Welfare reform, 96, 119, 134, 136
What's the Matter with Kansas? (Frank), 71–72
Whigs (American), 5–6
Whigs (British), 152
Whitewater, 94
Wilson, Joe, 193
Wilson, Woodrow, 8, 125
World War I, 8
World War II, 9, 24, 109, 147, 149, 154, 158
Wright, Jeremiah, 176
Wright, Jim, 16, 130, 132, 133

YouTube, 180

About the Authors

Donald C. Baumer is a professor of Government at Smith College. He is the co-author, with Carl E. Van Horn, of *The Politics of Unemployment* (CQ Press, 1985) and three editions of *Politics and Public Policy* (CQ Press, 1989, 1992, 2001), co-authored with Carl E. Van Horn and William T. Gormley, Jr., and several articles on employment policy, Democratic leadership in the Senate, and party images held by the electorate.

Howard J. Gold is a professor of Government at Smith College. He is the author of *Hollow Mandates: American Public Opinion and the Conservative Shift* (Westview Press, 1992), and several articles on partisanship, third parties, and voting behavior.